THE NORTHWEST GARDENS OF

Lord & Schryver

THE NORTHWEST GARDENS OF

Lord & Schryver

Valencia Libby

Oregon State University Press ➤➤➤ Corvallis

Library of Congress Cataloging-in-Publication Data

Names: Libby, Valencia, author.
Title: The Northwest gardens of Lord & Schryver / Valencia Libby
Description: Corvallis : Oregon State University Press, [2021] |
Includes bibliographical references and index.
Identifiers: LCCN 2021033356 | ISBN 9780870711527 (paperback) | ISBN
9780870711534 (ebook)
Subjects: LCSH: Lord & Schryver (Firm : Salem, Or.) | Lord,
Elizabeth, 1887–1976. | Schryver, Edith, 1901–1984. | Landscape gar-
dening. | Gardens—Northwest, Pacific—Design.
Classification: LCC SB469.9 .L53 2021 | DDC 635.9—dc23
LC record available at https://lccn.loc.gov/2021033356

♾ This paper meets the requirements of ANSI/NISO Z39.48-1992
(Permanence of Paper).

First published in 2021 by Oregon State University Press
Printed in the United States of America

Oregon State University Press
121 The Valley Library
Corvallis OR 97331-4501
541-737-3166 • fax 541-737-3170
www.osupress.oregonstate.edu

Facing title page: The lower terrace looking west, Charles and
Mildred Robertson's garden, Salem, Oregon (c. 1945). Courtesy
University of Oregon Libraries, Special Collections and University
Archives, Coll 098, Lord & Schryver architectural records

Dedicated to the memory of our dear friend

Ruth Sprow Roberts and to all the ardent supporters

of the Lord & Schryver Conservancy

Contents

Foreword, Bill Noble   ix

Introduction   1

➤➤➤

1   Families, West and East   7

2   The Lowthorpe School of Landscape Architecture for Women   18

3   The Cornish Colony and Ellen Shipman   32

4   A Venture Launched   46

5   Against All Odds   65

6   Onward   93

7   Plantswomen   113

8   Cultivating the Profession   130

9   "Yard Architects" for Period Gardens   140

10   Salem Pride   152

11   Final Years   173

➤➤➤

Acknowledgments   183

Notes   185

Bibliography   205

Index   211

Plates follow page 124.

Foreword

"This is the real deal." These were the words spoken to me by landscape historian David Streatfield as we stood in the flower garden admiring the boxwood edged allee of lilacs and camellias glowing in the late afternoon sun. It was 2002, and we had been invited to see Gaiety Hollow in Salem, Oregon, by the newly formed Lord & Schryver Conservancy, who hoped one day to restore the garden and make it available to the public. As we strolled through its intimate spaces, created beginning in the 1930s by the pioneering landscape architects Elizabeth Lord and Edith Schryver, we began to realize that there was nothing like it on the West Coast, and very few examples elsewhere in the country. It was the home, studio, and garden of two prominent landscape architects that showcased their superb design skills and radiated the kind of charm that was cherished by their clients. The house and garden were in good shape, having been lovingly maintained by the subsequent owner. A huge Garry oak anchored one end of the garden and the modestly scaled house inhabited the other corner of the lot. A classically inspired series of garden rooms edged in boxwood and connected with brick paths and wooden arbors set the scene. There was no question that such a jewel of a garden should be preserved and shared with the public.

Now, more than a decade and a half later, the dreams of purchasing the house, repairing and restoring parts of the garden, and opening it to the public have been realized. But this is not all the Lord & Schryver Conservancy has accomplished over the years; it has also tracked down and documented many of the two hundred commissions the two women worked on during the forty years of their professional practice in residential, civic, and historic preservation design. It has gathered an archive of historic images, oral histories, billing records, and other information that adds telling detail to this book; it has also engaged with the current owners of Lord and Schryver gardens to document the gardens and in some cases advise on their maintenance and preservation.

All the while there has been the dream of a book to tell the story, to inspire and educate a wider public about the special character of gardens designed by Lord and Schryver from the 1930s to the 1960s. To this task, Valencia Libby brings the knowledge and perspective of a historian of twentieth-century American landscape architecture, with an acute eye for how women developed and shaped the profession. She tells the story of two women—one from an established Salem family, the other from a striving working-class New York background—who built and sustained a professional practice in a region not accustomed to making use of landscape architects, through years of an economic depression and world war at that. They faced challenges of clients who did not always recognize the worth of landscape architecture, and nurserymen and contractors who were not accustomed to working with women practitioners. What comes through in a way seldom encountered in books about garden design is how Elizabeth Lord and Edith Schryver inter-acted with clients and colleagues with grace, often with genuine friendship, and always with the desire to do the best possible work the situation would allow. We enjoy glimpses of how they developed and maintained collabora-tive, friendly, and horticulturally rich associations with other women whose interests were in plants and garden beauty.

We learn how these two landscape architects promoted good design to the public by using the new medium of radio to reach rural and ur-ban listeners, and how as writers they articulated their design principles in a series of articles in the Sunday newspaper. As educators they brought their insights into the classrooms of Oregon State University and lecture halls throughout the state. Their dedication to civic improvement is seen in their long-standing service to the Salem Art Association and on many city and state committees. We see how they shared the tasks of the busi-ness, from client relationships to the development of grading and plant-ing plans to plant selection, contract supervision, and ongoing stewardship of gardens. As the first female landscape architectural partnership in the Pacific Northwest, they created enduring gardens and a lasting legacy of civic improvement.

Of their own house and garden at Gaiety Hollow, one of their colleagues wrote, "There is a charm and unity about all your gardens. . . . Of course your own garden is one of the finest pieces of landscape design and composition I have ever seen, . . . not from the point of view of breath-taking expanses, but from a point of view of design with a particular emphasis upon circu-lation and unity." This is what motivates many of us to take an interest in their work: through their training at the Lowthorpe School and especially Edith Schryver's five years of employment in Ellen Shipman's office, they learned how to imbue gardens with a sense of proportion, scale, unity, and charm.

So many of their gardens have remained viable because they were thoughtfully designed and constructed to match the resources available. Their approach to design was crafted within a tradition that valued understanding and working with a site, creating a design that suited the living needs of the client, and relied on time-tested materials and plants suited to the climate and year-round interest. As one who has looked closely at the work of Charles Platt and Ellen Shipman, I see a continuity of design principles adapted for the Pacific Northwest. Their gardens are intimately connected with their surroundings—whether they be on a wooded hillside or in a residential neighborhood—but above all are made for gracious living. The preservation of gardens and the care that goes into maintaining them is a theme throughout this book. More than once they returned to gardens they had designed and reworked them for new clients, or recommended new planting schemes after the passage of time and the loss of trees had altered the original design.

I know you will share my enthusiasm for Val Libby's investigation into the way these women created gardens of lasting quality as well as furthered a broader appreciation for gardens and civic landscapes. Salem was fortunate to have these two civic-minded practitioners involved in helping the city grow into the livable place it is today. And now we can enjoy this fuller explanation of their accomplishments, while also exploring the verdant world of Gaiety Hollow.

Bill Noble
AUGUST 2020

Introduction

We were free-swinging career girls, and no one questioned us.
In the '20s everyone trained for a career. All the girls in my class
[at Lowthorpe] did; we all had careers.
   —Edith Schryver, 1980

On 10 June 1927, the SS *Andania II* eased away from the dock in Montreal harbor and sailed for Great Britain. As the passengers settled in for the nine-day transatlantic voyage, the usual travel thrill was heightened by the ongoing excitement over Charles A. Lindbergh's record-breaking flight from New York to Paris, landing on May 21. But for Edith Schryver, a twenty-six-year-old landscape architect working for Ellen Shipman in Manhattan, any regret about leaving the city before Lindbergh's historic ticker-tape parade on Broadway must have faded with the knowledge that she would soon be visiting the great gardens and monuments of Europe.[1]

Schryver was one of twenty people, mostly women, on the European Travel Course sponsored by the Cambridge School of Architecture and Landscape Architecture for Women and the Lowthorpe School of Landscape Architecture for Women.[2] She had received her certificate from Lowthorpe in 1923, and was working in Shipman's office when she decided to take a sabbatical tour of Europe. One evening on the ocean liner, the petite Edith was mistakenly seated at the children's table in the dining salon. When her request for a glass of wine was refused, she insisted on being moved to another table. The steward seated her next to Elizabeth Lord, then thirty-nine, from Salem, Oregon, another member of the European study tour and a student at Lowthorpe.[3] Thus began a lifetime friendship, a domestic partnership, and the first landscape architecture firm founded by women in the Pacific Northwest.

After landing in Glasgow and crossing Scotland to Edinburgh, the tour group traveled south through England and on to France and Italy for

0.1 Elizabeth Lord with the airplane to France during the European tour (1927). Courtesy University of Oregon Libraries, Special Collections and University Archives, Coll 098, Lord & Schryver architectural records.

almost three months, visiting numerous historic sites, estates, and gardens. Schryver later recalled, "We came to the wonderful gardens of mid-England and then we [Elizabeth and I] found that we really related very closely to our reaction to gardens, our feelings about garden[s]. I found out that her mother was a great gardener, so was she."[4] Schryver and Lord separated from the group in London and flew to Calais in a twelve-passenger plane with wicker seats, an experience that Edith described as "one of the best thrills of a lifetime"[5] (figure 0.1). They continued on through Germany and Austria together and reunited with the tour group in Italy. At the end of three months, Schryver invited Lord to join her on a journey to see the magnificent Moorish palaces and gardens of Majorca and Spain (figures 0.2 and 0.3). They traveled on their own for another month and arrived back in New York in October 1927.

Schryver returned to her employment in Shipman's office, and Lord resumed her studies at the Lowthorpe School in Massachusetts. Over the following year, they corresponded, and by the autumn of 1928, they had decided to move to Salem, Oregon, and open their own landscape architecture firm. They understood that it was an experiment and it held risks. But Schryver was ready for change and had "always wanted to see the West Coast, Alaska and Japan," even though it meant leaving an excellent professional position in New York.[6] Lord, having completed her studies at Lowthorpe, was ready to return to her home in Salem, Oregon, where her parents had been prominent citizens in a region that was rapidly developing. As Lord later commented, "I met Edith and she wanted to come west and forget the crowds of New York City."[7] They launched the firm of "Lord and Schryver, Landscape Architects" on 1 January 1929.

Introduction

The 1920s had been a time of great prosperity, with the Northwest's cities and industries growing quickly and the rate of real estate development accelerating. Those who had recently moved to the region and acquired great wealth from timber, agriculture, banking, and new businesses were keen to build prominent houses and establish their position in society. The middle class was also beginning to view landscape architecture in a new light. As the Oregon landscape historian Wallace Kay Huntington stated, "In the 1920s landscape architecture in the Northwest began to evolve from an elitist state and . . . became concerned with more modestly scaled, domestic architecture."[8] Lord and Schryver would excel at designing spacious country estates as well as the compact residential gardens that were much in demand.

Lord and Schryver were among the second generation of American women to take up careers in landscape architecture, following the path forged by Beatrix Farrand, Ellen Shipman, Annette Hoyt Flanders, Elizabeth Leonard Strang, Marian Cruger Coffin, and others. But almost all of these forerunners remained based in the East. On the West Coast, Florence Yoch and Lucille Council established a very successful practice in 1925 designing California's private estates and Hollywood stage sets. Yoch and Council enjoyed both a domestic and a business partnership.[9] Often, the earlier generation mentored young women and helped them to advance. Lord's mother, a strong and forward-thinking woman, had served as her daughter's role model, while the independent women of the Cornish,

0.2 Elizabeth Lord in Spain during the European tour (1927). Courtesy Lord & Schryver Conservancy, Anne M. Kingery Library.

0.3 Edith Schryver
in Spain during the
European tour (1927).
Courtesy University
of Oregon Libraries,
Special Collections
and University
Archives, Coll 098,
Lord & Schryver
architectural records.

New Hampshire, art colony had been Schryver's. And like many of those
figures that preceded them in landscape architecture, Lord and Schryver
never married or had children. They followed the "pioneer" ethic of the
founders of the Northwest's first Anglo-American communities: they went
west. They brought their expertise, energy, and enthusiasm to Oregon,
where their commitment to a younger and still-growing region of the nation was unparalleled.

   Lord and Schryver became the first women to create a landscape architecture firm in the Pacific Northwest, building a new professional model.
They were not the first women to practice landscape architecture in Oregon,
however, as Florence Holmes Gerke had established her career as the City
of Portland's landscape architect and opened a practice with her husband. It
was still a time when few women in Oregon worked outside the home, and
Edith would later admit, "It was not easy to be businesswomen in Salem."
They had to work hard, applying all the business techniques they had learned
from the professionals who had trained them. They joined the regional garden clubs, entered their plans in design exhibitions, and publicized their business through marketing efforts. They became active in the prominent social
circles in which Lord had grown up, using her connections to promote their
design services. They did not hesitate to pursue a lead to a good client. When

an article appeared in the Salem newspaper about a new resident, Daniel B. Jarman, building a substantial house, they followed up with a letter promoting their services and obtained their first major project.[10]

Over the course of four decades, the firm of Lord and Schryver completed approximately two hundred landscape designs for sites in Oregon and Washington. These included many residential gardens, public parks, school grounds, institutional landscapes, college campuses, two historic buildings, and a wilderness resort. They became widely known and well respected for the unvaryingly high quality of their landscapes and their extensive plant knowledge. Their garden designs had an identifiable style, adapted from the prevalent style in the Northeast. It was not the naturalistic style of Frederick Law Olmsted nor the Italianate formality of the large eastern firms, but a refined synthesis of the two styles, defined by the size of the property. Their residential style was similar to that most often used by Ellen Shipman, Marian C. Coffin, and similar practitioners during the first half of the twentieth century, but knowingly adapted to the climate and flora of the region.[11] It relied on a strong sense of scale and proportion in connection with the architecture and an excellent knowledge of plants. Lord and Schryver's gardens provided privacy, with trees and shrubs or fences and walls for enclosure. They incorporated formal areas—terraces, patios, walls, arbors, and the like—extending from the architectural dimensions of the house to provide spaces for outdoor living. As one moved farther away from the building, the garden spaces became less and less formal and more naturalistic. Each "garden room" had a distinct character and a planting plan created with a lush informality. Each plant composition might be based on a particular color scheme or season of bloom or the unique forms and textures of the plants. Axial sight lines between the areas drew one farther into the landscape and offered places to set decorative garden features as focal points. Low boxwood hedges, an element often adopted from New England's Colonial Revival style, outlined beds and borders, further defining the edges of each space. They became a recognizable hallmark of a Lord and Schryver garden.

The highly varied and spectacular natural landscapes and the flora of the Northwest provided Lord and Schryver with an endless source of inspiration. A distant view of a mountain or valley, framed by woodlands, a low fence or a garden hedge, became borrowed scenery in their designs, while a handsome tree or cluster of wild evergreen shrubs might form the basis of a plant composition. The wealth of wildflowers in Salem was such that they did not have to go far for Lord to educate Schryver on the many beautiful native species. They prized each spring the sight of the majestic Garry oaks in Bush's Pasture Park, the ground underneath carpeted with sky blue camassia (plate 1). To the great diversity of plant materials they had learned in the East, they incorporated the native species and the specialties grown by the Northwest's fine nurseries.

Lord and Schryver distinguished their practice from that of many of their predecessors and contemporaries by their exemplary commitment to civic improvement and public education. They made an exceptional effort to describe the process of fine garden design through lectures, newspaper and journal articles, and exhibits of their plans. As soon as the new technology of the radio came to their attention, they were producing educational programs for live broadcast from a studio at Oregon State College (today Oregon State University). These efforts, naturally, enhanced their visibility and attracted clients, but Lord and Schryver had a deeper desire to raise the overall standard for design and horticulture in the Pacific Northwest. During World War II, Schryver served on the faculty in landscape design at Oregon State College for three years, while few faculty men were available. Both women participated in the founding of the Oregon Society of Landscape Architects in 1940, the first professional organization for landscape architects in the Northwest. They knew they had a valuable asset—their shared knowledge and professionalism—to contribute.

Individually, and as a team, the two women volunteered countless hours of professional service to government advisory boards, historical societies, educational and cultural organizations, and regional garden clubs. They created landscapes for several properties that have now been preserved as part of Oregon's public realm: their own garden at Gaiety Hollow, Deepwood Museum and Gardens, Bush's Pasture Park, the McLoughlin and Barclay Houses (National Park Service), and the Hoover-Minthorn House. Well before the federal government formally recognized the need for historic landscape preservation, Lord and Schryver were providing appropriate period plans for the McLoughlin and Barclay Houses in Oregon City and the Hoover-Minthorn House in Newberg.[12] In 1969, when they decided it was time to retire, both Lord and Schryver continued their deep involvement with public projects, such as the Salem Art Association and Bush's Pasture Park, that have benefited Salem's citizens immensely.

As W. K. Huntington concluded, "One of the milestones in the history of Northwest garden design was the 1929 founding of the office of Lord and Schryver in Salem. . . . They brought to Oregon an intellectual Eastern command of craft and style combined with an instinctive sense of taste."[13] Describing the unique appeal of their style, he further stated, "Their color schemes were like impressionist paintings, their garden decisions were logical and appealing and their sense of scale was impeccable. Although their style may have seemed old-fashioned in the later twentieth century, like antiques and works of art their legacy is becoming more valued as reawakened interest and appreciation of their place in Northwest landscape architecture grows."[14]

1

Families, West and East

I have never come in contact with anyone who had such utter faith
in Oregon as my mother and father.
—Elizabeth Lord, 1944

Despite having grown up three thousand miles apart and in very different
regions of the country, Elizabeth Lord and Edith Schryver recognized they
possessed a deep compatibility as they gradually became acquainted during
their European garden tour. Over time they would share a profound love
of nature and the arts, an enthusiasm for adventurous travel, and a passion
for the creation of landscape beauty. Where they began their lives, and their
family backgrounds, are important to this story.

Elizabeth B. Lord (1887–1976)

To some people in the community of Salem, Oregon, Elizabeth B. Lord
appeared austere, stern, or unapproachable. To others, she was warm and
generous. She was tall, handsome, and well-mannered: a true patrician.
And Salem was her world. Her family was as much a part of Salem's fabric
as the Garry oaks (*Quercus garryana*) that grew throughout the city, the tall
old trees that her mother had so greatly admired when she first came to
Oregon as a bride in 1880. Elizabeth ("Bess" or "Bessie") Lord was born on
12 November 1887 in her parents' home on the corner of High and Mission
Streets in Salem. She was the youngest of their three children (figure 1.1).
Her father, William Paine Lord (1838–1911), was a justice on the Oregon
Supreme Court, and her mother, Juliet Montague Lord (1844–1924), was
active in both the social and the political scenes.

Elizabeth's father had led a very distinguished career in the United
States military before he settled in Oregon (figure 1.3). Born in Delaware
in 1838, Lord graduated from college in New York State and enlisted in the

1.1 Elizabeth Lord, age sixteen (1903). Courtesy Lord & Schryver Conservancy, Anne M. Kingery Library.

1.2 Juliet Lord, Elizabeth's mother (1903). Courtesy Lord & Schryver Conservancy, Anne M. Kingery Library.

Union Army at the start of the Civil War. He rose to the rank of major in the Delaware Cavalry at the young age of twenty-four. Following the war, he attended Albany Law College in New York State, graduating in 1866. He returned to the military and served in the West: California, Washington, and Sitka, Alaska, where his commission was to take formal possession of the territory from Russia. Having seen the great opportunity afforded in the Northwest for growth and prosperity, he resigned from the military in 1868 and moved to Oregon to practice law, settling in Salem, the state capital. In 1878 Lord was elected a state senator (Republican) and two years later he became a justice on the Oregon Supreme Court. He served twice as chief justice during his fourteen-year tenure. Lord was elected the ninth governor of Oregon in 1895, and while holding this office he directed the State Land Board to investigate corruption by land speculators and reclaim state properties.[1]

Elizabeth's mother was born Juliette Cooke Montague in Lenox, Massachusetts, in 1844 (figure 1.2).[2] After the early loss of her mother, Juliette was raised by her aunt, Fanny Eliza, (Montague) and uncle, Henry Stockbridge, in Baltimore. Henry Stockbridge was an esteemed lawyer, and his position in society assured young Juliette's. She grew up in a cultured and sophisticated world. Juliette was tall, dark-haired and dark-eyed, poised and charming, and she was often the belle of the ball. Juliette Montague and Major Lord often met at parties and balls in Baltimore during the Civil War.[3] A romantic account claimed that they first met at a Union League Ball held in Baltimore for President Lincoln.[4] At that event, in 1864, President Lincoln invited twenty-year-old Juliette to join him on the platform and be his companion for the entire evening, thus denying all the officers a dance with the beautiful young lady. Major Lord, however, must have made an impression on her because they corresponded for the next fifteen years. On 14 January 1880 they were married in Baltimore and then traveled west to establish their home in time for Lord to begin his service on the Oregon Supreme Court.

The couple settled in Salem, where their three children were born: Montague in 1881, William Paine in 1884, and Elizabeth in 1887. The Lords lived in a small house on the corner of High and Mission Streets, where they occupied a large double lot on the southern edge of the city (figure 1.4).[5] The surrounding area was quite undeveloped and rural at that time. Elizabeth Lord would later describe Salem as having only four thousand inhabitants in the 1880s. "The streets were muddy, the sidewalks were made of boards, and it wasn't an unusual sight to see cows grazing on the curbs in the business district."[6]

Asahel Bush, founder of Salem's Ladd & Bush Bank, and his daughter "Miss Sally," lived directly across Mission Street from the Lords in a large Italianate house, set within one hundred acres of farmland that Mr. Bush and his late wife had purchased in 1860. The house sat on a rise, and large stands of Garry oaks throughout the property made it a veritable parkland. Because they kept a few grazing animals in the meadow, many of the locals called it "Bush's Pasture."

"Miss Sally," a graduate of Smith College and an accomplished amateur photographer, managed her father's household. She loved children, revered nature, and used her photographic talent to document her family and friends (figures 1.5, 1.6, 1.7). Both Elizabeth and her mother often crossed the

1.3 William P. Lord Sr., Elizabeth's father (c. 1890). Courtesy State Library of Oregon.

1.4 The Lord family home, Salem, Oregon (c. 1885). Courtesy Oregon Historical Society Research Library.

unpaved road to visit with her and wander among the wildflowers that grew prolifically beneath the stands of Garry oaks. Elizabeth later recalled her mother being "passionately fond of wild flowers," admiring the lady's slippers (*Cypripedium*), lamb's tongues (*Erythronium*), and violets that grew in abundance.[7] Mrs. Lord collected specimens of the flowers to press and send to her Aunt Fanny in Baltimore. According to Elizabeth, it was not long before her mother was "digging in her own backyard, sending for seed catalogues and getting fine results from her labor of gardening." With her daughter's help, Mrs. Lord created a beautiful natural world that many came to admire.[8]

Elizabeth later recalled, "We youngsters played down in the pasture and our main enjoyment was picking wildflowers and now I think of it in shame. They had so many varieties of wild violets down there just before you came to a creek. One called Voika [vukia]. . . . It had a divided stem. . . and the flower was brown and white and the sweetest smelling violet of all. It is now extent [extinct]. . . . It was one of the rare varieties and grew no further than the Willamette Valley."[9]

During the summer months, the Lords joined a few other families from Salem on the Pacific coast at Seal Rock (or Seal Rocks), where a rustic summer colony developed after the town was platted in 1887. Although it was an arduous trip to make at the turn of the twentieth century, Elizabeth, her mother, and her brothers loved their adventures at Seal Rock. As Elizabeth later explained,

> My father purchased a small cottage at the new resort called Seal Rocks. My mother loved the freedom of the place and its scenic beauty, and as it was a new development not many people lived there. Indians were still making the place their home on account of the deepsea fishing and trout streams abundant with trout and young Salmon and clams were abundant in the sandy spits and rock oysters in the soft kind of rocks. My father, not being a fisherman, did not care so much for the place as it was difficult to get there. Having to take a train to Albany, thence to Newport, stay all night and leave early next morning [in] a big country wagon down to the beach and carry our own baggage.[10]

Mr. Lord came out less frequently. In later years, when they had established their firm in Salem, Elizabeth and Edith would enjoy the cottage immensely, especially the beauty of the natural scenery, the peacefulness and visiting with their friends and relatives during the summer months.

Elizabeth began her education in the Salem public schools, where she recalled the other pupils made fun of her because she was the governor's daughter.[11] In 1899, when she was twelve years old, her father was appointed by President McKinley to be the "minister to the Argentine Republic."[12] The family, except for the eldest son Montague, moved to Buenos Aires for two years. There, Elizabeth was enrolled in a language school for girls. In the summer

1.5 Elizabeth and her brother, William Lord Jr., covered in wildflowers on the front porch of the Bush House, Salem, Oregon (c. 1892). Courtesy Bush House Museum.

1.6 Elizabeth's brother, Montague Lord, with a friend on the stone wall at the Bush House, Salem, Oregon (c. 1887). Courtesy Bush House Museum.

1.7 Elizabeth Lord posing with a friend on the front porch of the Bush House, Salem, Oregon (c. 1903). Courtesy Bush House Museum.

of 1901, Elizabeth, her mother, and brother William journeyed back to Salem. They planned to return to Buenos Aires, but her mother's poor health prevented that.[13] Instead, Elizabeth attended St. Helen's Hall in Portland, graduating in 1904.[14] Her father wanted her to have a year at a Swiss finishing school, all the fashion for American girls, but it proved too expensive.[15] Instead Elizabeth spent one year at the Anne Arundel Academy, a prestigious private school founded in 1854, not far from Annapolis, Maryland.

Mr. Lord remained in South America until 1903 when he retired.[16] Although his health was impaired after he returned, William P. Lord still worked, with the assistance of his son William Jr., to codify the laws of Oregon, known thereafter as Lord's Oregon Code. The *History of Oregon*, published in 1922, credits Lord: "His name deserves a foremost place upon the pages of Oregon's history for he contributed much to the shaping of its judicial record and its public policy."[17]

William P. Lord died in 1911 at the age of seventy-three, leaving a substantial estate of $69,270 ($1,850,057 current value) in a trust for his wife and children at the Ladd & Bush Bank in Salem. Montague moved to Manila in 1911 to work for the Hawaiian Sugar Planters' Association and William Jr. left Salem to study, and then practice, law in Portland. Elizabeth, Mrs. Lord's youngest child, became her mother's constant companion; her mother affectionately called her "my chum and comrade."[18] They traveled together, often visiting Montague in the Philippines (figures 1.8, 1.9). In 1917, when the United States became involved in World War I, their ambitious plans to circle the globe on their way home from Manila were hastily cast aside as Montague worried that passenger ships would be requisitioned. Once safely home, Elizabeth wanted to become a nurse's aide with the Red Cross and serve overseas, but she could not secure a place because of a congenital hearing problem. Instead, she briefly attended a business college to study typing and shorthand and then volunteered for two years with the Willamette Valley chapter of the Red Cross.[19] Elizabeth later commented, "It was the very beginning of women['s] activities and I remember it and will never forget how much we had to do."[20] This is one of the very few times she commented on women's growing role in American public life.

Elizabeth gladly took up her mother's interest in gardening, helping her with events for the Salem Floral Society (later the Salem Garden Club), founded by her mother in 1915, which was the first garden club in Oregon (figure 1.10). The two led a very active life as Mrs. Lord became involved with a number of local organizations and joined the Congregational church. Her New England family lineage entitled Mrs. Lord to membership in the Colonial Dames of America, and she helped organize the Oregon chapter.[21] Mother and daughter attended social events including the "silver teas,"

1.8 Elizabeth and Juliet Lord in the
Philippines (1913). Courtesy University of
Oregon Libraries, Special Collections and
University Archives, Coll 098, Lord &
Schryver architectural records.

1.9 Montague and Juliet Lord in the
Philippines (1913). Courtesy University of
Oregon Libraries, Special Collections and
University Archives, Coll 098, Lord &
Schryver architectural records.

a Salem tradition in which society ladies sponsored a tea party at an elegant home. A silver tray was placed on a table by the door where visitors
could leave their donations for a charitable cause.[22] But it was clear to her
daughter that Mrs. Lord valued the civic side of life more than the social.
Elizabeth recalled, "She thought and talked greatly of making Salem one
of the loveliest towns in the West, . . . but it all fell on deaf ears."[23] Mrs.
Lord gave her support to causes that she believed would increase Oregon's
prosperity. She was a strong advocate for certain state initiatives, one of
which was to promote flax farming in the Willamette Valley. Flax would
help farmers diversify their crops away from their previous dependence
on wheat. Elizabeth believed that the idea came from her mother's Aunt
Fanny in Baltimore.[24] Mrs. Lord campaigned, sent letters to politicians and
newspapers, gave speeches, and sought to educate all the farmers she met.
Her perseverance for this cause very much impressed her daughter.

Elizabeth always credited her mother's love of nature and gardening as
being the greatest influence on her choice of a career, and her mother's

courage, energy, and sense of civic responsibility as her inspiration for performing public works throughout her life. When Mrs. Lord died in 1924, her younger son William was appointed the administrator of his father's trust, which provided his sister with an income. Elizabeth was now thirty-seven years old and free to chart her own life. She traveled extensively for the next two years in the Far East and Europe. When she returned home to Salem, the deep love of plants and gardens she had learned from her mother motivated her to pursue a career in landscape architecture. On the advice of Florence H. Gerke, the first woman to become a landscape architect in Oregon, she chose to begin her education at the Lowthorpe School of Landscape Architecture for Women in Groton, Massachusetts.[25] It was a decision that would change her life in many ways and bring her into contact with Edith E. Schryver, her lifelong companion, closest friend, and business partner.

≫≫≫ Edith Eleanor Schryver (1901–1984)

Edith ("Nina") Eleanor Schryver was proud of being "Hudson River Dutch." She was born in Kingston, a small city on the west bank of the Hudson River, approximately ninety miles north of New York City.[26] Both of Edith's parents had been born in towns along the Hudson. Her mother, Eleanor (nee Young) Schryver (1871–1920), came from a German Lutheran family, while her father, George J. Schryver (1872–1955), came from a Dutch Reformed Church family with ancestry in colonial New York dating back to the early eighteenth century. (The Schryvers pronounced their name with a hard "sch" to sound like Skriver.) Edith's paternal grandfather established the Second Dutch Reformed Church of Kingston, splitting away from the original church.[27] Edith, as an adult, had no interest in either religion, but she did celebrate her heritage, if asked.[28] At the end of her life, despite having lived in Salem, Oregon, for more than half a century, Edith wanted to be buried with her parents in the old Wiltwyck Cemetery in Kingston. And she was.[29]

Edith was born on 20 March 1901 at 14 Warren Street in Kingston. In 1903 her brother Harry George was born. When Edith was about six months old, the family moved to an apartment over the Kingston railroad station, where her father managed the West Side Restaurant (figure 1.11). At five years old, Edith survived typhoid fever, which she caught from milk stored in cans along the back of the station building. According to her younger cousin, Kathyrn (Kay) Heavey, Edith's childhood was a happy one. She was friendly, outgoing, and artistic, and she loved to read. She also loved hair ribbons, dolls, Christmas decorations, and animals, especially animals (figure 1.12). In later years, when Edith and Elizabeth Lord came

1.10 Elizabeth and Juliet Lord in the Lord family garden, Salem, Oregon (early 1920s). Courtesy Lord & Schryver Conservancy, Anne M. Kingery Library.

to New York for the Christmas season, Edith always wanted to see the holiday decorations at Rockefeller Center, even though Elizabeth had little interest in them.[30]

Edith's family was hardworking, and as soon as she was old enough, Edith became a waitress in her father's restaurant. George Schryver was an accomplished entrepreneur who took advantage of the new opportunities associated with automobiles. Before World War I, he opened the area's first taxi service and then its first auto dealership, staging colorful and dramatic demonstrations to promote his vehicles. Edith recalled that, "on Sundays, in those early days, my father had a car [figure 1.13]. There was always a Sunday expedition in nice weather by many families over to Stockbridge, Massachusetts, to the Red Lion Inn for dinner. . . . We passed through Westfield, Massachusetts to get to Stockbridge. So the

1.11 Eleanor and George Schryver with young Harry and Edith (c. 1910). Courtesy Lord & Schryver Conservancy, Anne M. Kingery Library.

1.12 Edith Schryver with pet dog (c. 1919). Courtesy University of Oregon Libraries, Special Collections and University Archives, Coll 098, Lord & Schryver architectural records.

houses and gardens there are very familiar to me." During those outings she would have seen the charming formal gardens associated with grand historic New England homes on tree-lined avenues.[31] Otherwise, Edith made little mention of gardens or gardening in her youth.

By her senior year in high school, Edith was both popular and successful (figure 1.14). She had a steady boyfriend named Channing Clapp and was president of the Junior Audubon Society. Under Edith's leadership, Elizabeth Burroughs, the granddaughter of the famous naturalist John Burroughs, took the students on an outing to see the great man's home at "Slabsides." Edith also served as class secretary and assistant editor of the yearbook "Maroon," coauthored a musical piece with a combination of "old and familiar songs and several aesthetic dances" for the senior year production, and delivered a commencement speech titled "The Lost Battalion," from World War I (figure 1.15).[32] Sadly, throughout this time, Edith's mother was suffering from a chronic illness that grew progressively worse. In November 1920, while Edith was away from home at the Lowthorpe School in Massachusetts, Mrs. Schryver died. Her obituary was brief and identified her contribution to the church auxiliary and several charitable organizations in Kingston. George Schryver soon remarried, and Edith remained on good terms with her stepmother, although her brother Harry did not approve.[33]

1.13 Schryver family camping (c. 1919). Courtesy University of Oregon Libraries, Special Collections and University Archives, Coll 098, Lord & Schryver architectural records.

EDITH E. SCHRYVER,
191 Tremper Avenue.

RECORD—G. A. A., 1; A. A., 2, 3, 4; Pres. Junior Audubon Society, 1, 2; Glee Club, 1, 3; Prisma, 3; Author, Maroon Play, 4; Executive Committee, Senior Class, 4; Secretary, Senior Class, 4; Assistant Editor, Maroon, 4; Commencement Speaker.

HISTORY—It is just natural that Edie should be interested in automobiles. She says the latest thing is a warning device on the front of cars which says—"Dodge Brothers." They say she is going to France—that may be so—at any rate we all wish her luck and even a French man if she wants him.

1.14 Edith Schryver's senior portrait in the Kingston High School yearbook (1919). Courtesy Lord & Schryver Conservancy, Anne M. Kingery Library.

1.15 Edith Schryver at home (c. 1919). Courtesy University of Oregon Libraries, Special Collections and University Archives, Coll 098, Lord & Schryver architectural records.

After high school, Edith wanted to study art, which had always been her passion.[34] In the fall of 1919, she entered Pratt Institute in Brooklyn, a college established in 1887 for the study of art, where nominal fees allowed working men and women to attend. Edith is likely to have taken several classes in the freshmen general art course, which included portrait or figure drawing, anatomical drawing, freehand perspective and sketching, color, commercial illustration, art history, and physical education. The following autumn, Edith did not return to Pratt. Instead, she entered the freshman class of the Lowthorpe School of Landscape Architecture. Why she made this change, or whether anyone advised her, is unknown, as her father neither encouraged nor discouraged his daughter from pursuing her interests.[35] Tuition at Lowthorpe by the early 1920s was $300 per year, and room and board were $500 per year. It was an expensive venture for the young woman to undertake—however, it proved to be an excellent choice.[36]

2

The Lowthorpe School of Landscape Architecture for Women

A school of the standing of Lowthorpe deserves the support of
those who are aiming to make this country more beautiful through
its gardens and the encouragement of those who appreciate the
opportunity women have in landscape architecture.
—Richardson Wright, 1926

A photograph of Edith Schryver with her freshman classmates at
Lowthorpe, circa 1920, shows a group of six young women posed in a garden with five older women—the resident faculty—standing behind them
(figure 2.1). At the left side of the picture, the school's senior faculty member, Miss Hetzer, is restraining a large shaggy dog.[1] Schryver, on the right
side of the group, gazes intently at the camera.[2] In 1927, four years after
Schryver had graduated from Lowthorpe, Elizabeth Lord would become
a student at the school. Although their attendance did not overlap, the
fact that they both had graduated from this unique school created a strong
bond between them.

Few American colleges in the early 1900s had programs in landscape
architecture; fewer still admitted women. Only Cornell University, the
University of Illinois Champaign at Urbana and the University of California
Berkeley accepted women for degrees in landscape architecture. The earliest
and most famous women to enter the profession, Beatrix Farrand (1872–
1959) and Ellen Shipman (1869–1950), had pieced together their educations,
combined with years of practical experience. In 1900, Harvard University
created a program in landscape architecture associated with architecture, but
it did not admit women. In 1901, the Massachusetts Institute of Technology
(MIT) created a program that did accept women, but it operated only from
1901 to 1904, when, in competition with Harvard, it briefly became a graduate program before closing. The Pennsylvania School of Horticulture for
Women in Ambler, Pennsylvania, founded in 1910, offered an education in

"landscape design" and all aspects of horticulture; however, the program placed less emphasis on spatial design, engineering, and construction than was required in landscape architecture. Finally, in 1916, two members of the Harvard faculty opened the Cambridge School of Architecture and Landscape Architecture for Women. This might have been an option for Edith Schryver or Elizabeth Lord, but they chose instead to attend the residential program at the Lowthorpe School, where they could live and study in an attractive and inclusive environment.

Judith Eleanor Motley Low (1841–1933), a wealthy widow from Boston, founded Lowthorpe in 1901 to prepare women for professional lives and economic independence. She recognized the opportunity that all aspects of horticulture and design offered women who wished to succeed in careers outside their homes.[3] Mrs. Low modeled her school on Swanley Horticultural College in Kent, England, which she had attended. Swanley was one of several "gardening colleges" for women established throughout Europe in the late 1800s and early 1900s. They offered programs that combined theoretical knowledge, business skills, and practical training. Students were expected to live on campus, participate in classes and studios,

2.1 Edith Schryver, seated third from the right, with Lowthorpe School classmates and faculty (c. 1920). Courtesy Robert Melnick, FASLA.

and work on the grounds during outdoor practicums. The standards were rigorous, and students had to pass multiple exams before receiving a certificate of completion.

Lowthorpe was the first school in the United States to offer such an education just for women. Mrs. Low purchased a large, Federal-era house on seventeen acres in Groton, Massachusetts, that had once served as a private school for "young ladies" (figure 2.2).[4] The property was in a picturesque New England setting already famous for Groton School, a private academy for boys. It was just thirty-five miles northwest of Boston and connected to the city by a railroad line. An easy commute from Boston and Harvard to Lowthorpe by train encouraged professional specialists to teach at the school. Its physical facilities were particularly attractive. The stately white house provided classroom, administrative, library, and dormitory space for the women attending its two-to-three-year programs. A paved terrace decorated with potted plants ran across the back of the house, the perfect area for reading or conversing on a sunny day. By 1910 the faculty and students had already developed the acreage into an orchard, vegetable and flower gardens, a meadow, and a small arboretum of more unusual trees and shrubs. Charming plantings, maintained by the students, surrounded the outbuildings, which consisted of all the practical structures necessary for growing plants: cold frames, hot beds, a greenhouse, and a vinery.[5]

In 1909, the school was legally incorporated in Massachusetts with a board of trustees. Mrs. Low wisely secured the patronage of many important figures in higher education and horticulture for the school: Charles Sprague Sargent, director of the Arnold Arboretum; Charles W. Elliot, president of Harvard University; Mary E. Wooley, president of Mount Holyoke College; Ellen F. Pendleton, president of Wellesley College; and Bertha M. Moody, dean of Radcliffe College. Their prominence was important in developing the school's finances and attracting the best students.[6]

To gain acceptance at Lowthorpe, applicants needed to demonstrate an interest in plants or gardens, have "a high school education or its equivalent, and be in good health."[7] The coursework for a major in landscape architecture was intensive and lasted three years. It included architectural drafting, freehand and perspective drawing, construction, surveying, site engineering, history of architecture and landscape architecture, soils, plant materials, elementary forestry, botany, and entomology. It was a program worthy of any modern department of landscape architecture and included an emphasis on horticulture that is rarely found today. What usually set the women who completed landscape architecture programs apart from their male colleagues was, in fact, their superior plantsmanship. Upon completion of the program, students received a certificate rather than a degree or diploma. Regrettably, the school was unsuccessful in several attempts to affiliate with a college and thus gain accreditation.

2.2 Lowthorpe
School of Landscape
Architecture and
entry gardens
(c. 1925). Courtesy
Lord & Schryver
Conservancy, Anne
M. Kingery Library.

Schryver seemed to enjoy every moment of her three years at Lowthorpe.
Being introduced to the tools and techniques of a professional discipline,
learning how to draw and draft artistic plans, and becoming acquainted with
the proper use of "plant materials"—as well as working with such leading
professional women as Elizabeth Leonard Strang—all these opportunities
were thrilling to the young artist (figure 2.3). So was the sheer pleasure of
working and living with a small group of young women. Schryver and her
five classmates took on pet names; made up skits, jokes, and cartoons for
each other's entertainment; and chatted away in the studio while working
on their plans. It was a most congenial sisterhood, and Schryver lovingly
recorded their shared moments in her notebooks. Many years later, she
remembered three of them best: Joanna C. Diman who became a lifelong

A COUNTRY ESTATE
CROSS SECTION THRU A-A
LANDSCAPE EXCHANGE   CLASS-B PROBLEM-II
SCALE ONE INCH EQUALS EIGHT FEET

2.3 Edith Schryver's class assignment "Country Estate" cross section (c. 1922). Courtesy University of Oregon Libraries, Special Collections and University Archives, Coll 098, Lord & Schryver architectural records.

friend, Florence Stroh, and Mary Lawrence.[8] Edith typed up lengthy lecture notes from each of her courses, added handwritten comments and sketches, and then placed them in binders; she kept these binders in the office of Lord and Schryver for the rest of her life.[9] They are now preserved in the University of Oregon's archives.

At Lowthorpe, Schryver was free—free to extend her artistic talents, to make new friends, to study hard, and to impress the faculty (figure 2.4). With her fellow students, she went on guided fieldtrips to public and private gardens, explored numerous sites of horticultural excellence such as the Arnold Arboretum, and viewed exhibitions at the Massachusetts Horticultural Society. She undertook part-time employment in Boston with Elizabeth Leonard Strang (1886–1948) and two other well-established landscape architects who taught at Lowthorpe: Harold Hill Blossom (1879–1935) and Elizabeth Greenleaf Pattee (1893–1991).

Strang was an excellent role model for the young women students. She was born Elizabeth Leonard in New York State in 1886, and in 1910 became the first woman to graduate from Cornell's "Outdoor Art," or landscape architecture, program. After working for short periods with two firms in the United States and one in London, she returned to America and joined the city planning office of John Nolen in Cambridge, Massachusetts. At that time, city planning was a very unusual field for a woman to enter. Nolen was on the board of Lowthorpe, and, immensely impressed by Leonard's work, he recommended her for a teaching position there, which she accepted in 1913. She also worked as an assistant for Ellen Shipman in her Plainfield, New Hampshire, office.

Strang transformed Lowthorpe's design program by adding courses in history, design theory, engineering, and planting design, to make it more challenging and comprehensive. She strove to inspire enthusiasm and confidence in her students. In 1915, she married the writer Robert Strang and changed her name to Elizabeth Leonard Strang. They moved to Leominster, Massachusetts, where she opened an office in her home. Strang wrote extremely well and published four dozen articles on design issues often faced by middle-class homeowners. One of the aspects she frequently addressed was "a certain quality that went beyond good design and adequate planting . . . called the 'garden's personality.'"[10] In 1923 she wrote, "A garden correctly designed may still fail in that touch of charm which calls forth a responsive thrill from the heart of every true garden lover."[11] Creating a garden with charm was to become a notable theme in Lord and Schryver's practice, too. When Strang retired from teaching in the late 1920s she was a well-respected member of the American Society of Landscape Architects (ASLA).[12]

2.4 Edith Schryver as a student (early 1920s). Courtesy University of Oregon Libraries, Special Collections and University Archives, Coll 098, Lord & Schryver architectural records.

Schryver performed well in her Lowthorpe courses, and her work was highly regarded. For her project in Senior Planting Design, during her final year, Schryver created a plan for a seaside garden that was so beautifully rendered the school chose to reproduce it in their annual catalog for 1925–1926 (figure 2.5).[13] Her senior thesis was also impressive—an idealized master plan for a school of landscape architecture for women in a similar location and of a similar size as Lowthorpe. She named her school "Wynndie-Lea" and provided a general design for its very complex sequence of spaces as well as a number of highly detailed planting plans (figure 2.6; plate 2). Following her second year at Lowthorpe, Schryver successfully completed a summer internship at Brook Place, Ellen Shipman's office in Plainfield (near Cornish), New Hampshire. In 1923, when Schryver graduated from Lowthorpe, Shipman immediately recruited her for the Manhattan office as a junior draftsperson.

Elizabeth Lord's experience at Lowthorpe may have varied somewhat from that of Schryver's: Lord was older—thirty-nine—more worldly and more widely traveled when she arrived. And yet, the school still presented her with new and challenging experiences. Only two other students from west of the Mississippi were in her class year.[14] Lord arrived at Lowthorpe in the autumn of 1926, joined the European summer tour of 1927, and returned to do some of the 1927–1928 coursework. She enrolled in the summer course of 1928, which may have allowed her to complete the program by November 1928, even though she had not been there a full three years. Lord received her graduation certificate with the class of 1929.[15]

Prior to Lowthorpe, Lord had already gained significant practical experience in horticulture by working with her mother. Elizabeth's talent had been recognized in 1922 when she was appointed by the Illahee Country Club of Salem to improve the club grounds.[16] She won a second prize from the Oregon Floral Club in March 1923 for an herbaceous border design combining shrubs, bulbs, and perennials in a balanced planting scheme (figure 2.7). The border received high praise from garden journalist Jesse A. Correy, who described the composition, which "embraces a wide number of subjects, but they are so arranged to bring out the individuality of each plant, provide a continuity of blooms and well-arranged color groupings, with effective backgrounds of shrubs and tall growing perennials.... All the plants for the garden ... are raised by Mrs. Lord or her daughter."[17] And in July 1924, *House & Garden* magazine published two photographs that Lord had submitted of a perennial border she and her mother had designed. The caption read, "Two Seasons in a Western Garden: The Garden of Mrs. William P. Lord at Salem, Oregon."[18] Mrs. Lord saw the publication on the last day of her life, 4 July 1924, while hospitalized in Salem.[19]

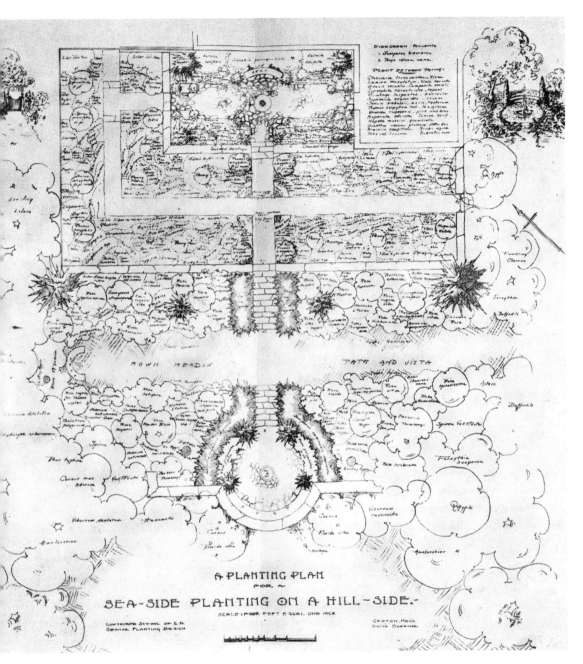

2.5 Edith Schryver's class assignment "Sea-Side Garden" planting plan, in the 1925/1926 Lowthorpe School catalog (1923). Courtesy Lord & Schryver Conservancy, Anne M. Kingery Library.

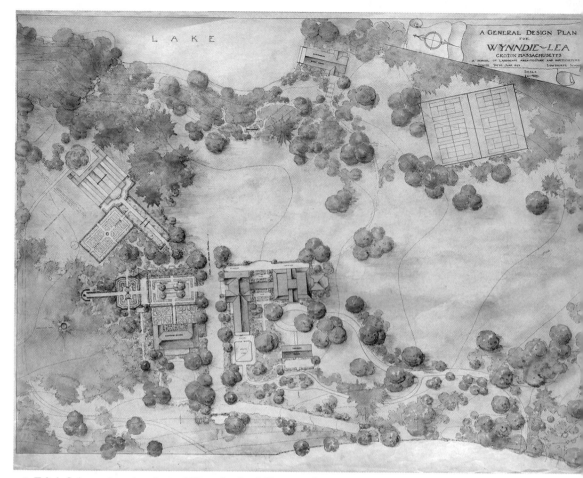

2.6 Edith Schryver's senior thesis, "Wynndie-Lea" (June 1923).
Courtesy University of Oregon Libraries, Special Collections and
University Archives, Coll 098, Lord & Schryver architectural records.

Schryver is likely to have seen the article, too, as she subscribed to *House & Garden* as well as several prominent garden magazines during her time working for Ellen Shipman. She later had the volumes bound as references and kept them in the office at Gaiety Hollow, where they remain to this day.

Lord received good grades for her projects at Lowthorpe, although her graphic design skills did not display the delicacy and sophistication of Schryver's (plate 3). There is no senior thesis project among the plans she saved, and fewer of her notebooks survived, so we must rely on Schryver's records from Lowthorpe for an account of their experiences during the 1920s.

May in this border brings the Darwin Tulips, edged with Royal Blue Forget-me-nots. For a background there is the lattice and the up-springing growth of healthy perennial clumps. Against these the Tulip colors, in all their variations, show to advantage

The Tulips go and in their place Foxgloves, Pyrethrums and Columbines flower. June brings Delphiniums, Lupins, Canterbury Bells and Sweet William. July claims Hollyhocks and Phlox and the autumn gaily colored Asters, Dahlias, Zinnias and Marigolds

TWO SEASONS IN A WESTERN GARDEN

The Garden of Mrs. William P. Lord at Salem, Oregon

2.7 "The Garden of Mrs. William P. Lord at Salem, Oregon," *House & Garden* magazine (July 1924). Courtesy Lord & Schryver Conservancy, Anne M. Kingery Library.

By 1927 Edith Schryver had decided to take a sabbatical from Shipman's office. She was busy planning her own "grand tour" of European gardens when she saw the advertisement for a program jointly sponsored by the Cambridge School of Architecture and Landscape Architecture for Women and the Lowthorpe School. She signed on with encouragement from the tour's director Henry Atherton Frost, a faculty member at Harvard and cofounder of the Cambridge School.

The faculty of the two design schools for women, the Cambridge School and Lowthorpe, wanted to create a more collaborative relationship by offering the joint European study tour. Like the grand tours of the eighteenth-century British aristocracy, the study tour would introduce the participants to the great historic monuments of Europe, including country houses, villas, and palaces, and their associated gardens. The tour was limited to twenty women, most of them students at the Cambridge School. They came from around the United States, as well as Hawaii.[20] Mr. Frost, Mrs. Joel H. Metcalf, and Mrs. Edward Unwin from England would lead the group. The tour offered the students the opportunity to not only visit sites, but also to sketch, measure, and photograph them, a classical training method for the design fields.

Elizabeth Lord, completing her first year at Lowthorpe, also enrolled, and the storied meeting between Lord and Schryver took place while sailing toward Europe on the SS *Andania II*. In the coming weeks, the two grew closer as they recognized that they shared very similar tastes and interests. Although both Lord and Schryver's notebooks from this adventure have survived, it is difficult to determine exactly which itineraries they followed and which were "wish lists" of sites they hoped to see. Their attention was focused on the monuments and gardens they were visiting, and almost all their notes refer to their personal responses to the locations, the designs, and occasionally to each other. These are incorporated with sketches and measured drawings.

Arriving in Glasgow on 19 June 1927, the group traveled overland to Edinburgh. From there they departed in vans for a tour of the English country houses, historic villages, cathedrals, and landscapes that included a wide variety of historic sites: from the seventeenth-century Charlton House in the picturesque Cotswolds to the early-twentieth-century masterpiece Hidcote Manor designed by its owner Lawrence Johnston (an expatriate American). Johnston's estate included a small village, substantial farmland, and extensive gardens renowned for their beauty. He placed formal "garden rooms" based on specific color and planting schemes near the manor house and gradually merged them with wild gardens on the periphery, leading to views of the countryside's rolling meadows.

On 16 July the rest of their group continued to France, while Schryver and Lord flew to Calais and then on to Belgium. They traveled overland through Germany, stopping at Cologne, Bonn, to see Beethoven's House and in Heidelberg, Rothenberg, Nuremberg, and Munich to enjoy the opera and the art galleries. They were able to rejoin their tour in Venice. Lord, however, went on by herself to Vincenza because she greatly admired the Renaissance architect Palladio and wished to see his buildings. She met the tour in Florence, and the two friends were happy to be reunited. They visited art galleries, the Boboli Gardens, and the villas of Fiesole. For one day, the tour went to Siena to see the great black-and-white marble cathedral and to watch the traditional horse race, the Palio, held in the central piazza. In the following days, the group traveled to Lucca, Perugia, Assisi, Orvieto, Viterbo, and Rome.

Early in September, Schryver and Lord again left the group to visit historic Spanish and Moorish sites together. While working in Shipman's office, Schryver had been asked to draft two Spanish-inspired garden designs.[21] How exciting to finally see them in reality. She carefully arranged their agenda to travel first to the island of Majorca, where they had received permission to visit several private estates. At La Granja, Lord commented, "famous old estate belonging to the Fortunys ... garden in rear too crowded and rather grotesque."[22] They returned via ferry to Barcelona and continued overland to Madrid and then south to Andalusia. Here the beauty of the grand Moorish palaces, exquisite gardens, and mosques overwhelmed them. In Granada they toured the Alhambra and the Generalife. In Seville they visited the Alcazar, the Casa de Pilatos, the Casa de Americanos in which Washington Irving had resided, and the nineteenth-century park of Maria Luisa, where Schryver rejoiced, "Drive through park. Almost fell out of carriage. Every detail of pergola, fountains, hedges, just as they have been pictured" (figure 2.8).[23] Of the Court of the Oranges (Patio de los Naranjos) in Seville, Schryver perceptively observed, "In Spain all trees are surrounded by wells ... connected by rills for irrigation." She was referring to an ancient Middle Eastern technique brought to Spain by the Moors, where plantings are linked by irrigation channels and watered by periodic flooding. Not every observer would have noted the difference from European techniques of watering.

Both Lord and Schryver were enchanted with the gardens and architecture of Moorish Spain and created more notes, photographs, and diagrams of them than those of any other country. Their firsthand study of these gardens would greatly enhance their future design of Spanish-inspired gardens in the Northwest, especially that of the Jarmans' garden in Salem.

Whether Lord and Schryver returned to northern Europe by traveling through France, to engage in more sightseeing, we cannot be sure. Their itinerary is unclear. They sailed home to New York in October 1928 and

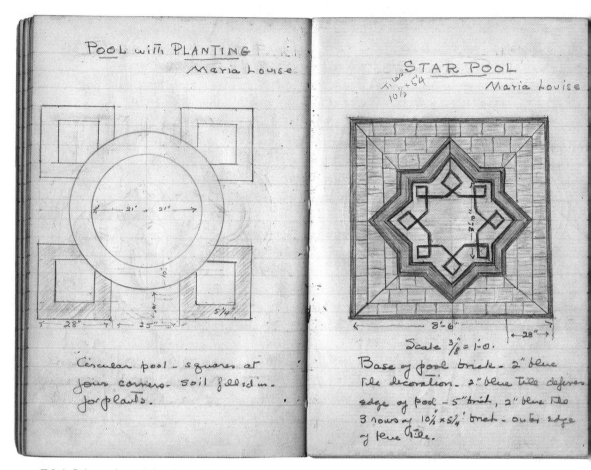

2.8 Edith Schryver's pool sketches in Maria Louisa Park, Seville, Spain, during the European tour (1927). Courtesy University of Oregon Libraries, Special Collections and University Archives, Coll 098, Lord & Schryver architectural records.

returned to their previous positions working and studying—Schryver in Manhattan and Lord in Groton. Having formed a close bond, they maintained a correspondence and occasionally visited each other. By 1928, they had made the decision to move to Salem, Oregon, and open their own practice. They brought with them their travel journals, school projects, beautifully rendered plans, multiple notebooks, photograph albums, and Schryver's senior thesis. In April 1929, only four months after they had arrived, the Monroe Gilbert Studio in Salem mounted an exhibit of their landscape plans, bringing public attention to the artistry of their work and to their new business (figure 2.9).[24] They would pursue the career that Richardson Wright, the influential editor of *House & Garden* magazine, had enthusiastically promoted when he declared, "Landscape architecture is one of those professions into which women, when suitably trained, fit with harmony and grace."[25]

Mr. and Mrs. Monroe Gilbert

invite you to view an

Exhibit of Garden Plans

the work of

Miss Elizabeth Lord and Miss Edith Schryver

Landscape Architects

MONROE GILBERT STUDIO   THURSDAY EVENING, APRIL 4. 1929
UPSTAIRS AT 147 N. COMMERCIAL ST.   SALEM, OREGON

2.9 Lord and Schryver's garden plan exhibition announcement card (1929). Courtesy Lord & Schryver Conservancy, Anne M. Kingery Library.

3

The Cornish Colony
and Ellen Shipman

One of the most hopeful spots which any believer in the future of American garden art can visit is the little New Hampshire town of Cornish.
—Frances Duncan, 1906

Their tour of European gardens had inspired the two women with a wealth of ideas that would enrich their work for years to come, but prior to that trip Edith Schryver had already had the opportunity to be immersed in a community of artists and to work with several important professional designers. These experiences would prove fundamental to the development of the professional style embraced by Lord and Schryver.

During the summer of 1922, Edith Schryver accepted an internship with Ellen Shipman's practice in Plainfield, New Hampshire, near the famed art colony of Cornish, New Hampshire.[1] The young designer had much to learn from a recognized master in her field. Schryver's immersion that summer in the world of artists, architects, writers, and musicians of Cornish gave greater depth to her formal education at Lowthorpe. It exposed her to a community where women valued creative work and seriously pursued professional aspirations.[2] She was influenced by design ideas from such garden aficionados as the artist Stephen Parrish, his son Maxfield Parrish, the architect Charles A. Platt, and the landscape architect Rose Standish Nichols. For each of them, the view of the broad Connecticut River Valley and the steep hills with Mount Ascutney in the distance became "borrowed scenery" for their gardens, scenery that no one person owned but all could enjoy (figure 3.1).

Located in the hills of western New Hampshire, the upper Connecticut River Valley was pervaded with an atmosphere of serenity. In 1885, the sculptor Augustus Saint-Gaudens (1848–1907) and his wife Augusta were among the first to "discover" the region (plate 4). Soon other artists, writers, and

musicians followed, and Cornish became more of a year-round community with a vibrant social life and stimulating culture beyond the workday routine. The members of the Cornish Colony bought and restored the town's older houses and then created gardens around them according to their own personal tastes. Frances Duncan, one of the literary members of the colony, brought national fame to their gardens in her articles for *Century Magazine* and other popular periodicals. She described the Cornish gardens as "livable, lovable spots, on very intimate terms with their owners, . . . [each] an outgrowth of the house, an out-of-door living room, to be used and changed if one pleases, until one finds the best possible arrangement" (figure 3.2).[3] Schryver absorbed this notion of the garden as an extension of one's home, designed for living as well as for viewing, a space that might possess a personal character.

When Schryver came to New Hampshire in 1922, Ellen (Biddle) Shipman had been part of the Cornish community for almost thirty years. Shipman and her husband, Louis Evan Shipman, a playwright, had first visited Cornish in 1894, initially renting, then buying an old farmhouse in the nearby town of Plainfield. They named their home Brook Place, and

3.1 Charles Platt's garden design, High Court, Cornish, New Hampshire (2018). Courtesy of author and Max Blumberg, owner.

3.2 View from the front of Charles Platt's house, Cornish, New Hampshire (1910s). Courtesy Platt Family.

Mrs. Shipman oversaw its restoration and interior décor, as well as the design of its gardens. Unlike many of the famous homes in the area, Brook Place lay in the valley and had a very limited view. Shipman divided her landscape into garden rooms, separated by low stone walls. She edged the beds with wooden planks and used small hemlocks, sheared into cubes, to mark their corners. The beds were densely planted with an abundance of herbs, flowers, vines, and shrubs in the spirit of the Colonial Revival so popular in New England at that time.[4]

In 1910, Louis Shipman moved to London, leaving his wife and three small children behind; the couple divorced in 1927. Forced to support her family, Ellen Shipman began to practice landscape design from her home. She already had significant experience creating her own much-admired gardens. The artist and architect Charles A. Platt (1861–1933), another very influential member of the Cornish Colony, agreed to teach her how to draft professional plans and construction details, perhaps recognizing her potential value to his practice.[5] Shipman, in return, designed planting plans for his projects. By 1912, Shipman was working closely with Platt on many large properties across the country from Philadelphia to Seattle.[6]

It was the height of the Country Place Era, 1890 to 1930, and wealthy Americans, aspiring to the lifestyle of the European aristocracy, built grandiose homes with elaborate landscapes in rural areas. These "country houses" were the epitome of American style and taste. Proud owners employed architects who had learned Beaux-Arts principles by training in Boston or Paris. They designed according to a formula that created a hierarchy of spaces, often symmetrically arranged, and with exaggerated classical detailing. The plan required both house and garden to be firmly related through structural lines that extended into the landscape, creating spatial continuity between the two. Axial lines from the principal windows or doors into the garden created a further visual connection between architectural and landscape elements.

Charles Platt's influence was everywhere apparent in Cornish. In 1890, Platt designed his first residential commission, High Court, for the art patron Annie Lazarus, bringing a vision of the Italian Renaissance villa, his architectural ideal, from the Roman hills to the New England countryside. Platt had carefully studied villas on two extensive tours of Italy. He organized his gardens around architectonic features such as terraces, walled compartments, and pavilions to serve as a transition between the house and its site. To explain the motivation behind his design of High Court, Platt revealed his underlying philosophy of garden design, a philosophy to which Schryver would subscribe: "One still wished to be at home while out-of-doors; so the garden was designed as another apartment, the terraces and groves still others, where one might walk about and find a place suitable to the hour of the day and the feeling of the moment and still be in the sacred portion of the globe dedicated to one's self."[7]

Platt's enthusiasm overflowed in his publications, first in journal articles and then as a book, *Italian Gardens* (1894). Together with Edith Wharton's *Italian Villas and Their Gardens*, published in 1905, with illustrations by Maxfield Parrish, they established a marked taste for Italianate formal design among the American elite. Platt's work for many affluent clients made him one of the leaders of America's return to formal landscape design.[8]

Schryver would certainly have seen Charles Platt's own home in Cornish. The house was one of his most beautiful and tasteful designs, a hybrid of an Italian villa and a spacious nineteenth-century New England home (figure 3.3). Platt classicized the building with a piazza, or porch, on the west side accented by Doric columns, and painted the building a pure white, in stark contrast to the lush greenery of the landscape. His own garden was far less formal than those he designed for his patrons. It lay in the valley below High Court, but still retained a stunning view of the Connecticut River and Mount Ascutney. Plantings were contained in narrow terraces below the front of the house, looking out to the view, with flower beds separated by small brick paths. On the hillside, well below the house, a grove of stately white pines rose above the field, providing a shaded destination for their

3.3 Charles Platt's house, Cornish, New Hampshire (2018). Courtesy of the author.

outings. And Platt employed a device that appeared frequently in Cornish gardens—a low stone wall, a hedge, or a fence to create a line separating the middle ground from the distant background (plate 5). Schryver would adopt this technique for Lord and Schryver's practice when they designed larger properties with distant views.

Shipman's design style derived elements from Platt and all the Cornish gardens she knew so well, from the Colonial Revival to the Italianate.[9] The Colonial Revival encouraged the creation of lushly planted "dooryard" gardens close to the house, laid out along a simple geometrical plan. Stephen Parrish's garden at Northcote was a perfect example (figure 3.4). Where the climate allowed, these beds were frequently edged with clipped boxwood, a hallmark of the Colonial Revival. Such gardens held an abundance of "old-fashioned" herbaceous plants, both annuals and perennials. Often the line between so-called old-fashioned and Colonial Revival gardens was hazy. Both held a nostalgic view of the past and promoted the peaceful charm of gardens as an antidote to the haste and noise of modern life. Many of the plants used were not, in fact, from the colonial period but were first used by gardeners in the late nineteenth century.[10] Shipman believed she had seen a return to the ideals of "early traditional gardening," when New England dooryard gardens expressed domesticity and simplicity.[11]

Shipman's plans for her clients often began with a formal axial garden similar to Platt's Italianate formula. However, her expert knowledge of

Chapter 3

3.4 Stephen Parrish's house and garden, Northcote, Cornish, New Hampshire (1910s). Courtesy Dartmouth College, Rauner Special Collections Library.

plants and artistic compositions set her work apart, more so than her skill at spatial design, as she had never received formal training in architecture or landscape architecture. Her solo work often involved replanting or restoring older gardens, bringing new vibrancy to them with sophisticated planting plans. Shipman also worked on many "country house" projects of an impressive scale, as well as public and institutional sites, completing a remarkable array of approximately six hundred projects during her thirty-five years in practice.[12]

An advocate of women in landscape architecture, Shipman employed only women in her office (figure 3.5). She offered them opportunities to advance that they were often denied in the male-dominated profession. She preferred to employ graduates of Lowthorpe, where she served as an adviser, because she believed they received a superior education. At times the women who came to work as Shipman's assistants had more formal education in spatial design than their employer, but it was always clear who was in charge. In 1914, Shipman hired her first assistant, Elizabeth Leonard Strang, to draft plans for an estate garden in Bennington, Vermont. Strang

3.5 Ellen Shipman
in her Beekman
Place office, New
York, New York
(1920s). Courtesy
Cornell University
Library, Division of
Rare and Manuscript
Collections.

developed the distinctive style of graphic layout that became the standard for Shipman's office. Around the edges of the plan, she drew small vignettes of the architectural features—dovecotes, gateways, arbors, and so on. She also added handwritten notes regarding horticultural needs and seasonal changes. This gave her landscape plans a charming appearance that was much appreciated at the time.[13] Strang later taught this technique to her students at Lowthorpe, and Schryver would utilize it for Lord and Schryver's clients.

After spending her summer internship with Shipman, Schryver returned twice to Cornish in the autumn of 1922 with her Lowthorpe classmates (figure 3.6). On their first visit, the students toured Saint-Gaudens' Italianate gardens at Aspet.[14] On their second trip, they visited The Oaks, the home of artist Maxfield Parrish (1870–1966), whose landscape was far less formal than that of Saint-Gaudens. The house lay along a ridge shaded by ancient white and red oaks. A series of shallow terraces on the hillside below the house offered a dramatic view of the river valley. The terraces were enclosed by low stone walls built by craftsmen who imbedded them with decorative patterns (figure 3.7). Thus, Parrish expressed a combination of formal and rustic, or local, traditions in his garden.[15] He had no large flower garden, but narrow borders overflowed with shrubs and perennials. And at the edge of the garden, he built a large, plain Tuscan arch to form the boundary with the natural wooded landscape beyond, a singular Italian gesture. Schryver was quite impressed by The Oaks and wrote in her journal, "Very delightful. Large house set upon a hill with a broad outlook over valley of [Mount] Ascutney in the distance. No formal display of flowers. Small division of lower terrace especially effective. Large pool, very simple, flat coping set almost flush in simple turf. . . . Iron grill set in opening in wall to suggest an[d] invite inspection of the view beyond." Inside the front cover of her notebook, she pasted a newspaper photograph of the handsome artist.[16]

Shipman's practice grew steadily, and by the early 1920s she decided to move her principal office to Manhattan, a location that was more prestigious and more convenient for her clientele, while keeping her house in New Hampshire. She purchased a brick townhouse at 21 Beekman Place by the East River; it was large enough to provide a home and an office, a studio on the third floor, and two apartments. In 1923, Edith Schryver became a full-time member of the practice; she moved to New York and rented one of the apartments. A visiting journalist described a glimpse into Shipman's studio, "of girls in blue smocks bending over drafting tables," one of whom may have been Schryver.[17]

3.6 Edith Schryver, second from the left, picnicking with her friends (1922). Courtesy University of Oregon Libraries, Special Collections and University Archives, Coll 098, Lord & Schryver architectural records.

3.7 Maxfield Parrish's house and garden, The Oaks, Cornish, New Hampshire (1910s). Courtesy Dartmouth College, Rauner Special Collections Library.

Schryver was delighted to be living in Manhattan. Her classmate and friend from Lowthorpe, Joanna C. Diman, spent two years in the office, as did an earlier Lowthorpe graduate, (Ellen) Louise Payson.[18] When Payson left the firm in 1927 to establish her own office, Diman went to work for her.[19] Schryver later recalled, "We were free-swinging career girls, and no one questioned us. In the '20s everyone trained for a career. All the girls in my class [at Lowthorpe] did; we all had careers. You didn't get married in those days until 26 or 27, so we didn't have any trouble being accepted. We were career women first."[20] She relished the ready access to concerts, theater, opera, cinema, and dance and budgeted very carefully in order to indulge in them. Each summer, Shipman and some of the office staff packed up and headed back to Brook Place in New Hampshire. For five years, Schryver was part of this seasonal migration.

Schryver refined her design skills in Shipman's office and learned how to manage clients with sizeable projects. Her expert draftsmanship and project management skills were much appreciated. After an initial site visit and consultation with the client, Shipman would make rough sketches of the design concept and send them back to the office.[21] She also shared her field notes and photographs with the staff. Professional engineers usually provided the site survey, and the grading and drainage plans, while Schryver and her colleagues had to work out the design details and draft the finished drawings, including the construction and planting plans.

The 1920s was the very height of Shipman's landscape practice, and her staff of five to ten women worked hard to maintain the productivity. One of the many large projects Schryver drafted in 1926 was the landscape for Mrs. Henry V. Greenough's estate in Brookline, Massachusetts (figure 3.8).[22] Shipman located a formal garden with axial paths close to the house and a naturalistic garden farther away. Schryver's "sketch plan" defined the areas, the circulation (paths) and an intensive planting scheme to provide seasonal color. She drew the final plan on linen with black ink, adding five vignettes to illustrate special garden features such as the naturalistic pond and waterfall. Her lengthy horticultural notes about the "wild garden" occupied the rest of the plan. Intended to look completely natural, the wild garden included ornamental exotics as well as native species. High brick walls gave the garden privacy and formed the backdrop for informal groups of trees and shrubs.

Schryver also created plans for two Spanish-themed gardens: the Evander B. Schley estate in Far Hills, New Jersey (1924–1926) and the Mrs. Henry D. Shelden estate in Grosse Pointe, Michigan (1927).[23] For the Schley estate, Schryver encircled the plan with vignettes of Spanish-inspired features such as a tiled wall fountain. In 1929, Lord and Schryver would incorporate an identical wall fountain in the Jarmans' garden in Oregon. For the Shelden estate, Schryver generated numerous sketches of a Spanish-style garden before settling on an octagonal form (figure 3.9).[24] In each of these cases, it was necessary for her to create garden areas with the correct proportions and scale to complement the architecture. Although she would not see an actual Moorish garden until her European tour of 1927, she was able to achieve this with remarkable accuracy based on her studies.

Over time, Schryver became a valued member of Shipman's team, an office manager and a trusted employee. When she left the practice in 1928 to move to Oregon, Shipman not only allowed her to take twenty-five blueprints of designs that she and others had drafted—plans now archived at the University of Oregon—but also generously recommended that her former clients, the Merrills of Seattle, now work with Lord and Schryver, Landscape Architects.

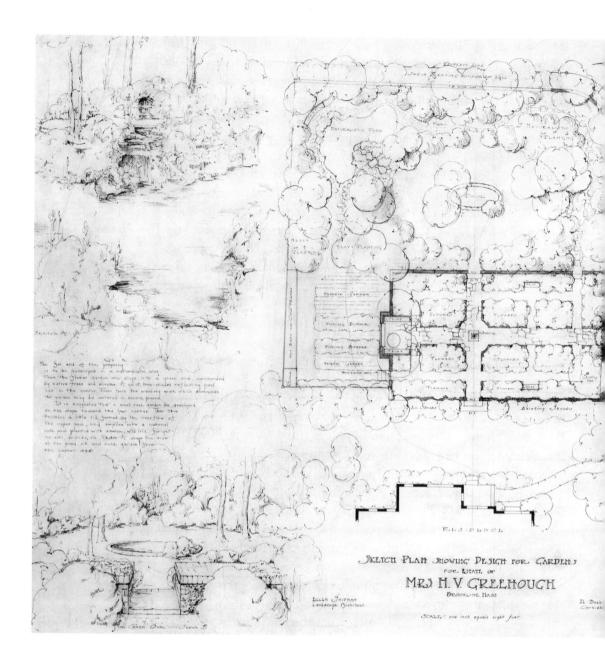

The far end of the property
is to be developed in a naturalistic way.
From the flower garden one steps into a green oval, surrounded
by native trees and shrubs. A quiet, tree-shaded reflecting pool
lies in the center. From here the woodsy walk which surrounds
the garden may be entered in several places.

It is suggested that a small rock garden be developed
on the slope toward the far corner. Thru this
trickles a little rill formed by the overflow of
the upper pool, and empties into a natural
rock pool planted with azaleas, wild iris, forget-
me-nots, orchids, etc. Sketch A shows the view
of the pond, rill and rock garden from
the corner walk.

SECTION A

THE GREEN OVAL — SKETCH B

SKETCH PLAN SHOWING DESIGN FOR GARDEN
FOR ESTATE OF
MRS H. V. GREENOUGH
BROOKLINE MASS

ELLEN SHIPMAN
Landscape Architect

SCALE: one inch equals eight feet

21 Deck
Cornish

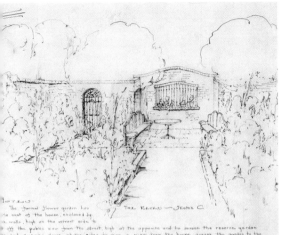

THE RECESS — SKETCH C

[handwritten text block, largely illegible]

The formal flower garden lies
to east of the house, enclosed by
...walls, high on the street side to
...off the public view from the street, high at the opposite end to screen the reserve garden
...and curving down at the sides to give a view from the house across the garden to the
...and trees beyond. Crossing the lawn from the house, the garden is entered by a flight
...few brick steps, giving into the main cross path, along which there is a vista over the
...up another few steps and into the green area with its tree-shaded pool, and beyond a
...of the door in the wall (Sketch B) It is suggested that a sundial or other appropriate fea-
...to be placed in the circle at the intersection of the main garden paths. In the high wall at the
...is a niche and a wall fountain, with its continuous trickle and suggestion of coolness in
...summer. In the niche is a narrow ledge for growing vines, and a pedestal on which a figure
...to be placed. It is suggested that the basin and the ledge be cut to suitable shells as shown
...Sketch D. The north wall of the garden is recessed, providing a paved terrace for table
...seats. A grilled window at the back gives a glimpse into the reserve garden with
...bright picking border, and so creates an illusion distance to the garden and the
...greenery. A wide brick window ledge provides a place for pots of flowers and
...vines. An apple tree on either side of the terrace shades the recess, and
...makes it a pleasant place for serving afternoon tea.
...Behind the garden is a small reserve and vegetable garden, with a picking bor-
...of annuals on axis with main garden path where flat beds and cold frames are
...in against the high white lath fence. If desired, it is suggested that the fence at the
...here be formed into a small tool house with a flat roof. Such a shelter would be
...convenient for keeping flats, small tools, stakes, etc. A grilled door in the garden wall,
...a ramp for wheelbarrows gives easy access for carrying on the necessary upkeep
...in the garden

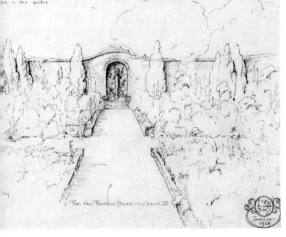

THE WALL FOUNTAIN NICHE — SKETCH D

JANUARY 1926

3.8 Edith Schryver's garden plan for Mrs. M. V. Greenough, in Ellen Shipman's office (1926). Courtesy University of Oregon Libraries, Special Collections and University Archives, Coll 098, Lord & Schryver architectural records. Frank Miller photo.

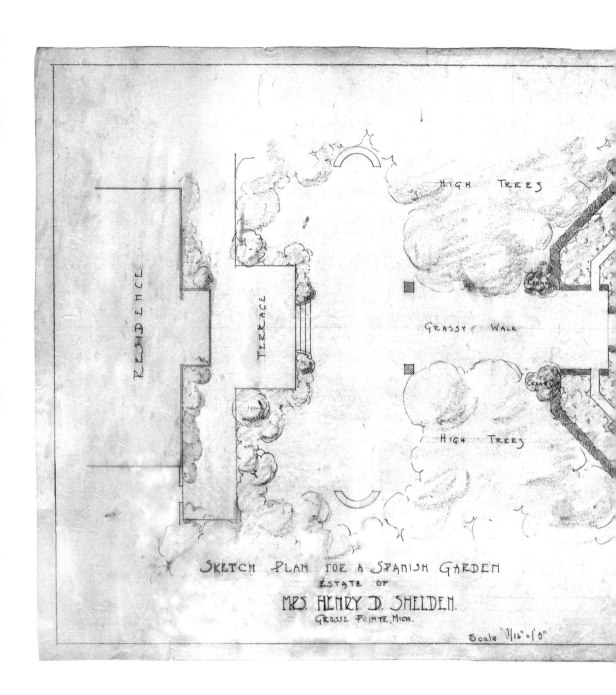

RESIDENCE

TERRACE

HIGH TREES

CEDAR

GRASSY WALK

CEDAR

HIGH TREES

SKETCH PLAN FOR A SPANISH GARDEN
ESTATE OF
MRS. HENRY D. SHELDEN.
GROSSE POINTE, MICH.

Scale 1/16" = 1' 0"

44

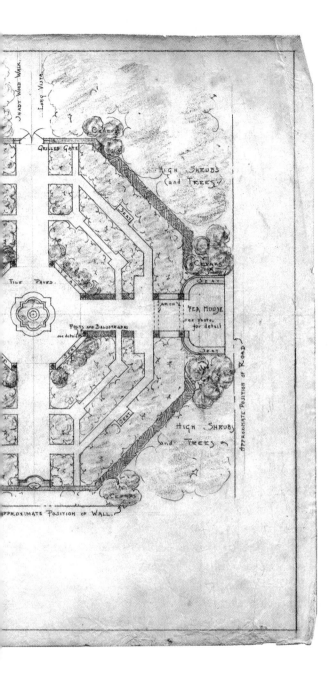

3.9 Edith Schryver's Spanish garden plan for Mrs. Henry Shelden, in Ellen Shipman's office (c. 1926). Courtesy University of Oregon Libraries, Special Collections and University Archives, Coll 098, Lord & Schryver architectural records.

4

A Venture Launched

> We are having quite a lot of work here. We are greatly encouraged
> and are as happy as two girls could be. What everybody has called a
> venture is becoming a profitable business.
> —Elizabeth Lord, 1929

For Elizabeth Lord, returning to Salem, Oregon, meant going home. After traveling for two years following her mother's death in 1924, and then spending two years in Massachusetts at Lowthorpe, she would make a new beginning with Edith Schryver in the old family home. For Schryver, the move to Salem from New York was an adventure with great potential for exciting personal and professional challenges.

The two traveled from New York to San Francisco in November 1928, probably by train. Two of Lord's more adventurous friends from Salem, Mrs. Bernard O. (Agnes) Schucking and her mother, Mrs. A. N. Gilbert, drove to San Francisco to meet them and bring them home.[1] After several days in the Bay Area, their party drove north on the Redwood Highway and the Roosevelt Highway (today's Route 1), giving Schryver her first direct experience of the spectacular western scenery. Although there is no record of her impressions of the Pacific Coast from this trip, it must have affected her strongly—the sheer drama and scale of the landscape, the mountainous shoreline with huge, angular rock outcroppings and the forests of towering redwoods and Sitka spruce.

After several days of travel, Schryver at last saw the broad Willamette Valley spreading to either side of the Willamette River. Unlike the Hudson River of Schryver's childhood, the Willamette River flows south to north through a 150-mile-long valley to join the Columbia River near Portland.[2] The valley is bound on either side by mountain ranges—to the west the Coast Range and to the east the Cascades—which would sometimes appear faintly in the distance. Small hills of ancient volcanic rock occur randomly throughout the valley, rising like islands above its floor. These hills remained forested while level areas of oak savannah had been burned by the Kalapuya tribes to maintain the openness for hunting. Later, farmers cleared the level land for their agricultural fields. These spread to a width of seventy-five miles near Oregon's capital city, Salem. Both north and south of Salem, the river forms and reforms braided channels and sloughs, shallow backwaters that fill in times of high water. It was this valley, with its forests, grasslands, deep rich alluvial soils, and the availability of land, that attracted Euro-American settlers to the area in the mid-1800s and led to the creation of the state of Oregon.

In 1928, Salem was still a young and evolving city. Founded in 1842, it became the state capital in 1859. State government, along with water-powered textile mills and processing plants for the valley's abundant agricultural products, provided a solid economic base for the city's growth. With a population around twenty-four thousand in an area of six square miles, Salem had been laid out on a grid pattern similar to most western cities. The downtown commercial center was small, but generous hundred-foot-wide avenues framed space for future growth. Residential neighborhoods surrounded the impressive capitol building and boasted a few large mansions; most of Salem had modest-sized homes on smaller lots. A network of many creeks and rills drained the relatively level landscape. They gave to the city a unique natural character and beauty that Lord's mother, Juliet Lord, had recognized and sought to preserve.

Lord and Schryver arrived in Salem just before Christmas 1928. Having left the Lord family home empty for almost four years, Lord needed time to ready it for their occupation. Estelle (Bush) Thayer, an old family friend and the eldest daughter of Asahel Bush, invited them to stay in her home while these preparations were under way. On their second evening in Salem, Lord and Schryver were invited to dine at Bush House, where Schryver met Miss Sally Bush for the first time. The two women quickly became close friends, and as Schryver later explained, "Miss Sally, Elizabeth and I were related in an entirely different way than most other people because we all loved plants."[3]

When Lord and Schryver came to the Northwest in anticipation of opening their practice, the architectural profession had been expanding rapidly. Since the end of World War I, formally trained architects built the larger homes and commercial buildings applying Beaux-Arts principles. Many modest-sized houses were built according to less formal patterns, including the popular bungalow. Landscape architecture in the Northwest, however, was viewed as an "elitist service—the prerogative of the wealthy."[4] The smaller homes of the middle class might be architecturally designed, but typically they were landscaped by their owners.[5] The front yards were for civic beauty, and great effort was made by proud owners to enhance them. Foundation shrubs screened the base of homes while rockeries were popular additions to sloping property edges. Residents valued the existing trees and planted many shade and flowering species to create attractive settings for their homes.

By the 1920s, the Northwest's residents had become more interested in the services of a landscape architect.[6] Between 1911 and 1929, four to seven professional firms listed their businesses in Polk's Directory of Portland each year. The only woman practicing landscape architecture in Oregon was Frances Holmes Gerke, whose office was in Portland. For several years, she listed her practice separately from that of her husband, Walter H. Gerke, even though they worked together.[7] Lord and Schryver were the first landscape architects in Salem to advertise, using Polk's Directory in 1929. This was only one of many ways they promoted their new business.

Wasting no time, Lord and Schryver compiled a list of 117 of Lord's social connections and designed a handsome announcement card (figure 4.1).[8] Lord wrote to one potential client on New Year's Day 1929, saying, "We have just arrived in Salem, which is my old home, and we intend to make this city our headquarters. . . . We are both enthusiastic over the great advantages which the Northwest has to offer in this profession, as the climate and the varied plant material is so favorable to the development of gardens which could be as beautiful and interesting as the older established ones in other parts of the country."[9] They decided on a fee schedule based on Schryver's experience in Shipman's office, but with lower pricing, as they recognized that most potential clients in Oregon were unfamiliar with the profession and its customary fees. To market their business, they composed

4.1 Lord and Schryver's business announcement (1929). Courtesy Lord & Schryver Conservancy, Anne M. Kingery Library.

ELIZABETH LORD
EDITH SCHRYVER
LANDSCAPE ARCHITECTS

ANNOUNCE THE OPENING OF AN OFFICE AT

796 SOUTH HIGH STREET

SALEM, OREGON

JANUARY 1ST, 1929   TELEPHONE 1124-J

several illustrated garden lectures to offer garden clubs and civic organizations. The Monroe Gilbert Studio, a Salem gallery and craft shop owned by Lord's friends, scheduled an exhibition of their landscape plans in April 1929, presenting the works as both visual art and graphic communication.[10] The society editor of the *Statesman* noted the opening reception alongside photographs of both women and a short announcement of their plans to live in Salem.[11] In May, the Art Institute of Seattle also invited them to exhibit their work in their annual architectural show, an invitation they accepted.[12] Without the support of a large firm or a professional network, Lord and Schryver had to work hard to launch their new business. They were tireless in their efforts.

➤➤➤ The Daniel B. and Edith M. Jarman Garden, 1929–1930

Next came the search for Lord and Schryver's first major client. In March 1929, Lord spotted a newspaper article in Salem's *Capital Journal* announcing that Daniel B. Jarman, a wealthy businessman from California, planned to build a villa for $75,000 (equivalent to $1,140,000 in 2020) in their neighborhood, Gaiety Hill.[13] The lot was only two blocks away from their home and a little more than half an acre in size. Mr. Jarman was moving his family from Santa Barbara, California, to Salem to manage a new J. C. Penney department store. But what interested them most was that Jarman had chosen to build his home in the Spanish Colonial Revival style, which was unique in Salem and unusual for Oregon at that time.

Lord and Schryver had delighted in the many Spanish gardens and parks they visited during their 1927 study tour of Europe, particularly the historic Moorish gardens of southern Spain. They found them extraordinarily beautiful for their integration of interior and exterior spaces, elegant architecture, and division of the landscape into garden rooms. They also admired the gardens' sophisticated use of water features and decorative elements, such as the colorful tilework, and their privacy. Their notebooks, sketches, measured drawings, and photographs from 1927 are testament to their enthusiasm and careful observation of this style. While in Shipman's employment between 1923 and 1928, Schryver was quite pleased to design an intricate "Sketch Plan for a Spanish Garden" for the estate of Mrs. Henry D. Shelden in Grosse Point, Michigan. She completed six renditions of the theme.[14] And one of the first illustrated lectures they gave, based on their European travels and photographs, was on Spanish gardens.

The Jarmans' proposed new residence presented a perfect opportunity for their fledgling business and Lord immediately wrote to Mr. Jarman on the very same day she read the article, describing their backgrounds and the advantages of employing their new practice.

Dear Mr. Jarman:

The Capital Journal this evening gave the news that you are intending to erect a home of Spanish architecture on the Hughes property on south High Street. Naturally this announcement is of great interest to Salem people and it is particularly to us—the reason I should like to explain.

Miss Schryver and I have entered the field of Landscape Architecture—both having received our education in the East. Salem is my old home; my interest in gardens covers many years. Miss Schryver has been associated for six years with Mrs. Ellen Shipman of New York City, one of the most prominent landscape architects. Much fine work has gone through her hands, gardens of all types including Spanish and Italian.

We both traveled five months abroad studying European gardens and remained over a month in Spain, devoting our time measuring garden details and studying the characteristics of Spanish garden design and planting with the architecture of the home.

If you would be interested in seeing our work in the past and examining our Spanish details we were able to obtain we would take great pleasure in showing them to you. I have been a neighbor and friend of Mr. and Mrs. Fry—your future neighbor—for many years. I am sure they would be glad to give you any information concerning me. We are greatly encouraged by the reception we have received in Salem. We find people greatly interested in our work and we are most enthusiastic over the possibility of beautifying many gardens.[15]

How could he fail to be impressed?

Less than a week later, Mrs. Jarman responded with a letter expressing the couple's interest.[16] By August of that year, Lord and Schryver, Landscape Architects, had presented them with a design, "Suggested Garden Treatment Plan," in a Spanish Colonial Revival style, with a square, four-part garden and a formal entrance court. This large-scale plan is a fine work of art executed in ink with a watercolor background, a technique Schryver had long practiced and now perfected. As they went forward, they developed a more complex plan for the site. Their final simplified design, "General Design Plan," seems to have been the one carried out (plate 6).[17]

The Jarmans selected Glen C. McAlister, an architect from Beverly Hills, to design their new home after admiring ones he had built in Southern California. McAlister catered to California's elite and specialized in building the Spanish Colonial Revival architecture so popular there at the time.[18] William F. Wyatt, the contractor hired to build the house, was also from California, and he brought his own crew to Salem. The Jarmans' house was very large and occupied two city lots, with a scenic view of Salem from the top of the hill. It had two wings extending at right angles from a stylized round tower, white stucco walls, and a red tile roof. The architect surrounded the lot with a low brick wall. It, too, was covered with stucco, painted white, and articulated every ten feet with short posts, a treatment that immediately distinguished the property from all the others in the neighborhood.

Lord and Schryver's plan drew the principal lines of the building out into the landscape to frame garden rooms, thus creating a cohesive spatial pattern. They laid out four formal areas adjacent to the house: an entrance court, a large flower garden with a traditional four-part plan, and two small terraced patios tucked neatly against the house. A narrow, curving drive extended from the southern boundary on Oak Street to the main entrance on the east side of the building.

McAlister had designed a very unusual entrance to the Jarmans' home. The front doorway was formed by a parabolic arch with a metal overhang and a heavy custom-made door. The entrance court by Lord and Schryver was elliptical in shape and had two sets of steps from the driveway up to the house, which were interrupted by a paved terrace with a Moorish-inspired fountain. Surrounding the entrance court were tiled posts with boxwood bushes planted on top of each one. A saucer magnolia (*Magnolia × soulangeana*) provided a vertical accent and shade. On the west side of the house, adjacent to the library, was a small paved terrace, and to the south of the living room was a paved court.

The largest garden was walled, almost square, and divided into four quarters, the oldest and most symbolic of ancient garden forms from the Middle East and the Moorish empire (figure 4.2). Measuring 80 feet by 90 feet, it centered on a large octagonal fountain. Each of the four surrounding beds was outlined in low boxwood, with the centers planted in grass (plate 7).[19] Schryver made the walls of this garden room almost seven feet high to create more privacy for the family. On the northern wall, Schryver located a tiled wall fountain (plate 8). The design was identical to a wall fountain she had created for the Evander B. Schley estate while in Shipman's office.[20] Along the western wall, she placed a wooden pergola, to be covered by two grape vines to shade the tiled benches below, like a Spanish ramada (figure 4.3). On the south wall was a seating niche with two tiled benches facing each other. In between them, a carved wooden grill offered a screened view of the street (figure 4.4). All the brick walls were stuccoed, painted white, and inlaid with panels of colorful tiles. The overall effect was subtly dramatic.

Lord and Schryver intended to keep the plant palette for the Jarmans' landscape rather simple, but a review of just one 1929 order to Mountain View Floral Company in Portland, Oregon, reveals its diversity. They ordered trees and shrubs ranging from Oregon grape holly (*Mahonia aquifolium*) to Southern magnolia (*Magnolia grandiflora*), along with Spanish-themed plants such as Mexican orange (*Choisya ternata*). They selected

4.2 Construction of Daniel B. Jarman's Spanish-styled garden (1930). Courtesy Lord & Schryver Conservancy, Anne M. Kingery Library.

4.3 Daniel B. Jarman's garden and pergola with Edith Schryver on left (c. 1930). Courtesy Lord & Schryver Conservancy, Anne M. Kingery Library.

4.4 Central fountain of Daniel B. Jarman's garden (c. 1930). Courtesy Lord & Schryver Conservancy, Anne M. Kingery Library.

predominantly evergreen shrubs and ones with scented flowers.[21] In keeping with their design training at Lowthorpe, the plantings were color-schemed to complement the architecture. Schryver went one step further by using many plant containers that, like their floral contents, were brightly colored to accent each area. In consultation with Mrs. Jarman, the colors she recommended were yellow, orange, red, bronze, and a touch of pink. She called the Jarman project "a dashing garden—very Spanish!"[22]

When Lord and Schryver returned to visit the site in February 1930, after a particularly harsh winter, they were able to reassure Mrs. Jarman that the new plantings had fared well. "The Jasmine was in full bloom, the Quinces showing buds and the Lilac tips swelling rapidly. The grand old one from your former home acts as though it had never been moved. Even the big leaved Aralia in the front Court withstood the winter freeze and that is the most tender of all your plants."[23] The frost had not damaged any of the tile work. Nevertheless, Lord admitted, "We have to modify our ideas somewhat when jumping from Spain to Oregon."[24] They asked for permission from Mrs. Jarman to use slides of her garden in the lecture they planned to present on Spanish gardens.

The Jarmans' sloping hilltop site with its narrow serpentine driveway challenged Schryver's skill as site engineer. She had to design a complex grading plan as well as many of the walls, steps, terraces, patios, and walkways. Fortunately, she was able to work closely with the contractor, and together they succeeded in building garden features that have stood the test of time.

The magnificent Jarman garden immediately brought attention to Lord and Schryver. It proved that they could accomplish landscape design on a significant scale and in a style that was rather exotic for Salem. It stood out from the typical residential landscapes and was especially prominent on top of the hill, perhaps as the owners had hoped it would be. For this property, the two women had designed a landscape that looked inward, creating a world within a world, rather than a garden relying on borrowed scenery. Lord soon shared her sense of pride in this first big success with the contractor Mr. Wyatt, informing him, "The house has been very much admired and a steady line have gazed as they have driven by. We finished some time ago with the garden. The box edgings gave the garden the design and character so many have spoken about it. And the tiling is really very lovely. Anyway, there isn't a house or garden like it in the state of Oregon and that is something."[25]

The design of the Jarman garden remains relatively unchanged to this day, eighty years later, demonstrating how well its design has been maintained and valued by a series of owners. Although only a few of the original shrub selections remain, huge trees now shade the patios and contribute to a timelessly elegant effect.

➤➤➤ The Richard D. and Eula Merrill Garden, 1929–1940s

When Edith Schryver left Shipman's office in 1928, Shipman recommended that Mr. and Mrs. Richard D. Merrill, her former clients in Seattle, might be better served by Lord and Schryver. Upon their arrival in Salem, Schryver was quick to inform Mrs. Merrill of their new office, saying, "Salem is a beautiful town and we feel that for the present it will be a very convenient center from which to work. The field seems quite promising and tho it may be slow at first, we are looking forward to our venture with a great deal of pleasure."[26] The Merrills would be their second major client of 1929.

In 1909, Charles A. Platt had designed the Merrills' stately home and formal garden on a steeply sloping site in the Capitol Hill neighborhood of Seattle (figure 4.5). Mr. Merrill owned a large lumber business, as did many of the Northwest's wealthiest residents. The house was sited close to the street in order to create a garden behind it, overlooking the city and Puget Sound. Platt made a level garden, approximately one hundred feet square, with a central circular pool on axis with the centerline of the house.[27] In 1915, Shipman, recommended by Platt, went to Seattle to enliven his original geometrical design with her planting genius.[28] The result was so striking that the garden was featured in the June 1927 issue of *House & Garden* magazine (figure 4.6). The article described "a series of gardens on different levels," including a narrow brick terrace running the width of the garden facade, furnished with benches. From this vantage point, one could view "a garden of quiet and restrained beauty," enclosed by a low wall. The author

4.5 The Richard D. Merrill garden prior to Lord and Schryver's involvement (c. 1920s). Courtesy Cornell University Library, Division of Rare and Manuscript Collections.

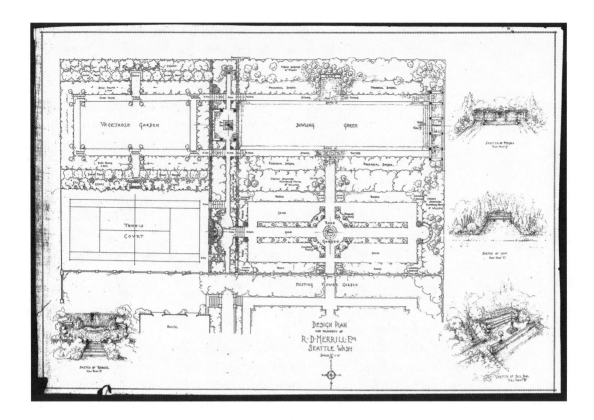

noted, "Infinite variety in the planting constitutes the ornamentation and decoration. But the restrained beauty of straight lines, good proportion, balance and rhythm is never confused or obliterated. A round pool like a huge mirror lies in the middle of a square panel of greenest turf. Four Box-bordered beds of flowers occupy the space between the house and the colonnaded loggia terminating the main axis."[29]

When Lord and Schryver were hired by the Merrills, they did not find it easy to make improvements to "a garden [that] has been lived with for years."[30] This was one of the first designs they were asked to refresh rather than create anew. As Schryver explained to Shipman, "the garden is a conglomeration of ideas, rather than one complete conception with the charm of your gardens."[31] Schryver was the primary on this project, while Lord collaborated with her on the planting plans. Mrs. Merrill was an avid gardener with very changeable interests. They did their best to satisfy her particular tastes and create a result Shipman would have approved. Schryver ordered 180 feet of boxwood to be shipped by rail from Delaware (for a freight charge of $1,200) and $873 worth of shrubs and perennials from the Bonnell Nursery in Seattle.[32] She replanted much of the original boxwood edging, renewed the evergreens along the west wall and installed the

4.6 Ellen Shipman's plan for Richard D. Merrill's garden, Seattle, Washington (1915). Courtesy University of Oregon Libraries, Special Collections and University Archives, Coll 098, Lord & Schryver architectural records.

perennials and shrubs called for in Shipman's plan. However, instead of placing perennials in the four central beds around the pool, Schryver had them planted with tea roses, "a drastic change."[33]

In February 1930, Schryver reported to her former employer on the first year's results: "It proved to be the most difficult to carry out satisfactorily of any of your gardens on which I have worked." She went on to say that finding an expert gardener to maintain the gardens was impossible and that "Studley, the young gardener who came out from the East, was there for part of that time but he became dissatisfied and left before the perennials went in." Complicating matters further was "the fact that in the past various nurserymen had worked on the garden and hence their advice and suggestions were sought aside from your plan."[34] She reassured Shipman that if they found a trained gardener, and the gardens received the proper care, the plantings might give a lovely effect in July 1930 when the Garden Club of America would visit. "Mrs. Merrill is having quantities of soft colored annuals raised to set in. The garden has not yet had an opportunity to show what it can be."[35]

In her reply, Shipman admitted that she had had concerns and gracefully removed herself from any future debate by saying, "I was afraid you would have difficulties, because the Merrills have been so undecided for years as to just what they would do. I do not believe there is anything further I can do in the matter, but if at any time you feel that my opinion on any part of the garden would help you to carry the ideas that you know I would like, please let me know, and I shall be very glad to write to Mrs. Merrill."[36]

The Merrills were very satisfied with Schryver's work, as she remained their landscape architect for many years. She even designed a Victory Garden of vegetables and fruits for them during World War II to replace the formal flower garden, although it seems that this last plan was never implemented. In the 1960s, the California landscape architect Thomas Church remade the formal garden again, this time with French-style parterres in boxwood scrolls and colored gravel.[37]

According to Salem historian Ruth Roberts, "It's very likely that Lord and Schryver's association with the family influenced the next generation as well. The two Merrill daughters, Virginia Bloedel and Eulalie Wagner, were to carry on the family involvement with gardens by developing the Bloedel Reserve on Bainbridge Island [Washington] and Lakewold Gardens in Tacoma, respectively." Both landscapes are now greatly enjoyed by the public.[38]

While they were still working for the Jarmans and the Merrills, Lord and Schryver were commissioned to design a comprehensive development plan for a twenty-acre wilderness resort. This was a significant change from their residential projects and demonstrated the breadth of their abilities, although it is not clear whether the design was actually carried out as planned. Dr. Mark Skiff and his wife Ada of Salem requested a landscape plan for the rustic health resort they intended to build at Breitenbush Hot Springs, near the foot of the Cascade Range. The Breitenbush area had been called one of Oregon's natural wonders. It was famous for having forty springs that released water as hot as 180 degrees Fahrenheit.[39] Native Americans had revered the site's healing powers for centuries. The Skiffs' resort was located in the Santiam National Forest (now known as Willamette National Forest) on land leased from the US Forest Service. It included a section of Breitenbush River, a prime fishing area for salmon. Any plans Lord and Schryver made had to be approved by the supervisor of Oregon's Forest Service. The Skiffs hoped to attract tourists looking for a wilderness experience as well as people seeking a cure from the hot springs "amidst the pines and primeval forest—conducive to rest and health."[40]

Late in 1929, Lord and Schryver made two trips to Breitenbush before any of the resort's structures had been completed.[41] Working from a rough survey provided by Dr. Skiff, they divided the twenty acres into several "distinct areas which will be in accordance with the existing natural conditions."[42] Schryver drafted the plan at a much larger scale—1 inch equal to 50 feet rather than 1 inch equal to 8 feet—than she normally used for garden designs (figure 4.7). Seeking to preserve the natural beauty of the site, they laid out a rustic village with a store, hotel, and community center located directly off the main highway. There were parking areas, a gently curving circulation system with a hierarchy of vehicular and pedestrian trails, and sites for rustic cabins that would rent for $7 to $12 a week. At a greater distance from the central building, they located an "auto camp," a bathhouse, and a swimming pool.[43] The property necessitated construction of a small bridge across the river to reach the bathhouse (figure 4.8). Nearby, they provided places for fishermen to access the river. Their plan also indicated where trees and shrubs would be massed to create privacy and give maximum scenic effect.

Breitenbush Resort was the most naturalistic of Lord and Schryver's many designs. They carried out the entire plan, down to the rustic fence details, following the principles of naturalistic landscape design first laid down by Frederick Law Olmsted. Their plan for the resort demonstrated a reverence for the natural environment as fine as an Olmsted master plan.

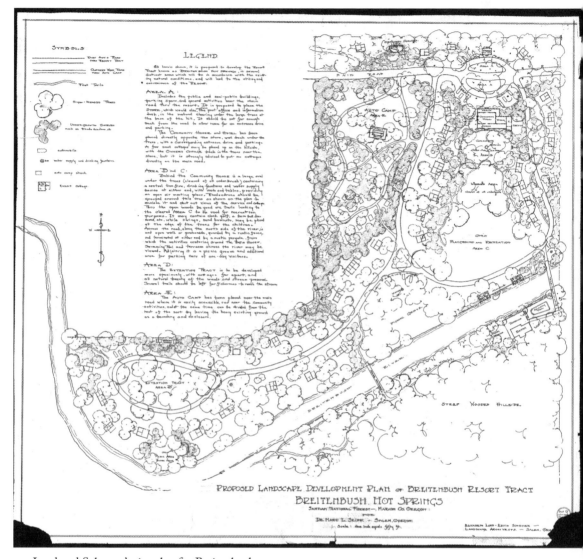

4.7 Lord and Schryver's site plan for Breitenbush
Hot Springs Resort (1929). Courtesy University
of Oregon Libraries, Special Collections and
University Archives, Coll 098, Lord & Schryver
architectural records.

4.8 Edith Schryver's photo of bridge and bath house construction at
Breitenbush Hot Springs Resort (1929). Courtesy University of Oregon
Libraries, Special Collections and University Archives, Coll 098, Lord
& Schryver architectural records.

4.9 Elizabeth Lord at the Lord family home (1930). Courtesy Lord & Schryver Conservancy, Anne M. Kingery Library.

The only formal element Schryver included was an oval village green near the community center as a gathering place for the guests, to be screened with rhododendrons. This was quite unlike her other garden designs, which typically established a formal or axial order to the site before the addition of plantings. Lord and Schryver were pleased with this project. In 1931 they referred to the Breitenbush design in their correspondence regarding a park design for the City of Pendleton, Oregon.

As sometimes happened, the client was not happy with the final bill of $100. Lord stood firm and defended their position, citing all the work they had to put into the design, including their travel to Breitenbush (figure 4.9). In the end, she said they had made about $8 per day, the same rate, in 1929, as a good gardener.[44] The Skiffs built the primary components of the resort in 1929–1930, although we cannot be sure to what extent they followed the Lord and Schryver plan. Breitenbush Hot Springs Resort drew hundreds of tourists from the mid-Willamette Valley, only seventy miles away, and beyond. In the 1960s, new owners took over the facility, and it continues to be a recreational and health resort today.

➤➤➤ Professional Outreach

Florence Holmes Gerke (1896–1964) was one of the first landscape architects to welcome Lord and Schryver to the Northwest and one of the constants in their professional lives (figure 4.10).[45] Before applying to Lowthorpe in 1925, Elizabeth Lord had asked for her advice about the two eastern schools of landscape architecture for women. It is not certain which one Mrs. Gerke recommended; she had studied at the Cambridge School. Mrs. Gerke greeted Lord and Schryver, upon their arrival in Oregon in January 1929: "My very best wishes to you for a successful & happy pursuit of landscape architecture."[46]

Florence Holmes was born in Portland and spent the majority of her professional career there. She attended the Portland Art Museum's school and went on to study "landscape gardening" (the first program in landscape architecture) at Oregon Agricultural College (now Oregon State

4.10 Florence Holmes Gerke, landscape architect, Portland, Oregon (c. 1950). Courtesy Marianne Ott from the *Oregonian* ©2012. All rights reserved. Reprinted with permission.

University), graduating with honors. With World War I in progress, Holmes secured a position with the federal government's Seattle office working on town planning projects for the Bremerton Air Force Base. At the time, a Portland newspaper highlighted her accomplishments: as a "Prominent Oregon Agricultural College Student, . . . she is one of the few girls in the West who has taken up this line of work [landscape architecture], which includes surveying, civil engineering, drafting, study of plant materials and horticulture. With this, she has taken French and English and has received high grades in all her work."[47] This was a striking achievement for a young woman of that era.

Following the war, Holmes studied and traveled in Europe. When she returned to the United States, she enrolled in the Cambridge School of Architecture and Landscape Architecture in Massachusetts on a scholarship. Unfortunately, she ran out of funds and was unable to finish the program.[48] Returning to Portland, she established an office and led an active career designing both private and public landscapes. In 1922 she married the horticulturist Walter H. Gerke (1891–1982), and together they ran a highly respected firm. In a small professional world, they knew and worked with several of the architects Lord and Schryver would collaborate with, including Ernest Tucker, Glenn Stanton, and John Storrs. The couple, along with Lord and Schryver, were founding members of the Oregon Society of

Landscape Architects (OSLA). Mrs. Gerke served a term as president of the OSLA, chaired the Portland Art Commission, and was an active member of the Portland Garden Club.[49]

While employed by the City of Portland, Mrs. Gerke designed a number of prominent public spaces including the International Rose Garden and Amphitheater and the Shakespeare Garden, both located in Washington Park. She also landscaped Grant, Irving, and Dawson Parks. Working together, the Gerkes landscaped the Lloyd Center (a shopping mall) and the Shriners Children's Hospital, both in Portland, and the Dammasch State Hospital in Wilsonville, Oregon. During the Depression, they were hired to landscape the headquarters of the Bonneville Power Navigation Project.[50]

Florence Holmes Gerke was also an accomplished journalist, writing about topics related to her practice. As the garden editor of the *Oregon Journal* she wrote thirty-eight articles in one year, 1932–1933, the same year that Lord and Schryver published nine garden articles in the Portland *Oregonian*. Mrs. Gerke published articles in popular national magazines such as *Sunset, American Home, House & Garden*, and *House Beautiful*.

In March 1929, Mrs. Gerke invited Lord and Schryver to help judge Portland's citywide garden competition held in June and July and sponsored by the garden clubs and the First National Bank. "We are most anxious to have you and Miss Schreiber [*sic*] act as judges for the Competition. You realize as I do that there are relatively few persons qualified to judge garden design and some of the subtleties of taste which make a planting distinguished. Since this is the first Garden Competition to be held in Portland, we have an open field in which to set a rather high standard of endeavor."[51] To promote the contest, the *Oregon Sunday Call* featured an article in early May introducing all seven judges, with a portrait of each. Lord and Schryver were the only professional landscape architects. In the photograph, they wore outfits they considered their "working clothes" and looked strikingly young.[52]

After the judges had viewed all of the gardens in June, Schryver wrote a joint report to Mrs. Gerke, as she and Lord had reached the same conclusions. First, she qualified her comments by stating, "We were more lenient in our verdicts than if all the judges had been professional, as naturally amateurs and professionals do not always see things with the same mind and eye." Then she continued,

> In general, the Portland gardens which we saw, whether pretentious or simple, were excellently maintained, with very good lawns, and all the plants in excellent horticultural condition; but not enough thought and study has been given to color combination, association, leaf texture, etc. to make interesting flower border and shrub planting with any definite character. There was a tendency in quite a few gardens toward design in the distribution of areas, tho

very few service yards were screened. To us, the greatest point to be stressed in the development of the garden was an enclosed, out-door living room with that essential requisite, privacy."[53]

Having stressed the points of good design that Lord and Schryver consistently proclaimed, for reasons unknown, they did not return for the second round of judging in July.

Inquiries quickly began to reach Lord and Schryver as other professionals learned that they were in Oregon and wanted to enlist their help. In January 1929, Lou Richardson, the editor of *Sunset* magazine, wrote to Lord inviting her to compose an article on garden design for them.[54] Lord politely declined by explaining she had only recently returned to the area and was busy establishing their business.[55] As word spread, Lord and Schryver received another invitation from the director of the Art Institute of Seattle to contribute photographs of their work to an annual exhibition showcasing projects by architects, interior decorators, and landscape architects. Schryver responded that they could send several sketch plans but "our gardens have not progressed far enough as yet to have any photographs of them."[56] They did send a roll of their drawings, including a few renderings from Lowthorpe.[57] One can assume their work was displayed in the exhibit and further helped to promote their firm.

It does not appear that Lord and Schryver ever hired employees, certainly not full-time assistants. They managed to handle all the details of their projects themselves, although at times they may have felt overwhelmed. They did receive at least one letter from a young woman hoping to find employment with them. Edith Loomis, who had been working on her own in Oregon, heard about their firm and contacted them to see if they had an opening. Schryver answered the letter with kindness and encouragement; however, she said that she was unable to offer immediate employment. She urged Miss Loomis to consider the program in landscape architecture at Oregon Agricultural College, explaining that the new director, Frederick A. Cuthbert "is an Ann Arbor [University of Michigan] graduate and he is introducing the very latest methods and ideas right up to standard."[58]

One year later, Miss Loomis wrote to them a second time, and this time Lord responded, "We were glad to hear from you again and to know that you had ventured out in the field of the 'L.A.' It takes courage, I'll admit, especially when you are alone and we admire you for launching forth. When people have confidence in you, you should not worry—especially when they do not argue. The trouble is making them see what you are trying to express."[59] Perhaps the latter was a frustration Lord and Schryver frequently experienced as well.[60]

By the end of their first year, Lord and Schryver would reflect back with satisfaction on all they had accomplished in establishing their firm in the

Pacific Northwest. They had completed work on at least two major residential projects, the Jarman and Merrill residences; designed a master plan for a resort community; and begun work for at least eight other clients. They were becoming known for their expertise in the Northwest's professional design community, and they had exhibited their work in two public venues: the Monroe Gilbert Studio in Salem and the Art Institute of Seattle. Others now sought them out to lecture, to consult, and to volunteer their services. Lord considered their rising status when writing to a potential client: "Both Miss Schryver and I are greatly enjoying our work in the West. Miss Schryver is from New York and has been associated with Mrs. Ellen Shipman for five years prior to coming out West with me—I think she is becoming a Westerner rather quickly. As much as I have been away from Salem, I am always happy to return and now that I have entered this profession, I feel more content as I think there is a great opening for our line of work in the West."[61]

5

Against All Odds

It was not easy being business women.
—Edith Schryver, 1983

Were Lord and Schryver aware that by the end of their first year in business, serious financial trouble was brewing for the nation? If they were, they made little mention of the Great Depression in their correspondence until 1931. It was an uncertain time to start a business. The stock market crashed in late October 1929, and the government's lack of response set in motion the events that led to the worst economic depression in the nation's history to date. At first, Salem's civic leaders believed that the capital city would not suffer a setback. It had the government services, agriculture, and food processing industries, along with major institutions and manufacturers to sustain the economy. But as the economic devastation of the 1930s continued, it was clear Oregon and Salem would suffer along with the rest of the nation.[1]

During the Great Depression, many design firms that employed landscape architects closed their doors for good. The women who entered the professional field prior to 1930 tended to be sole practitioners. For them, it was necessary to take drastic steps to survive the leanest years. Marian C. Coffin (1876–1957), for example, closed her office in Manhattan, laid off her staff, and created a studio in her home in Connecticut. Her practice did outlast the 1930s, mainly because she had important social connections who were able to keep sending her a few clients until the economy improved. Similarly, Lord and Schryver certainly benefited from Lord's strong social network and financial resources during this decade.

Lord and Schryver had made an excellent start in 1929 that carried through the following year. By 1931 business began to slow, but Lord remained pragmatic, yet optimistic, about the situation. She admitted to a friendly nurseryman, "Work has been very scarce this spring. Our business is a luxury and one thing people can do without. We are hoping for a better lookout next fall."[2] One of the nursery owners in Maplewood, Oregon, told them, "Local business is very slim, in fact, none of the landscape gardeners are buying plants.... If it was not for our shipping to California and eastern points, we could close up shop and go fishing."[3] Considering how difficult this period was for design professionals, Lord and Schryver demonstrated remarkable success at bringing in new clients through the early years of the Depression. The fact that they continued to work steadily, consistently producing designs of high quality, is notable. Finally, by the end of 1935, Lord would write, "Work seems to be picking up a bit."[4]

Lord and Schryver operated their practice from the Lord family home and had not hired any staff; their overhead was minimal. By 1930, they had organized their business into a flexible division of labor. Schryver, with her superior artistic and engineering skills, carried out the site analysis and design, drafted the plans, and oversaw construction in the field. Her beautiful drawings were works of art. Despite her diminutive size, Schryver was very good at directing workmen and making them do things properly. She did not put up with any nonsense, having been well trained at Lowthorpe and in Ellen Shipman's office to hold her own when dealing with male contractors. Lord, using her superior knowledge of gardening in the Northwest, was the plant expert. She designed the planting plans and the seasonal flower schemes that many of their clients required. She, too, was in the field to oversee installations. In addition, Lord ran the office and took care of their correspondence, billing, plant orders, and the like. Lord's one problem was her increasing deafness, an affliction from which she had suffered since her youth. By 1930, her hearing problem made it difficult to hold telephone conversations. She preferred to have her partner take the calls.

➤➤➤ Pendleton Pioneer Memorial Park, 1929–1932

In November 1929, Lord learned through a friend that the City of Pendleton in northeastern Oregon was considering building a park on a site close to the Umatilla River. Lord boldly wrote to Mrs. Edna Hubbard McNary, a member of the Park Commission, to ask if Lord and Schryver might submit a design. She explained their process and asked if it would be appropriate to send an example of their work. Lord mailed Mrs. McNary a blueprint of their plan for the Breitenbush Hot Springs Resort.[5]

Mrs. McNary's response was complimentary but not encouraging. She wrote,

> The general ease and natural beauty [of the sketch] was well liked as was the use of native trees, flowers and shrubs. Much favorable comment was given and I hope much from the showing. The financial situation makes it

impossible for the Commission to make a survey of our park needs at the present time but we are hopeful that a generous-minded citizen will make a gift sufficient to employ an architect who will work out plans, looking to a complete park system for the future years. We will certainly let you know when we are able to employ the services of a firm such as yours giving you the opportunity to bid for the work.[6]

The following year, the Park Commission was able to employ Lord and Schryver to provide a "sketch plan" for the area the city was calling Pioneer Memorial Park. By October they sent off their design proposal. Although this would be one of their first civic projects, they demonstrated a fine understanding of both the public's needs and the civic budget process (figure 5.1).

The site was 2.5 acres at the edge of the affluent North Hill neighborhood near the Umatilla River. It contained a historic cemetery with grave markers that could not be removed. This was a challenging project. As Lord explained, "We have endeavored to leave all the existing memorials such as monuments, old lilac bushes, and trees, intact at the same time providing the easy circulation and accessibility, and division into separate areas for varied uses."[7] She stated that they had provided a quiet area for adults, a supervised sports field, and a separate playground for mothers with small children. Organized along a north–south axis, the plan gave "a sweeping vista of sloping lawn thru [through] the full length of the park."[8] The main

5.1 Lord and Schryver's proposed plan for Pioneer Memorial Park, Pendleton, Oregon (1930). Courtesy University of Oregon Libraries, Special Collections and University Archives, Coll 098, Lord & Schryver architectural records.

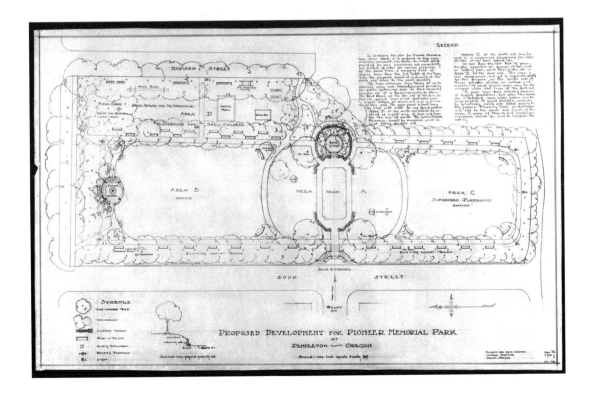

entrance led to a central area reserved for public gatherings and featured a raised bandstand. "Flowering Crabs [crabapples] or Hawthorns will add to the charm and finish the area." If the general scheme met with the commission's approval, Lord and Schryver would send detailed sketches of the architectural features, such as the bandstand.

The Park Commission was "quite charmed with the sketch" and informed Lord and Schryver that it was highly acceptable.[9] After spending the winter in California, they returned to their Salem office, and by mid-March 1931, they were able to send the design plan to Pendleton with the construction and layout plans for a fee of $100. The Board of Park Commissioners formally accepted their plans in May, but the extent to which they were ever carried out is unknown. In January 1932, the commissioners were still consulting them about its development. A park was eventually built on the site but not one that followed the overall design drawn by Lord and Schryver. Unfortunately, the Pendleton Parks Department has retained no record of the project, and the Oregon Historical Society was unable to clarify how much of the design came from the original Lord and Schryver plan or from other sources.

➤➤➤ Deepwood Museum and Gardens, Salem, 1929–1962

Lord and Schryver's longtime friendships with two of their neighbors would lead to the creation of landscapes that became lasting cultural assets for the City of Salem. The properties of both Sally Bush and Alice Brown Powell, on which Lord and Schryver had worked for a period of many years, would ultimately be transformed to city parks.

Lord and Schryver's study of the plant collections at Lowthorpe and the Arnold Arboretum gave them an encyclopedic knowledge of many species that were not well known in the Northwest. Early in their careers, Sally Bush gave them a monthly retainer to be her plant consultants. This arrangement lasted until 1935 and resulted in a very fine property with a diverse selection of flowering trees with many cultivars of ornamental cherries, plums, and crabapples.[10] These trees became a field of bloom in springtime that Lord and Schryver enjoyed from across Mission Street. Years later, after their friend's death, Lord and Schryver would be strong advocates for the preservation of the flowering tree collection as an arboretum for the public's enjoyment and education.

Another neighbor and good friend, Alice Brown Powell (1882–1971), was the owner of Deepwood, an eclectic Victorian mansion on five acres east of Lord and Schryver's home on Mission Street, adjacent to the Bush property (figure 5.2). Alice Brown Powell resided at Deepwood for forty-five years beginning in 1924. The original owner, Dr. Luke A. Port, a chemist, pharmacist, and land developer, had purchased the property at the corner of Mission and Twelfth Streets in 1893, when the area was on the rural fringe of the city. He spent an immense sum ($15,000) to build the rambling Queen Anne style house on a prominence near Pringle Creek, one of the several streams that wind through Salem. At the time, it was considered one of the most handsome houses in Oregon.[11] Within two years after he added a charming two-story carriage house, he sold the property to Judge and Mrs. George C. Bingham. The judge loved to grow fruits and vegetables in his garden and to compete in the local agricultural fair.

Following the deaths of the Binghams in 1924, Clifford Brown, a successful wool and hops broker, and his wife Alice, purchased the property from the Binghams' heir. In 1935, Alice officially named the property Deepwood, the name derived from the title of their two sons' favorite storybook.[12] Clifford Brown enclosed the original porte cochere with glass panels as a solarium and built a full-size tennis court for his sons. Alice loved gardening and nature; she spent almost every day outside, usually with a trowel in hand. She designed several informal garden areas by herself before calling on her friends and the new firm of Lord and Schryver to assist her.

Alice was a romantic. In front of the house and parallel to Mission Street was a large hillock of earth that may have resulted from the excavation of the house. She preferred to imagine that it was an Indian burial mound and would not let anyone disturb it.[13] (Local schoolboys claimed Mrs. Brown

5.2 Deepwood entry gate, Salem, Oregon (c. 1955). Courtesy Salem Public Library, Hugh Stryker Collection.

had buried a buffalo there.)[14] She loved to wander in the woods along Pringle Creek and admire the wildflowers that grew in abundance. Over time she made narrow pathways lined with stones that can still be followed today. She claimed these paths were for the fairies that lived in the woods.[15]

In 1929, two years after her husband's untimely death while boating in Alaska, Alice decided to employ her friends' professional talents to help her with the landscape.[16] She wanted an outdoor area for social gatherings and concerts and to transform Judge Bingham's vegetable gardens into flower gardens. On a level lawn just southeast of the house, Lord and Schryver created the Great Room (figure 5.3). They marked a formal entrance to the lawn with boxwood hedges and framed the terminus in the same manner. The design included a circular pool on the garden's main axis, but Alice did not install this. Instead she added a bench as the focal point and a small pool for koi, offset from the axis, a change from the design's formality that Schryver would not have approved.

To the east of the Great Room, Lord and Schryver replaced Judge Bingham's former vegetable garden with the Teahouse Garden, a rectangular flower garden within a wooden latticework fence (figure 5.4). It featured a hexagonal pavilion, or teahouse, which served as the focal point of the east–west axis with either a seat or an arbor terminating each of the brick cross paths (plate 9). They retained two old apple trees to lend a sense of age and character to the formal design. Alice envisioned it as a "moon garden" with flowers of pale colors releasing their fragrance into the evening, and all three women contributed to the plantings. The result was intimate and charming and complex, clearly drawing on the principles of garden design Schryver had learned from Shipman and the Colonial Revival gardens of Cornish, New Hampshire (plate 10).

Adjacent to the Teahouse Garden, Lord and Schryver created the Spring Garden, a less formal area sheltered beneath the twisted trunk of Judge Bingham's old quince tree (*Cydonia*). The quince added the proper note of ageless charm. Within the confines of a wooden fence, Lord and Schryver made curvilinear borders for spring-flowering bulbs and perennials such as peonies, iris, and poppies, and edged them with boxwood. Alice loved color, and one of her small pleasures was always to have flowers on the table that matched her many sets of china.[17] She had all her garden fences painted an unusual shade of blue-green, creating a cohesive theme that drew together the wide variety of colors and textures that so delighted the owner.

When Lord sent Alice the bill for their work at Deepwood in 1930, she wrote, "Both Nina [Edith] and I want to say how much we have enjoyed working with you and working on your garden. Your feeling for line, beauty and proportion is rare."[18] As work continued on and off at Deepwood, Alice would write,

5.3 The Great Room Garden at Deepwood (c. 1940). Courtesy Deepwood Museum & Gardens.

5.4 The Teahouse Garden at Deepwood in spring (c. 1940). Courtesy Deepwood Museum & Gardens.

Dear Bess [Elizabeth] and Nina [Edith], I'm happy to be sending you this check because I consider it much more than a check—it's really a promise of a garden that I feel myself is one day to become a very lovely thing. From the background of my long and valued friendship with Bess—rambles and companionable walks and intimate days along the bluffs at Seal Rock—it's particularly happy now to add her inspiration and artistic comprehension to my garden of today and then have added to that Nina's sensitive and delicate little touch. I'm entirely harmonious with all you've done and only hope now I can take it on to some little charm of its own that any garden must have in order to really live. . . . I'll never be satisfied just to have it please one's eyes—it must stir the imagination—or it's no real garden.[19]

In 1936, Alice invited Lord and Schryver to design another special garden area at Deepwood. This garden would feature a large Chinese tea jar that they had purchased for her while in Manila (figure 5.5). With help from Lord's brother, Montague, they had the three-foot-tall ceramic container shipped to Salem. The exotic Chinese jar, raised on a small brick plinth, served as the focal point at the garden's west end. Another, perhaps more unusual, gift became the inspiration for Schryver's playful design. Alice's sister, Vivien Bretherton, had given her a cast iron and steel balustrade that had been removed from Portland's Davis Building prior to demolition. They had it repaired and repainted a shade of burnt orange. Schryver used the balustrade to define a level, rectangular space in an open field edged by woodlands. She further outlined the interior beds with low boxwood

5.5 Alice Brown Powell, on left, with friends around the tea jar in Scroll Garden at Deepwood (c. 1940). Courtesy Lord & Schryver Conservancy, Anne M. Kingery Library.

5.6 The Scroll Garden at Deepwood (c. 1940). Courtesy Deepwood Museum & Gardens.

hedges that looked like unfurling scrolls, inspired by the curling lines of the balustrade (plate 11). To Schryver, the scrolls were her initials, and she called it the Scroll Garden; Alice preferred to call it the Chinese Garden (figure 5.6). Local history recalls that Alice planted the area with deciduous azaleas in cream, yellow, orange, and rust colors to contrast with the dark green of the boxwood.[20]

Large trees have grown up around the Scroll Garden today, shading out much of the planting. The effect is quite different from the earlier years when one could look down on the bold baroque pattern.

In 1945, Alice married her second husband Keith Powell and became Alice Brown Powell. It was around this time that she was able to add the perfect focal point to the Great Room: a gazebo of twisted wire they nicknamed "The Birdcage." The metal structure had originally been designed as an ornamental feature for Portland's 1905 Lewis and Clark Exposition, an event that young Elizabeth Lord had attended. For many years, Alice had admired the structure as it sat in the backyard of its Portland fabricator, knowing it would be perfect for her Great Room. Finally, in 1949, he agreed to sell it and transport it to Salem.[21] Alice had the gazebo painted a luminous white.

5.7 The "Birdcage" gazebo at Deepwood (c. 1940). Courtesy Deepwood Museum & Gardens.

Today its lacy texture stands out against the emerald foliage of the hedges and lawn, and it is a favorite place for weddings (figure 5.7).

One cannot overestimate the joy that Alice Brown Powell, Elizabeth Lord, and Edith Schryver shared in their friendship. They were all well-educated, passionate about their interests, imaginative, curious, and intellectual. They enjoyed reading and traveling and learning about new places. During the summer months at Seal Rock, they owned cottages close to each other and frequently socialized, enjoying hours in the relaxed atmosphere of picnics, casual dinner parties, walks on the beach, fun and laughter.[22]

In the early 1960s, Alice hired Wallace Kay Huntington, a landscape architect and young protégé of Lord and Schryver, to design the little Secret Garden close to the west side of the house. She was having trouble with vandalism on the grounds and wanted to bring her garden art into a safer place. In October of 1962, a powerful windstorm, memorably called the Columbus Day Storm, destroyed hundreds of trees throughout the City of Salem. The devastation was overwhelming to property owners. Deepwood lost more than thirty mature trees, and it brought to an end any new additions to the house and gardens. In 1968, Alice moved to a smaller and more practical house, and Deepwood became a city park through financial support from local foundations and a successful grassroots preservation effort.

Working with Alice had been frustrating at times for Lord and Schryver. Her taste in plants was very eclectic. She would never carry out the details of their carefully wrought plans exactly as intended. In later years, Schryver told Huntington, "Although Alice was a good friend, she just interfered too much."[23] Lord would claim that they had done little to create the gardens at Deepwood because Alice had changed it so much; but clearly they had. The more defined spaces, connections, and design details show Schryver's hand and eye at work. The plantings reflect Lord's knowledge. The original plans are further evidence of Lord and Schryver's involvement. The mixture of architectural styles combined in the Queen Anne house is reflected in the mixture of garden spaces around it. The gardens designed in 1929 by Lord and Schryver—the Great Room, the Spring Garden, and the Teahouse Garden—are clearly organized and spatially defined within the landscape, while the Scroll Garden, which they added later, seems to stand alone. Several pathways softened with plantings of perennials and shrubs were necessary to connect the parts into a complex but enchanting whole: Alice Brown Powell's fairyland.

➤ ➤ ➤ The Cambridge and Lowthorpe Schools' Exhibition, 1931

Schryver was suddenly taken ill in September 1930, and her condition required surgery. Afterward, Lord determined that they would spend a few months that winter in the more salubrious climate of California. They returned to Salem as winter was ending in 1931, to pick up their work again. In September of 1931, they received an unexpected invitation from Louise Leland, assistant to Henry Atherton Frost, the founding director of the Cambridge School and a professor of architecture at Harvard University. Miss Leland's inquiry to Schryver read, "The school is making a collection of professional work to be exhibited throughout the country this fall and winter. Mr. Frost asked me to write to you to find out if you would like to send some photographs of your work to be included in the exhibition. We are not limiting the collection to the work of Cambridge School graduates, for we feel that the exhibit is first and foremost to increase public interest in women's work in these professions."[24] Graduates of Lowthorpe were also invited to participate. If Miss Schryver were interested, Miss Leland asked for three mounted photographs of any gardens she had designed. Each exhibitor might submit three works, as the whole exhibition would feature no more than fifty mounts.

Lord took charge of sending their submissions to Miss Leland, and the firm soon received a wonderfully complimentary letter from Mr. Frost: "Miss Leland has just shown me the photographs of the work done by you and Miss Schryver . . . and I think they are extremely fine. I congratulate you on getting such fine work to do and handling it in such an excellent manner. We are delighted to have them to exhibit and indeed the whole exhibition is going to show that the practitioners are keeping their end up in professional work."[25] To receive this level of praise from a well-respected practitioner and professor must have been uplifting indeed, especially as the economic depression deepened.

The Cambridge School organized eight exhibitions that they shipped to garden clubs and other women's organizations around the nation to promote the accomplishments of the graduates and faculty of both the women's schools. They also mounted an exhibition of photographs of English houses and landscapes taken during the school's European travel courses. They publicized both the exhibitions and a lecture service in a special bulletin.

> > > The Charles G. and Mildred Robertson Garden, Salem, 1931–1932

The Robertson garden in the fashionable Fairmount Hill neighborhood of South Salem started off with a muddle but became one of Lord and Schryver's most refined and lasting designs. The muddle occurred over the cost of the landscape plan. When Mrs. Charles G. Robertson, the wife of a prominent Salem physician, first inquired about having Lord and Schryver do a garden plan for them in 1931, she stated that they did not have a great deal of money to spend on it. The Robertsons agreed to hire them to carry out a master plan for a total of approximately $75, but not more than $100. Lord and Schryver, however, were under the impression that they were to undertake the entire project from design to installation. This would include a site visit and a site analysis. But when the Robertsons received the preliminary "Sketch Plan" from Schryver, they wanted to purchase it outright for a lower sum without going any further. The firm did not work this way, and Lord patiently tried to explain this in a letter to Mildred Robertson:

> This would be a very unwise precedent for us to follow and would naturally do us a great deal of harm. Besides, it would not be fair to previous clients. I am sure that you will understand our point of view on this matter. . . . Naturally we are very anxious to carry out the ideas we have conceived for your garden and are awfully sorry that you feel that the price is more than you can afford. Under the circumstances the best that we can suggest is that we would make the price at $75.00 which could be paid at intervals during the year. . . . We could make the front design and planting plan, and later, when you wish it, draw up the rear part of the plan. We, also, want you to know we would purchase the foundation of front planting at regular nursery charges and oversee its planting. We should, also, give an occasional visit to the garden working, rockwall, etc. I do not see how we can possibly make the price less and we hope you and Dr. Robertson will consider this proposition.[26]

Lord and Schryver did not want to lose their clients, nor did they want to take a loss on the time and effort they had already invested in the project.

The site the Robertsons had purchased was one of the most challenging the firm would deal with in forty years of practice. The modest-sized residential lot was 90 feet wide by 160 feet deep, on Leffelle Street in South Salem. The street climbed a steep hill and ended at a sheer bluff overlooking the Willamette River. The lot itself had a steep slope, a grade change of 20 to 25 percent, angling the property from a high point on the south to a low point on the north, where it met the street. The Robertsons had already hired Salem architect Clarence L. Smith (1894–1950), a colleague and friend of Elizabeth Lord, to design their new home. Smith was a well-established design professional. He would later be described as "the capital city's leading designer of period houses during the late 1920s and early 1930s."[27] Smith was originally from Portland, Oregon, and had apprenticed in the Portland architectural offices of Charles W. Ertz and A. L. DuPuy. He left to study architecture at Cornell University for two years but did not complete the program. He worked for several firms in New York state before returning to Oregon. Eventually Smith settled in Salem and established his own firm. He designed several notable homes in the Gaiety Hill and Fairmount neighborhoods that were widely admired and were placed on the National Register of Historic Places. The Robertson house and garden was listed on the National Register in 1982.[28]

Smith centered the house approximately halfway up the slope from the street so that only the roof would be seen from street level. He designed it using a combination of revival styles, modeling it primarily on an English cottage, with a low one-and-a-half-story profile, a facade veneered with old brick, a steeply pitched roof, and mullioned windows. The house had lovely proportions and interior detailing, with the primary social rooms looking south over a very private rear garden screened from the adjacent homes with tall greenery.

Lord and Schryver's plan for the Robertsons' garden was strikingly similar in layout to a design they had made two years earlier for Mr. and Mrs. Raymond Brown of Portland. In October 1929, Lord contacted Mrs. Brown, having heard that the Browns wanted to make a garden on a lot they had just purchased adjacent to their house. The site tilted upward away from house in a steep slope, similar to the Robertsons' property. Following a site visit and consultation with the client, and the usual series of communications, Lord and Schryver were able to send the Browns a garden plan and construction details (figure 5.8). Their design divided the slope into three formal terraces of varying widths, leading to the topmost level, where a small lawn was enclosed with informal plantings. Schryver's construction

plan shows the elegant stone retaining wall, steps, and a gazebo (figure
5.9).[29] The Browns paid Lord and Schryver for their work, and their letters
continued until April 1931. After that, Lord and Schryver heard nothing
further from their clients.[30] They were left wondering whether the Browns
ever built their garden. A few months later, planning for the Robertsons'
new garden in Salem was under way.

For the Robertsons' property, Schryver designed the driveway on the
transverse, entering from the street and moving diagonally uphill to a parking area in front of the house (plate 12). Much of the slope near the street
was too steep to disturb and required a vegetative cover to prevent soil
erosion. Lord and Schryver's plan called for shrubs to be planted under
three existing trees that were saved to provide visual punctuation along the

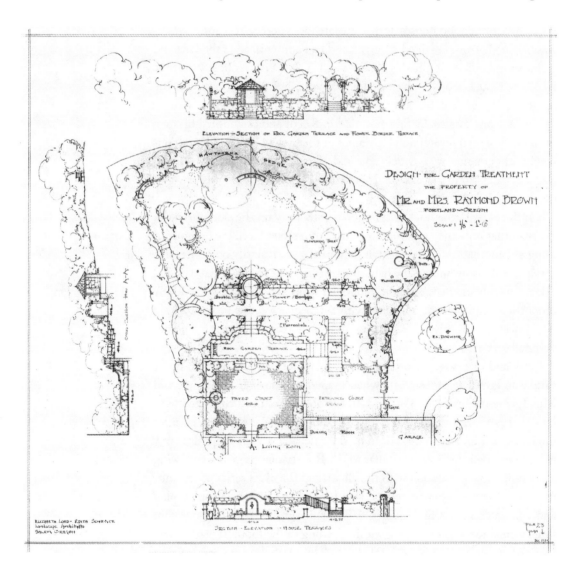

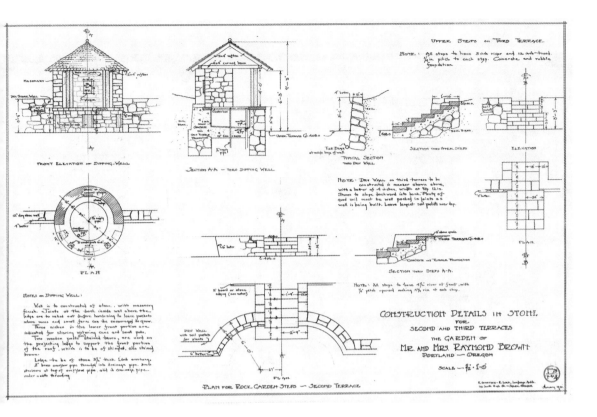

slope. Where the driveway widened into the parking area, there was a small section of lawn defined by low stonewalls and shrubs.

To the rear of the house was the main garden, compact and very carefully composed because of the slope. The main window of the dining room overlooked this garden, and Schryver aligned the garden's axis with the window's centerline (figure 5.10). Along this axis, she created three garden levels running parallel to the east–west alignment of the house. The first, a stone-flagged terrace twenty-four-feet long, was on the same plane as the house, giving easy access for entertaining (figure 5.11). Steps led up to the second level, a narrow terrace with flagstone paving, and a sundial. A few steps led from this to the third level, which opened onto a lawn. The boundary was informally planted with a selection of evergreen and flowering trees and shrubs (figure 5.12). The preferred color scheme for the garden was carried out in greens and lavenders.[31]

Lord and Schryver designed the central terminus of the garden axis to be a wall fountain framed by two trees, but the owners placed a seat there instead. The architect had tucked a small porch outside the study on the east end of the house. It looked out on a small pool set within a naturalistic rockery, designed by Lord and Schryver to form a cool, shady oasis. The

5.9 Lord and Schryver's construction details for Mr. and Mrs. Raymond Brown, Portland, Oregon (1929). Courtesy University of Oregon Libraries, Special Collections and University Archives, Coll 098, Lord & Schryver architectural records.

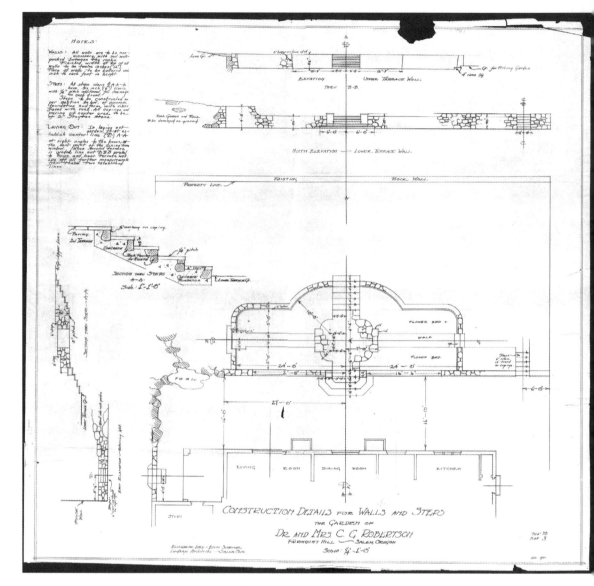

5.10 Lord and Schryver's construction details for Charles and Mildred Robertson's garden, Salem, Oregon (1931). Courtesy University of Oregon Libraries, Special Collections and University Archives, Coll 098, Lord & Schryver architectural records.

5.11 The lower terrace looking east, Charles and Mildred Robertson's garden, Salem, Oregon (c. 1936). Courtesy University of Oregon Libraries, Special Collections and University Archives, Coll 098, Lord & Schryver architectural records.

5.12 The lower terrace looking west, Charles and Mildred Robertson's garden, Salem, Oregon (c. 1945). Courtesy University of Oregon Libraries, Special Collections and University Archives, Coll 098, Lord & Schryver architectural records.

steep slope and narrowness of the terraces gave the garden the unusual appearance of being on a tilted plane facing toward the rear of the house. The effect was one of increased spatial intimacy, masterfully accomplished by the collaboration between architect and landscape architects.

The Robertsons' garden design has been much admired over the years, and two subsequent owners were fortunate in being able to call on the firm for assistance with garden restoration and refinement. In fact, Lord and Schryver often kept an eye on their garden installations and would notify a new owner, if they felt some improvements were necessary (plates 13, 14).

➢➢➢ The Garden Design Articles of 1932

Lord and Schryver were busy serving their clients and planning to build a new home for themselves when Edward M. Miller, the editor of Portland's *Sunday Oregonian* newspaper, invited them to contribute a series of articles on gardening. His original proposal was for twelve articles on subjects of their choice. Lord replied, "Both Miss Schryver and I feel the general garden public are interested in the development of a garden as a whole, rather than just garden snatches. In the three years that we have been here, we have noticed quite an advancement in that line and people are just a bit fed up on all these articles dealing entirely with plant cultivars."[32] They decided to write nine articles focusing on garden design for the average-size city lot, illustrated with simple plans as "something entirely different hereto published in Western papers."[33] The articles provided an excellent way to publicize their firm and, simultaneously, to educate the consumer. The editor at the *Sunday Oregonian* was enthusiastic, too, and assured them, "Your outline seems a most excellent one and . . . we will ballyhoo the series and I'm sure we'll have a large following."[34]

Lord and Schryver planned to lead the reader through a sensible step-by-step approach to residential landscape design, beginning with site analysis of the lot and the proper placement of the house. They emphasized that a topographic map and an accurate survey were necessary to form the basis for a landscape plan. Written in a straightforward, no-frills style, the authors discussed the design process and illustrated each article with a plan or plans. Did Lord write them and Schryver illustrate them, or did they collaborate on both aspects? It is impossible to know. The *Sunday Oregonian* published their articles weekly through the spring of 1932.

In their first article, "Essentials of Landscape Architecture for Average-Sized City Dwelling," Lord and Schryver defined five basic principles of garden planning: order, balance, composition, utility, and beauty. They encouraged homeowners to work from a plan: "There must be a floor plan before a house can be built; a good dress requires a pattern and a good meal means recipes and menu planning. We provide for all of these as necessities but when it comes to a garden plan we are very apt to think that all charm will be lost unless the garden is allowed to grow haphazardly."[35] They offered practical suggestions for locating both the house and garage and further explained the difference between building a garden on a level site or one on a sloping site, with the increased expense of the latter. They discussed the division of the landscape into areas, or garden rooms, and how important it was to create clear connections between them.

In subsequent articles, Lord and Schryver discussed using view lines from the house to locate special features in the landscape. They wrote several articles on the correct placement of trees, shrubs, perennial borders, and rose gardens. They even offered suggestions for how to make a rural property more attractive. In their final article, "Garden's Charm Heightened by Appropriate Features," Lord and Schryver talked about the quintessential quality of charm. They explained that "individual charm" was introduced by personalizing the garden with structures such as pergolas, arbors and summerhouses, ornaments or statuary, decorative pots, sundials, birdbaths, and the addition of pools and fountains.[36] Several of the plans they published had strong similarities to gardens they had previously designed or to the garden they were enthusiastically planning for Gaiety Hollow. To be sure, their own garden would begin with a plan; it would not grow haphazardly.

➤➤➤ Gaiety Hollow, Salem, 1932–1934

Between 1932 and 1934, Lord and Schryver completed a major personal project that brought them great satisfaction and further established their roots in Salem. Elizabeth Lord had decided in 1932 to sell her family's home facing High Street on a corner lot. She would build a new house on the remainder of the lot facing Mission Street. It was 130 feet deep by 108.25 feet wide, almost a third of an acre, and relatively level.[37] Most of the residential properties in the Gaiety Hill neighborhood had compact homes built close to each other. Their garden would be slightly larger. The Depression had greatly lowered the demand for new construction, and contractors were desperate for work. It was, therefore, an economical time to build, if one could afford to build at all. Lord had the financial means to undertake this project, probably using income from the family trust established by her father and managed by her brother William. It is likely this financial stream helped support the two women in a manner that their business earnings alone might not.

For the design of the house, Lord and Schryver selected architect Clarence Smith, with whom they had just worked successfully on the Robertson house and garden. Their views on design were compatible, assuring that the relationship between house and garden would be a complementary one. Smith knew how to make a refined dwelling of modest proportions, and Lord and Schryver knew how to transform the landscape into a private Eden.

The two women wanted a comfortable, but practical, home suited to their needs for living, working, and entertaining. In the event they might decide to sell the property, the design of the house would have to be equally suitable for a small family. Smith's design utilized an eclectic blend of Colonial and English Rural Revival styles (figure 5.13).[38] The house was two stories high, with a pitched roof and dormer windows on the front. The front facade of the house was rather flat and plain. The lower portion was brick, while the upper portion and all the other sides were shingled and painted white, including the attached garage. The house front faced south and was set close to Mission Street, allowing for a larger portion of the lot to be made into a private garden on the north and west sides of the building. The garage was also placed intentionally close to the street to minimize the driveway's length.

For the second floor, Smith designed the rear portion of the house in an unusual manner, with two gables to provide additional space for three bedrooms and a bathroom, along with a small office space. Over the garage, he tucked a studio under the sloping eaves. The entire cost of the house was approximately $6,500, according to a statement Lord and Schryver made when they entered the plan for their new home in a contest sponsored by *House Beautiful* magazine (figure 5.14).[39]

5.13 Lord and Schryver's home at Gaiety Hollow prior to landscape installation, Salem, Oregon (1932). Courtesy University of Oregon Libraries, Special Collections and University Archives, Coll 098, Lord & Schryver architectural records.

5.14 Gaiety Hollow submission for *House Beautiful*
contest (c. 1935). Courtesy University of Oregon Libraries,
Special Courtesy University of Oregon Libraries, Special
Collections and University Archives, Coll 098, Lord &
Schryver architectural records.

What a delight it must have been for Lord and Schryver to have their own landscape in which to showcase their talents. It would be a gallery of interconnected garden rooms, each with a separate but subtle theme, displaying their favorite plants and reflecting their two personalities. Naturally, they would continue to modify the garden over time until they were satisfied. But are gardeners ever satisfied? Schryver drew up the initial plan, "House and Garden for Miss Elizabeth Lord at 545 Mission St. Salem Ore" (figure 5.15). She never mentioned herself.[40] Since the property lay in the lower area of the neighborhood known as Gaiety Hill, they began to call it Gaiety Hollow. The first time this name appeared on a plan was 1938.[41]

The first step in laying out garden areas was to extend the architectural lines of the house and the garage into the landscape, creating a grid. Within this outline, they defined different garden rooms and centered each space on an axial view through an important window or door. In this manner the composition of the entire garden was linked to the spatial composition of the house and could be clearly viewed from inside.

5.15 Garden plan for Lord and Schryver's home and garden at Gaiety Hollow, Salem, Oregon (1932). Courtesy University of Oregon Libraries, Special Collections and University Archives, Coll 098, Lord & Schryver architectural records.

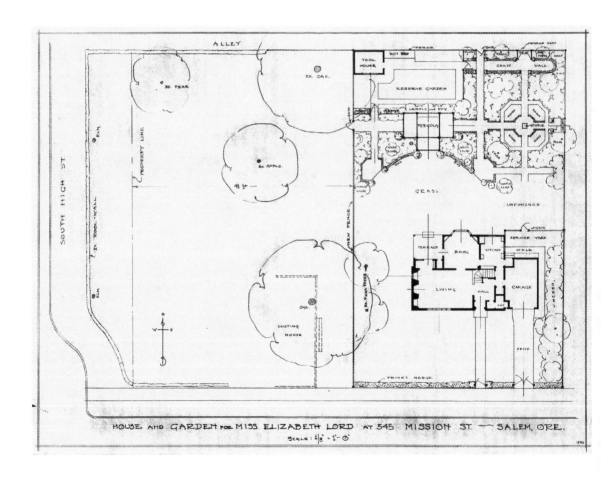

HOUSE AND GARDEN FOR MISS ELIZABETH LORD AT 545 MISSION ST. — SALEM, ORE.
SCALE: 1/8" = 1'-0"

Lord and Schryver believed, both personally and professionally, that privacy was absolutely essential for a residential landscape. They screened each boundary line of their property from their neighbors and planted a boxwood hedge along the front sidewalk, with openings for the entrance gate and the driveway. The gate was framed with two Lavalle hawthorns (*Crataegus × lavallei*), which would eventually arch over the opening (figure 5.16). They erected a tall fence around the north, west, and east sides, utilizing sections of the original fence that had enclosed Mrs. Lord's garden, with white latticework panels between dark green posts.

Along the front of the house, Lord and Schryver planted white flowering azaleas and evergreen shrubs against the white walls, creating a contrast so subtle that most designers would not have considered it. Eventually they had a Bosc pear tree espaliered against the facade. Today this area is known as the Entry Garden. To the west of the house, off the living room, a narrow space provided just enough room to create a small garden, known as the Evergreen Garden, with a circular reflecting pool featuring a cherub's statue (figure 5.17). This garden, visible from the living room's western window, was one they particularly enjoyed during the winter months. It also provided a pathway along the west side of the house. Here, evergreen shrubs were framed by white azaleas in spring. The concept of having a small area planted with evergreens that looked equally beautiful in midwinter became one they used for several of their clients.

5.16 Lord and Schryver's home at Gaiety Hollow, Salem, Oregon (c. 1945). Courtesy University of Oregon Libraries, Special Collections and University Archives, Coll 098, Lord & Schryver architectural records.

5.17 The Evergreen Garden at Gaiety Hollow, Salem, Oregon
(c. 1945). Courtesy University of Oregon Libraries, Special
Collections and University Archives, Coll 098, Lord &
Schryver architectural records.

Behind the house they retained an area of lawn, today known as the North Lawn, defined with an arc-shaped border at the back.[42] The central axis of this lawn began at the center line of French doors in the living room, crossed the terrace and terminated at a large wooden pergola (figure 5.18). The pergola, also remade from Mrs. Lord's garden, was a focal point for the entire landscape. Beneath it a brick-paved area contained seating, and a path ran at right angles to the geometric Flower Garden.[43] From the beginning, they had decided to preserve elements from Mrs. Lord's original garden. The four-part Flower Garden had a very traditional design of beds divided by brick paths. Here, they planted the inner beds with roses while the wider, outer divisions held a range of bulbs, perennials, annuals, and shrubs for a constantly changing display of bloom in a color-coordinated sequence.

5.18 Axial view west across the Flower Garden to the pergola at Gaiety Hollow, Salem, Oregon (c. 1938). Courtesy University of Oregon Libraries, Special Collections and University Archives, Coll 098, Lord & Schryver architectural records.

By 1938, Lord and Schryver had decided to expand the western perimeter of the gardens with a narrow walk between two large, old Garry oaks (*Quercus garryana*) (figure 5.19). The trees had grown on the site for several centuries, and Lord's parents had intentionally preserved them. Lord and Schryver created a long passage between the two great oaks, bordered with evergreen and flowering shrubs (figure 5.20). A narrow ribbon of low boxwood hemmed each side of the walk. Modifying in stages, they encircled the oak at the north end with a wooden bench and, later on, laid a brick patio beneath the bench to complete the design, using a string line to determine the visual center. Today a visitor may hear this garden referred to as the West Allee.

5.19 Laying out a line in the Oak Allee at Gaiety Hollow, Salem, Oregon (c. 1938). Courtesy University of Oregon Libraries, Special Collections and University Archives, Coll 098, Lord & Schryver architectural records.

Chapter 5

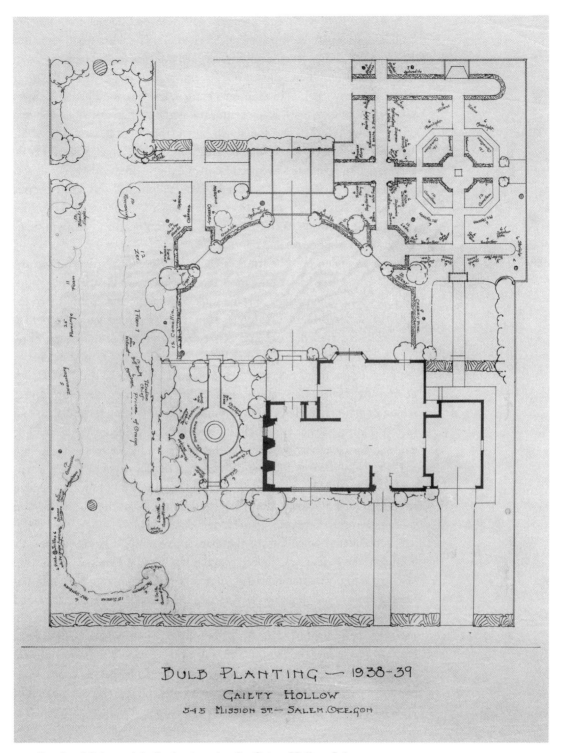

BULB PLANTING — 1938-39

GAIETY HOLLOW

545 MISSION ST — SALEM. OREGON

5.20 Lord and Schryver's bulb planting plan for Gaiety Hollow, Salem,
Oregon (1938). Courtesy University of Oregon Libraries, Special Collections
and University Archives, Coll 098, Lord & Schryver architectural records.

Lord and Schryver frequently used low boxwood hedges to outline, or highlight, the spatial compartments of a garden design. Boxwood remained green and attractive through all the seasons, and they loved boxwood for its traditional usage. They believed it gave "immediate age, charm and dignity where properly used."[44] In their own garden, low boxwood hedges framed the east–west cross path leading into the pergola, the path along the rear of the Flower Garden and the North Lawn. The use of boxwood to define garden sections became very popular during the Colonial Revival period and carried over into the twentieth century. Almost all the garden designers of the early 1900s used it, including Ellen Shipman. Lord and Schryver applied the technique to many of their clients' gardens. They called it "a heritage handed down to us from old English and colonial gardens, a heritage which we must preserve and continue."[45]

With an eye to practicality, they created a Reserve Garden behind the pergola at the very back of the property, screened from view by tall hedges. To the west of the pergola, a brick walk offset from the North Lawn led into the Reserve Garden through a uniquely designed gate over which a holly hedge arched. Lord and Schryver located a tool house, a potting bench, and a hot bed in this area. To create symmetry on the east side of the pergola, another brick walk led to a gated entrance to the service alley behind the garden. The garden fence and a laurel hedge created a privacy screen here. Service alleys were a common feature throughout Salem and kept less attractive activities behind the homes, while front yards could be adorned for civic beauty.[46] Behind the garage and close to the back door at Gaiety Hollow was a square of lawn reserved for drying laundry, a typical component of the domestic landscape at the time. It was separated from the North Lawn by a low hedge and connected to the Flower Garden through an arch. Later on, when electric dryers made a laundry yard obsolete, subsequent owners turned the space into a patio. It has more recently been restored to its original design as the Drying Garden.

A garden, no matter how beautiful, is never static, and the garden at Gaiety Hollow continued to evolve over the next forty years as Lord and Schryver practiced landscape architecture. Even after their retirement in 1969, they continued to refine the plant compositions without changing the basic arrangement. The design is complex yet unified. It contains intimate spaces that are of a perfect scale, appropriate to the house, each area separate but a part of the visual and thematic whole, and it preserved the best of Mrs. Juliet Lord's garden from Elizabeth Lord's past.

6

Onward

Dear Miss Schryver: If I am to go the poorhouse, I don't know
anyone I would rather have help me along the way, you do it so
pleasantly.
　　—Dr. W. W. Baum, 1937

By the summer of 1934, Lord and Schryver had worked for forty-one clients, completing numerous projects in Oregon and Washington.[1] During
their first five years, they had designed landscapes primarily for residential
properties. They had also worked on several institutional and commercial
sites throughout the Northwest and had been asked to advise on many
public projects in Salem. Their new home at Gaiety Hollow and their practice were in good order.

The World Tour, 1934–1935

As business slowed because of the Depression, they decided to accept the
generous offer made by Elizabeth Lord's brother Montague to pay for
them to join him in Manila and travel together, circling the globe by sea
and air. They had not traveled outside of the United States since the 1927
study tour of European gardens. The grand plan was to sail to Hawaii, then
on to Manila, where they would spend some time with Montague. All three
would then fly to South Africa, Argentina, Chile, and Mexico (figure 6.1).
Lord and Schryver would return via ship from Mexico to Los Angeles,
and from there home to Oregon.[2] It was a very ambitious trip. Although
Asia was reasonably familiar to Lord from previous journeys there, it was
completely new to Edith Schryver. The rest of their world tour would be
new terrain for both of them. On 2 November 1934, they departed from San
Francisco on the SS *Hoover*, bound for Hawai'i.

6.1 Elizabeth Lord, Montague Lord, and Edith Schryver, center, on their world tour (1934–1935). Courtesy University of Oregon Libraries, Special Collections and University Archives, Coll 098, Lord & Schryver architectural records.

Fascinating black-and-white photographs, taken by both women, capture a vivid record of their adventures (figure 6.2). They documented the scenery, architecture, and people they encountered; but they made surprisingly few photographs of exotic plants or landscapes.[3] One photograph captures Schryver with two Filipino workers in an area marked off with posts and twine, possibly directing the layout of a garden design (figure 6.3). Two years later, Lord and Schryver sketched a planting plan for Mrs. Fairchild, the wife of the director of the Hawaiian-Philippine Company, for whom Montague worked in Baguio-Benguet (figure 6.4).[4] Later on their trip, they reached South Africa and were fascinated by scenes in Kruger National Park, Kirstenbosch Botanical Gardens, and by the traditional Dutch houses built by white settlers. In 1936, when Schryver lectured about this journey, she declared, "The most interesting gardens in the world are found at Cape Town in S. Africa."[5] In South America, they traveled through the Andes Mountains and north along the Pacific coast. On the Yucatan Peninsula of Mexico, they explored and photographed the Mayan ruins, and in Mexico City, the public parks. By April 1935, they had safely returned to Salem.

Unfortunately, few of their journals or letters have survived to describe in detail their experiences or reactions to foreign places and exotic landscapes. Were they inspired by Asian gardens, for example, or by the lush vegetation of the tropics? We do not know. Nor do we know, as we do for their 1927

6.2 Elizabeth Lord in the Philippines, on their world tour (1934–1935). Courtesy University of Oregon Libraries, Special Collections and University Archives, Coll 098, Lord & Schryver architectural records.

6.3 Edith Schryver directing a garden installation in the Philippines, on their world tour (1934–1935). Courtesy University of Oregon Libraries, Special Collections and University Archives, Coll 098, Lord & Schryver architectural records.

6.4 Edith Schryver, Mrs. G. Fairchild, and Elizabeth Lord in the Philippines, on their world tour (1934–1935). Courtesy University of Oregon Libraries, Special Collections and University Archives, Coll 098, Lord & Schryver architectural records.

study trip, how much this expedition influenced their design work over the following years.

➤➤➤ The Gerald and Mary Beebe Garden, 1935–1940s

Upon their return, they continued with their previous connections. Among the first clients to receive their attention were Mr. and Mrs. Gerald Beebe of Portland.[6] Mary Beebe knew Lord and Schryver through the Portland Garden Club, as she was an active member and an enthusiastic plants-woman. Mrs. Beebe had sent them an inquiry in October 1934, right before they were to depart on their travels. "We have recently purchased four acres on the Boones Ferry Road, seven miles south of Portland. . . . Gerald and I hope to retire there someday and have a small farm—we may not build for ten years, but we would like to plant some trees this fall. . . . We would like to have some sort of a simple plan to work towards but we do not feel at this time that we can go to much expense."[7] Schryver politely explained the situation to Mrs. Beebe: "You can imagine that every minute is packed with at least two things waiting to be done. We had hoped to be all finished with our gardens by now, but there is still a great deal of work piled up ahead of us to be finished. So we feel that even tho we could make a hurried trip out to the farm we could not give you enough to make it worthwhile."[8] She assured her that they would be able to help them when they came back.

The Beebes were building their retirement house on a rural site in the Englewood community of Lake Oswego, south of Portland. Their architect, Ernest Fanning Tucker (1900–1976), specialized in residential design. He was not only Gerald Beebe's good friend but would also be their future next-door neighbor.[9] Tucker sent Lord and Schryver the plan for the proposed new house in October 1935, and the landscape architects went to work. The four-acre site was an open field on a sloping hilltop with a breathtaking view to the east of snow-covered Mount Hood. For Schryver, the advantages of such a view were reminiscent of Cornish, New Hampshire.

Schryver's first effort was to locate the building within the lot in order to take advantage of the view and the sloping topography (figure 6.5). In consultation with Tucker, she selected the best location for the L-shaped house, and the architect deferred to her decision. This was an unusual accommodation for an architect to make to a landscape architect, in recognition of her professional skills.[10] After several visits to the site, Schryver made extensive notes from which to generate the grading plan and the landscape design.

Schryver's plan for the area in front of the house included a graceful, semi-circular driveway and a parking court with adjacent plantings (figure 6.6). Along the south side of the house, she created a flagstone patio, eighteen feet wide.[11] She drew an imaginary axial line through the French doors of the living room, across the patio and beyond to a long garden walk, an allee of twelve small flowering trees (figure 6.7).[12] This leafy walk was twenty-six feet wide and extended eighty-two feet. It had a yew hedge behind the trees as a background and an inner hedge of very low boxwood for linear emphasis. No ornament or special view lay at the end of this walk, but the striking view from the house was enough to draw one into the garden (plate 15).[13]

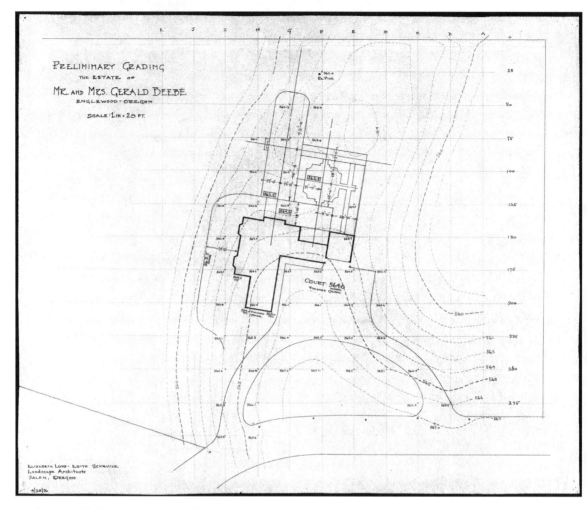

6.5 Lord and Schryver's grading and layout plan for Mr. and Mrs. Gerald Beebe's property, Lake Oswego, Oregon (1936). Courtesy University of Oregon Libraries, Special Collections and University Archives, Coll 098, Lord & Schryver architectural records.

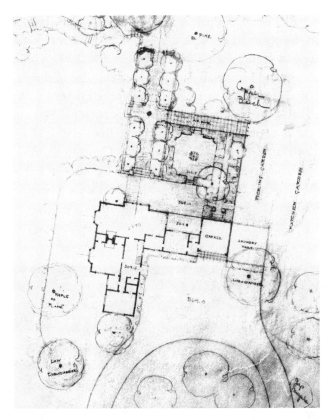

6.6 Edith Schryver's sketch plan for Mr. and Mrs. Gerald Beebe's garden, Lake Oswego, Oregon (1936). Courtesy University of Oregon Libraries, Special Collections and University Archives, Coll 098, Lord & Schryver architectural records.

6.7 Mr. and Mrs. Gerald Beebe's house under construction after the installation of the crabapple allee, Lake Oswego, Oregon (late 1930s). Courtesy University of Oregon Libraries, Special Collections and University Archives, Coll 098, Lord & Schryver architectural records.

Adjacent to the patio was a formal walled garden, a thirty-six-foot square. Schryver left the center of the square open for the Beebes to place a fountain or a sculpture (figure 6.8). She also created a walkway with a double border for shrubs and perennials along the western edge of the enclosure, and an arbor along the southern edge. The entire garden had an elegant eight-and-a-half-foot-high brick wall, with long openings beneath the arbor to allow the flow of air and light (plate 16). This detail is similar to that of Charles Platt's interrupted wall at High Court in Cornish, New Hampshire, which Schryver is likely to have seen. Her nuanced architectural sketch for the Beebes' formal flower garden included a charming roofed gateway and unique Craftsman-style gates (figure 6.9, plate 17).

6.8 Gerald Beebe's house from the doorway into the walled flower garden, Lake Oswego, Oregon (early 1940s). Courtesy Oregon Historical Society Research Library. Al Monner photo.

On the east side of the house, the windows of both the living room and the master bedroom looked out on a superb view of Mount Hood. Here the landscape around the house was a simple uninterrupted lawn with a few specimen trees. Below the lawn, the land sloped away to a field, the perimeter framed by woodlands.[14] The remaining landscape was planted naturalistically with trees and shrubs to balance the formal geometry of the flower garden and the allee, transitioning into the rural landscape.

Schryver's siting of the Beebes' house and her landscape design both recall Charles Platt's recommendations for the ideal landscape. As he stated in 1912, "To a house set high upon a hill, the ground falling away from it with some abruptness, the whole site chosen for the view, the landscape gardener will give surroundings of the utmost simplicity that they may not compete with or disturb the larger without."[15]

The Beebes were very satisfied with the landscape work, and Lord and Schryver remained their consultants throughout the following years. They became good friends, which was often the case in Lord and Schryver's relationships with their clients. Gerald Beebe held them in high regard,

6.9 The walled flower garden at Gerald Beebe's house, Lake Oswego, Oregon (early 1940s). Courtesy Oregon Historical Society Research Library. Al Monner photo.

complimenting Schryver by letter in 1936, "Indeed, in the quite short period of our friendship, I have developed a thorough respect for the good quality of your ideas and the gentle determination with which you succeed in having them carried forward."[16] Mary Beebe relished their expertise in plantsmanship.

Both visually cohesive and balanced, the landscape Lord and Schryver designed for the new house provided a great opportunity for Mrs. Beebe to express her taste in flowering and foliage plants. In 1941, Mary Beebe called on Lord and Schryver once again as she envisioned a planting of heather for a section of the east sloping bank behind their home. Lord replied by letter that they were working at the historic McLoughlin House in Oregon City and could not start immediately.

> We both are happy you want us to do the Heather bank for we think we can and believe it will be fun to work out—only to do it right now will be impossible. I have to speak frankly, for I do not believe in stalling off, making excuses because we are not there. Not knowing how you stood in the matter, we had not worked out any plan and being so snowed under with work, we have had to give our attention to work that demanded immediate supervision—especially construction work—which cannot be done late in the season. Moreover, we have not been able to study on varieties enough, or even visited nurseries yet! But please count on us doing the very best for you and Gerald.[17]

The following year they worked out the planting plan for the heather bank, and it perfectly suited the site. A carpet of lavenders and purples, the heather slope is beautiful almost eighty years later (plate 18). The entire Beebe garden is remarkably intact today and just as lovely as it was when designed in the 1930s. Natural growth and decline of plants will always transform a landscape; one cannot freeze them in time, a certainty that Lord and Schryver well understood. As Schryver stated in 1981, "A garden is never the same, but its characteristics should be preserved."[18] For this remarkable preservation, we must thank the conscientious and inspired owners who have appreciated and cared for the captivating beauty that Lord and Schryver created.

   ⇉⇉ The Home Garden Hour at KOAC, 1930–1950s

When Elizabeth Lord invited Florence H. Gerke to speak to the Salem Garden Club, she wrote, "The subject of your lecture, we, of course, would like to be 'Planning the Small Garden.' It is something they need so badly, but 'they' do not know it and we feel we have said about all that is possible on that subject."[19] It was August 1931, and Lord's statement was a slight exaggeration. They persevered in their efforts to educate others for many more years.

Lord and Schryver were grateful for having had the benefit of an excellent education in landscape architecture in the East. When they opened their Salem office in 1929, they aspired to share their knowledge with the gardening public, and particularly to educate homeowners about the finer principles of garden design. This motivated them to lecture and to judge garden competitions, to write articles for the *Sunday Oregonian* in 1932, and influenced their activities throughout their long careers. Sometimes they found the effort to educate the public daunting, as Lord had expressed in her letter to Mrs. Gerke.

Beginning in the 1930s, Lord and Schryver had the novel opportunity to use one of the most innovative new media—radio broadcasting. The Oregon Agricultural College (OAC) in Corvallis created a public service radio station in 1922, named KFDJ.[20] Funding for it came from the Cooperative Extension Service of the US Department of Agriculture. The intent was to disseminate the latest agricultural and technical information from the land grant colleges to farmers and their families across rural America. The first radio station at OAC was built as an experiment by the physics department. In 1925, the station was rebuilt with more powerful wattage and renamed KOAC, with the slogan "Science for Service."[21] A small, well-educated staff kept up an ambitious plan to develop programs. They were so successful in reaching the many farm families in the Willamette Valley that radio historian Hugh R. Slotten claimed KOAC was "the most important radio station in the western United States serving the needs of agriculture."[22]

KOAC took its audience's interests seriously. Although initially founded to serve farmers, the station became an extremely popular venue by the late 1930s for both rural and urban/suburban dwellers. Radio played a very important role in the lives of American women during the early to mid-twentieth century, when many women were still homebound, and Station KOAC was an excellent means of reaching that audience.[23] A significant part of their programming focused on domestic topics. It also provided cultural programs including classical music, art history lectures, literary readings, and the like. The underlying intent conformed to part of the Progressive Era agenda—to transform a traditional rural society into a modern, well-educated society.[24]

The leadership of the Oregon Federation of Garden Clubs quickly realized the enormous potential of the new technology to further their own mission, and their officers devised an innovative way to utilize it.[25] They arranged with KOAC to provide a weekly program for Oregonians interested in landscape design and horticulture. The *Home Garden Hour* was broadcast live from the studio in Corvallis, and its speakers were gardening authorities, often faculty from the agricultural college and the University of Oregon in Eugene. According to Thea Croman, a journalism scholar,

"From seed preservation to 'gardening for health and beauty,' messages endorsing scientific rationality were plied over the airwaves."[26]

In 1930, the federation enhanced their program by creating a series of "radio clubs." Each radio club, a group of five or more garden enthusiasts, mostly women, would register with the federation and gather at a specific time and location to tune in to the *Home Garden Hour.* The monthly speaker, the federation assured clubs, "will step into your meetings, via radio, to answer questions and talk with you informally about your garden problems and interests."[27] Each expert also prepared a reference list of books and articles for the listeners. The lecture lasted half an hour, followed by a brief, preplanned question-and-answer period. The federation encouraged each club to discuss the topics among themselves afterward, then to complete a questionnaire provided by the KOAC Garden Club organizers, and to file a report about their meeting. Members could include any questions they would like to have answered on the next broadcast. It was a brilliant idea, an adult education service that was free and available to anyone in Oregon willing to register and file the monthly report.[28]

Lord and Schryver were among the first professionals invited to speak on the *Home Garden Hour.* Louise E. Weatherford, chair of the federation's Radio Committee, contacted Lord in 1930 to ask if she would discuss either town planning for small cities or the design of rural highways. For an unknown reason, the program had to be cancelled. But in 1938, Lord and Schryver were both able to join W. Dorr Legg, assistant professor of landscape architecture, to present an extended series of seven talks, "Planning and Planting the Home Grounds." To provide an insider's view of how a landscape design practice worked, they presented the series as radio theater. They wrote scripts for several characters, including imaginary clients and office staff, while Professor Legg played the landscape architect.[29]

Lord and Schryver returned to the airwaves many times. In the spring of 1944, the title of Schryver's lecture was "Looking toward the Fall Garden." In 1946, Lord read from her script "Spring Flowers in the Garden," about early flowering plants, and then "Color Schemes in Late Spring Gardens," which included her selection of favorite plants for May and June. She discussed the value of using color schemes, sequence of bloom and plant associations to enhance one's garden. Varying their lecture topics, they gave approximately twelve presentations extending into the 1950s, a notable contribution.

What an exciting experience working in radio must have been for them. They understood how important this new medium was for educational outreach, especially for women, and they generously contributed their time and knowledge. The transcripts for their KOAC presentations are preserved in the University of Oregon's Special Collections and Archives.

≫ ≫ ≫ The Lyle B. and Anne Kingery Garden, 1938–1944

While Lord and Schryver were on the air at KOAC, they began work for significant new clients, Dr. and Mrs. Lyle B. Kingery.[30] The Kingerys' architect Ernest Tucker was designing a new home for them in the Dunthorpe suburb of Portland. In December 1938, Schryver wrote to Mrs. Kingery that they had learned about the project from Tucker, with whom they had collaborated on the Beebe property. She inquired whether the Kingerys were interested in "garden development."[31] Dr. Kingery confirmed that they were and set up a meeting at the architect's Portland office later that month.[32] Following the meeting and a site visit, Schryver repositioned the house by a few degrees to better align with the topography, with the architect's approval. She also recommended the place to dig the well. Even though it was January, Schryver arranged for the Kingerys to visit Gaiety Hollow to see Lord and Schryver's own garden and how the garden rooms had been arranged.

With the threat of World War II looming in Europe, Dr. Kingery wrote to Schryver of his desire to plant a variety of fruit trees, a grape arbor, and filberts, as "nobody can tell what the future holds."[33] By July 1939, she had provided them with a sketch plan for the landscape and two little sketches that included an arbor of "the simple, old-fashioned type," a tool house, an orchard, and a vegetable garden.[34] Construction on the house began later that month. Lord and Schryver planned to select plants in September and plant them in the autumn.

In early December, Schryver informed Dr. Kingery that the season had been too warm and too dry to safely plant his deciduous trees because there was no outdoor water outlet at the new house. They would have to wait for the January rains before going to the site and laying out the planting plan with stakes.[35] When Dr. Kingery commented on the expense, Schryver replied, "All we ask is that we can come from time to time to supervise the planting, . . . giving the garden a finish which we think is most important for such a beautiful home as your's [sic]."[36] Their fee of $50 plus travel expenses of $3 per trip would cover their layout work and supervision of the planting plan.[37]

The setting for the Kingerys' house on the far outskirts of the city was the crest of a hill with a commanding view of wooded hills falling away to the south.[38] This was the inspiration for Schryver's design. She considered the view and the sloping hillside below the house as most important to the overall composition (figure 6.10). For the front of the house, she planned a semicircular drive from the street to the garage and the service court (figure 6.11). The house itself faced north and was an asymmetrical J-shape. Schryver chose to extend lines from the outer edges of the house into the

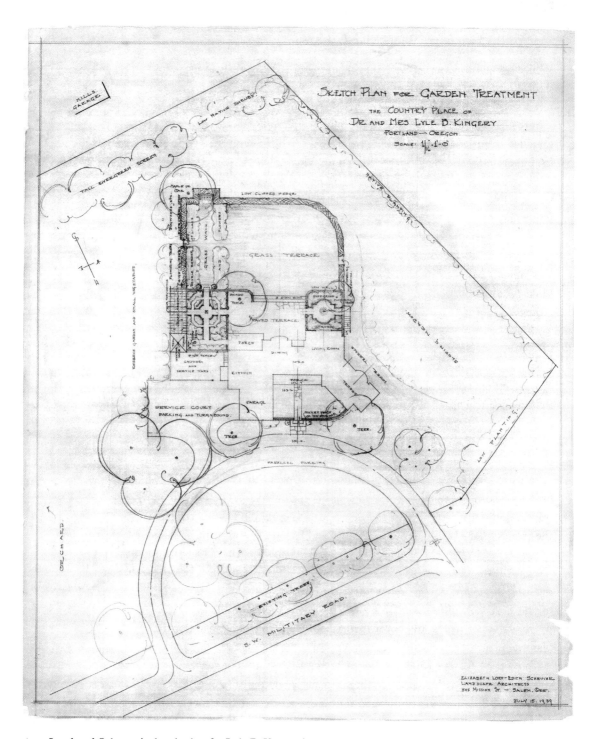

6.10 Lord and Schryver's sketch plan for Lyle B. Kingery's
garden, Portland, Oregon (1939). Courtesy University of
Oregon Libraries, Special Collections and University Archives,
Coll 098, Lord & Schryver architectural records.

landscape to define the sides of the garden area rather than use a central
axis. Within this large square, she placed three formal gardens, a paved
terrace, and a grass terrace.[39] To the east side of the patio, Schryver created
a sequence of two garden rooms somewhat reminiscent of her work for
the Beebes (plate 19). There was a four-part flower garden and a grass walk
with a double border of lilacs and flowers. On the west side of the patio,
Schryver proposed an "Evergreen Garden," a small, square garden with a
central fountain to be viewed from the living room. Regrettably, this space,
which bore a strong similarity to Gaiety Hollow's Evergreen Garden, was
never constructed. A low clipped hedge curved around the lawn, separating
the middle ground from background, a design detail Schryver had learned
from the gardens of Cornish. Beyond this was a sloping meadow where
Lord and Schryver had the boundary lines planted with evergreens and
native shrubs, referencing the natural landscape beyond. Each garden area
was very carefully composed, each space a part of a single unity.

The architect and the landscape architect disagreed about the size of the
Kingerys' terrace. Tucker argued that the one Schryver had designed was

too large and cost too much to build. Schryver stood her ground in their negotiations and insisted that the terrace, which was twenty feet wide, was not too much for the size of the whole house, and that their own ten-by-thirteen-foot terrace at Gaiety Hollow was "terribly cramped."[40] She prevailed, and the terrace remained as she had planned it.

Work on the Kingerys' landscape continued for almost five years. Anne Kingery very much enjoyed working with Lord and Schryver; they became good friends, sharing their ideas about the most desirable plants. All three women were very particular about their plant choices. When Lord and Schryver ordered evergreens for the Kingerys' boundary planting from Walsh and Rainwater's Nursery in Marshfield, Oregon, Lord made sure to specify, "when we do a mass planting, and for a boundary, we try to have different heights."[41] This would make the trees appear to have grown there naturally and blend into the scenery. Lord was also very particular about the color of the foliage, telling the nursery, "The Port Orford Cedars should be all one color, either the yellow green, or the blue-green, will you please keep this in mind."[42]

After America entered the war in 1941, many Oregonians became more concerned with potential shortages of food and materials than with ornamental gardening. Labor became scarce as men enlisted in the armed forces. In May 1943, Schryver wrote to Anne Kingery, "I see nothing but physical work till the war ceases. With no maid, and now our own gardener gone to the cantonment, we shall have to do the heavy work."[43] Fortunately, by December 1944, Lord and Schryver had completed the Kingerys' garden, and even the fine-tuning had just about ended.

➤➤➤ The Robert E. and Margaret Avison Garden, 1949–1955

Not far from the Kingery family in the Dunthorpe neighborhood south of Portland, Robert E. Avison, a prominent mill owner, built a new house for his wife and children in 1949. Margaret Avison had seen a neighbor's garden designed by Lord and Schryver, very possibly the Kingerys' garden, and had been impressed. She realized that their new property had several "knotty problems" and decided to employ Lord and Schryver to solve them (figure 6.12). She may also have met them at the Portland Garden Club. Either way, Lord and Schryver devised a masterful solution for how to transform a problematic site into a landscape enjoyed by the whole family. It required six years to design, install, and refine (figure 6.13).

They began with the visitor's approach from the main street to the Avisons' Colonial Revival home. Locating a "parking forecourt" off the street and a simple planting before the front door provided a formal entrance. The widest part of the property was the side yard to the east of the

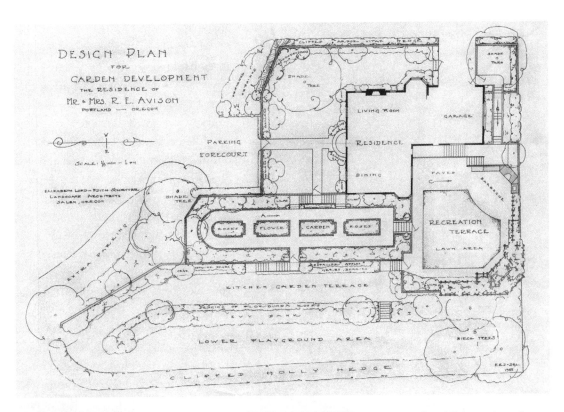

DESIGN PLAN
FOR
GARDEN DEVELOPMENT
THE RESIDENCE OF
MR. & MRS. R. E. AVISON
PORTLAND — OREGON

6.12 Lord and Schryver's garden plan for Mr. and Mrs. R. E. Avison, Portland, Oregon (1955). Courtesy University of Oregon Libraries, Special Collections and University Archives, Coll 098, Lord & Schryver architectural records.

6.13 Edith Schryver in Mr. and Mrs. Avison's landscape during construction (1956). Courtesy University of Oregon Libraries, Special Collections and University Archives, Coll 098, Lord & Schryver architectural records.

house (figure 6.14). It had a steep, downhill slope, at the bottom of which was an embankment and a busy state highway, creating both noise and privacy issues. To make this area usable, Lord and Schryver designed three terraces, each one longer than wide, stepping downhill. The uppermost level, adjacent to the house, was the Flower Garden Terrace, with roses in four central beds. Each bed was planted with a single color: white, yellow, pink and red, with 'Peace' roses to create the transitions because they contained all four colors (figure 6.15). They designed a border of shrubs and bulbs to encircle this terrace (figure 6.16, plate 20). The middle level, the Kitchen Garden Terrace, had espaliered fruit trees, berries, vegetables, and herbs against an east-facing wall, the perfect microclimate. The Lower Playground Area at the bottom of the hill was de-

6.14 Edith Schryver overseeing contractors during the construction of Mr. and Mrs. R. E. Avison's garden (1955). Courtesy University of Oregon Libraries, Special Collections and University Archives, Coll 098, Lord & Schryver architectural records.

signed specifically for the Avison children to race around freely. Schryver's love of children, observed by many of their friends, made her particularly sensitive to their needs. Lord and Schryver also made a fourth and larger terrace at the north end of the property, behind the house, and named it the Recreation Terrace, an outdoor space where the whole family could gather. Here, the Avison children had a paved circuit for riding their tricycles and a lawn for their swings and wading pool. There was a built-in barbecue, a vine-covered pergola, and tables and chairs for the adults, thus completing the scene for modern outdoor living.[44]

The terraces were constructed with concrete retaining walls faced with brick. Steps and walkways connected them in a comfortable pattern so people could circulate through all the spaces. In keeping with the Colonial Revival theme, Lord and Schryver had the brick walls, wooden fences, gates, and arbors whitewashed. They added traditional (historically reminiscent) plantings of lilac and boxwood. A clipped holly hedge of fifty-nine plants of ten different varieties were used to screen out the highway at the base of the garden. Mrs. Avison was so pleased with the design that, fifty years later, when members of the Lord & Schryver Conservancy visited her, the garden looked lovely. Mrs. Avison told them, "I tried to keep it just the way they designed it."[45]

6.15 Edith Schryver in Mr. and Mrs. R. E. Avison's newly planted rose garden (1956). Courtesy University of Oregon Libraries, Special Collections and University Archives, Coll 098, Lord & Schryver architectural records.

6.16 Mr. and Mrs. R. E. Avison's rose garden (1956). Courtesy University of Oregon Libraries, Special Collections and University Archives, Coll 098, Lord & Schryver architectural records.

A Seasonal Lifestyle

By the 1940s, Lord and Schryver's life together had developed a seasonal routine. From late winter into the summer months, they took on numerous projects, worked hard, and traveled from Salem to their project sites. In late summer, when heat and drought affected the Northwest, they enjoyed periods of relaxation at their cottage on the coast at Seal Rock in between periods of work. Many of their friends from Salem also owned cottages there, and they had a most pleasurable time with constant visitors. They would return to Salem in the autumn to complete projects before winter, when they enjoyed setting off on longer journeys together. They were intrepid travelers and had been since their first acquaintance. Their winter journeys sometimes brought them to New York and the East Coast to visit relatives, and sometimes to California for the sunshine and warmth. They also ventured further afield to Europe and the Far East. Visiting Lord's brother Montague in the Philippines was always an attraction. During World War II, however, the Japanese took him prisoner and requisitioned his property. He survived for three years in an internment camp, during which time his sister rarely heard from him.[46] After the Americans liberated the country, Montague continued to live in the Philippines. He had lost his home and most of his wealth, but he managed to obtain a house in Baguio, a mountain town.[47] Lord went to the Philippines to be with her brother during his final year, 1960.

Throughout the many years of their practice, Lord and Schryver had a keen interest in bringing new cultivars into the western trade to expand the plant palette available to gardeners. Their extensive experience with plants familiar in eastern landscapes and from their travels inspired them to encourage the Northwest's nursery industry to expand its offerings. Their expertise identified them as consummate plantswomen.

7

Plantswomen

As for flowers not requiring work, this is a difficult question to
answer, for I have yet to find any flower (or any plant for that
matter) that does not require attention.
    —Elizabeth Lord, 1945

Men tended to enter the profession of landscape architecture through the
portal of architecture, but women entered through the garden gate. From
the Victorian era through the early twentieth century, countless books, articles, and lectures encouraged women to consider gardening an important part of their domestic realm, and they accepted this assignment with
dedication. Having become expert amateur gardeners, a few considered
undertaking more—a professional career in landscape architecture. When
women entered the field, their work could usually be distinguished from
that of their male colleagues by their superior knowledge of plants and
horticulture, knowledge they had gained through long hours working in
their own gardens. As Shipman so famously stated, "Before women took
hold of the profession, landscape architects were doing what I call cemetery
work. . . . Until women took up landscaping, gardening in this country was
at its lowest ebb."[1]

Lord and Schryver's education at Lowthorpe ensured that they would
be accomplished "plantswomen," not only masters of design but thoroughly
knowledgeable about the proper selection and culture of woody and herbaceous plants. Lowthorpe emphasized the artistic aspects of plant composition, likening a gardener's use of plants to a painter's use of a palette of colors. By the early twentieth century, plant introductions, botanical exchanges,
and the growth of the American nursery industry had made available a vibrant selection of ornamental plants. In the gardens of Lowthorpe and the
estates, parks, and arboreta surrounding Boston—a mecca for American
horticulturists at the time—students could examine live specimens and

compare their flowers, forms, foliage, and growth habits, as well as consider how to use them in compositions. The Arnold Arboretum in particular featured a renowned and comprehensive collection of trees, shrubs, and vines, many of which were new introductions to the United States from around the world. The plants were labeled with their scientific names, enabling students to familiarize themselves with the plants' characteristics as they learned the correct botanical nomenclature and selected their personal favorites.

Lord and Schryver arrived in Oregon just as the profession of landscape architecture was beginning to develop in the Pacific Northwest. Although there were some fine nurseries in this part of the country, many did not grow the exact species or cultivars that Lord and Schryver were familiar with and preferred to use. At first, they placed their plant orders with eastern nurseries that Schryver knew well, such as Conwell's Nursery in Milton, Delaware, which specialized in superior quality boxwood. Schryver ordered 180 feet of small plants for the Merrills' garden in Seattle in 1929. The shipping cost by rail of $1,200 was far too exorbitant for most of their clients.[2] They soon realized that they would need to expand their search for the best nurseries in the Northwest through the network of local garden clubs.

Oregon's nurseries began to develop in the mid-1800s as nurserymen discovered the rich soils, abundant rainfall, and moderate temperatures that had already made the cultivation of fruit so productive in the Willamette Valley. Growers brought stock plants from the Midwest, and Oregon was soon renowned for its trade in fruit trees as well as for its orchards. In the 1880s, the Oregon Agricultural College (today Oregon State University) created a department of horticulture that helped support the nursery business, and 1893 saw the organization of the first Oregon Nurserymen's Association.[3] In the early years, Oregon's nurseries grew mostly orchard stock, but after 1918, as homeowners began to take a greater interest in their properties, the ornamental plant industry expanded. Professor Arthur L. Peck of the Oregon Agricultural College recalled the turning point in 1929, when Oregon's few growers of ornamentals began to flourish: "Nearly every grower was stampeded into the production of fruit trees but a few held their interest in ornamentals. . . . They have become the leaders in the production of an extensive line of ornamental trees, shrubs and vines today."[4] Propitiously, 1929 was the same year that Lord and Schryver opened their practice.

Many nursery owners in the Northwest struggled through the Depression. During the 1940s, as transcontinental transportation grew, these networks were able to link production with buyers in the rest of the nation and gradually build a stronger industry. In response to the boom in home construction that followed World War II, the Northwest's nurseries expanded and prospered. Smaller operations developed alongside the larger wholesale producers of standard trees and shrubs.[5] Numerous growers began to specialize in the newly hybridized cultivars of perennials, roses, bulbs, dwarf conifers, and alpine plants. Several of the wholesale nurseries made a significant contribution to horticulture by testing new plants for hardiness and adaptability before introducing them to the trade. In turn retail nurseries and their customers appreciated the fact that they received sound recommendations on what plants would grow well in their climate and soils.

Lord and Schryver made it their mission to increase the diversity of plants used to create landscapes in the Northwest and to make gardeners more aware of the wider range of choices available to them (figure 7.1). They had their own personal preferences and thought it desirable to cultivate display collections of particular plants at

7.1 Elizabeth Lord and Edith Schryver at Gaiety Hollow (1947). Courtesy *Capitol Journal.* Jesten-Miller Studio photo.

Gaiety Hollow to show their clients and visitors. When Schryver wrote to a nurseryman in Norwood, Massachusetts, in 1929 to order phlox for the Merrill garden, she admitted, "Miss Lord and I are very anxious to have a 'sample' garden of phlox on our place to show our clients as there are not many varieties in the nurseries out here."[6] By 1938, when Lord ordered seven hemlocks from Mr. Walsh of Walsh and Rainwater in Marshfield, Oregon, she sounded pleased with their progress at Gaiety Hollow, "I am most anxious to make a short hedge of Hemlock on my place. It would be good advertising for we have so many people come here to see the garden and we have a very good selection of all kinds of plant material on the place."[7]

Landscape architects depend on good nurseries to supply the plants they need. And yet nurseries will produce a new plant only if they are sure they will be able to sell a sufficient quantity. This often makes it difficult to bring new plants to market. Lord's frustration with clients who wanted only the "tried and true" slipped out in her comments to nurserymen, as in her letter to Mrs. Alice Case, who, with her husband Burton O. Case, owned a fine nursery in Vancouver, Washington, "We find people will not put in anything unless they know it and unless their neighbor has it. They are so sheep-like in selection of plant material. Everybody has to have a

Flowering Prune and a Pink Dogwood and we become beyond exasperated over their lack of imagination and originality."[8]

Based on their training in the East, Lord and Schryver viewed the Northwest's plant palette as limited, but sometimes the limitations were due to other cultural factors. Lord recognized this when she wrote to Hugh B. Barclay, a nurseryman in Narberth, Pennsylvania,

> We find people do not use Groundcovers extensively here, therefore we do not come across many varieties in the Nurseries. One trouble is everything grows so luxuriantly in the Northwest and spreading plants become a nuisance and in time they are difficult to obliterate. I believe we are the only Landscape Architects to use Pachysandra (that may be an exaggeration) but it really isn't known among gardeners and we like it very much. Miss Schryver was with Ellen Shipman of New York City for many years before coming West with me, so naturally she is more accustom[ed] to groundcover use than the run of Landscape Architects in the West.[9]

As their practice developed, so too did the nursery industry in the Northwest. In time, there were many more new cultivars and specialties available. Lord and Schryver came to lament the fact that they did not have sufficient time to prowl around nurseries examining the new plant introductions. In 1941 Lord wrote to their friend and client Mary Beebe to recommend a new cultivar of glossy abelia, *Abelia* × *grandiflora* 'Sherwoodii'; she stated, "I firmly believe our great trouble is that we do not have time to study more and see newer things, and we both miss it. Too much rush all the time—a la Americana."[10]

Nevertheless, Lord and Schryver developed strong friendships with some of the nurserymen. They particularly enjoyed Mr. and Mrs. Case, whose specialty nursery offered a wide variety of unusual flowering trees and shrubs. Early in the 1930s, they had considered buying a selection of lilac cultivars for Sally Bush, but later decided she was not really interested in having them. Lord then wrote to Mr. Case, "She [Sally Bush] is not as great an admirer of Lilacs as we are, thinks the bloom of short duration and the shrub not so attractive out of flower. On this point we do not agree with her for we think the Lilac has a most interesting and intriguing twig formation and the shape of the bush lends [blends] in so well with trees and landscape."[11] This was about the time that Lord and Schryver stopped working for Miss Sally on her landscape, as Lord explained, "We do not see her so often naturally because we are so busy elsewhere and she has not spent so much time in the garden across the way.... I am inclined to believe she does not want to take any more cultivated care in her garden and feels she has as much as her men can handle."[12]

In the spring of 1938, Mr. and Mrs. Case came to visit the garden at Gaiety Hollow. Afterward Lord wrote,

We are so happy you came to the garden and liked it. A week later it was much prettier for all the Darwin and Cottage tulips were in bloom and with the Lilacs we had a bower of flowers. The garden now looks rather sad for Iris and peonies are not so popular with us and they take so much room in the small garden we have to cut down on their planting. Perhaps we have over done the Lilac planting (we have 14 varieties on this piece of land). But we love them so we simply cannot give one up. It means we have to go without other shrubs which bloom later and give more succession. . . . I have a deep red purple [lilac] purchased by my Mother many years ago from Bertrand Farr [a specialist nurseryman] and the name is lost—but it is a lovely and fine keeper—I call it Juliet Montague in memory of my Mother and the name will last until some Lilac fanciere [*sic*] will come along and denounce me for fraud! Let us hope he never sets foot on my soil.[13]

Lord and Schryver asked for, and usually received from the nurseries, a 20 percent discount on plants they ordered for their clients, a standard practice. Sometimes they ran into difficulty when supplied with either mis-labeled or poor-quality stock. Occasionally, the issues were more serious, as when a nurseryman presumed to tell them how to run their business. This, they would not tolerate. In 1941 Mr. Lambert, the owner of Lambert Gardens in Portland, Oregon, advised them by letter, "Ladies, If you will pardon me for the suggestion, if you want your jobs to look nice, you must insist on your customers spending more money as you cannot get an effect with small shrubs where large ones are needed."[14] Annoying as this unso-licited advice was, Mr. Lambert made the further and even worse mistake of telling Lord and Schryver's client, Mrs. Gattie, when she phoned him, that the plantings were too small. Lord's reply was direct, "Your letter of last week criticizing our planting on the Gattie place quite surprised us for we feel that it was uncalled for and not professional. A great deal of trouble can come between the Landscape Architect and the client under such circum-stances and it was only thru my friendliness with the party that nothing serious happened by your remarks. I am sure you did not intentionally do it to hurt [our] reputation for you must realize we have had a pretty dif-ficult time in Oregon and at times most discouraging." She continued, "It may seem strange to you that we do not order more Rhododendrons and Evergreens for our gardens, but frankly speaking, we do not have that type of client. It may be due to the fact that we, ourselves, are not fond of just sweeps of such heavy planting, so naturally we do not force it upon our prospective clients."[15] It is doubtful that Mr. Lambert made the mistake of crossing boundaries again.

Boxwood was a plant with a special pedigree. Lord and Schryver used so much of it in their designs that they at first had trouble finding sufficient supplies in the Northwest. Lord consulted at length with nursery owners Mr. and Mrs. V. A. Goode about this early in their careers. "My dear Mrs.

Goode," she wrote, "We wanted to talk to you about the Box situation. We have tried to get people more interested in having it, but so many speak about the scent, which we both like, and it seems to be objectionable to so many and people here are so silly about the thought of a hedge of any kind. However, I know we have made some impression in that line in this last year and my advice is to keep on growing it and the time will come when it will be very popular."[16] Their order for two hundred small plants of boxwood followed, but only those that Lord had specifically marked in the Goodes' nursery with little sticks, because she was very particular about size and quality.

Later that year, Lord confided to Mr. Goode, "I do feel there is more interest in box in the last few years, but we have quite a tussle with a lot of our clients. Sometimes, we have to work the idea [that] Box is used in 'the very best circles' and thru [through] such an argument, it has effect. We have planned a fair-sized order of Box for Mrs. Clifford Brown and shall do all we can to have the order come to you."[17]

As their correspondence continued over the years, Mr. Goode offered his own assessment of boxwood, "This plant, as an ornamental has earned its position of aristocracy by a quality that practically borders immortality. I mean by this that once established, the plant will live on through many generations of man, and under the most adverse circumstances."[18]

In 1929, when Lord discussed ordering boxwood from the East with their new client, Mrs. A. Scott Bullitt of Seattle, her thoughts regarding the superiority of "true English Boxwood" (*Buxus sempervirens* 'Suffruticosa') were very clear: "To my mind there is nothing which gives so much charm, dignity and distinction to a garden as this true small leaved boxwood of the old colonial southern gardens. As far as I know, there is no such hedge in a Northwest garden, and would give yours a very distinct character. . . . The ordinary box which they grow out here in the nurseries does *not* give the right effect, or the same effect."[19]

The boxwood required for Mrs. Bullitt was to make a hedge two feet high as the background for an allee of eight crabapple trees. This walk would lead to a rectangular flower garden with masses of shrubs and perennials. Lord was able to assure Mrs. Bullitt, "The color schemes, combinations and quantity of bloom from season to season have been carefully worked out, with blue as the dominant note always."[20]

➤➤➤ Cooley's Gardens, Silverton, Oregon, 1931, 1951–1952

In 1931, Lord and Schryver had the unusual opportunity to design a display garden for Cooley's Gardens, a specialty iris nursery in Silverton, Oregon. Iris species and their cultivars were among the most popular perennials for home gardeners early in the twentieth century. In response, iris hybridizers created hundreds of new cultivars in a rainbow of colors and forms, the best of which were registered with the American Iris Society.[21] Hybridizers depended on nurseries such as Cooley's to propagate the new cultivars and bring them to market.

Rholin and Pauline Cooley had started hybridizing iris as a backyard hobby in the 1920s, and it soon became their passion. Dr. R. E. Kleinsorge, a local physician and iris breeder, encouraged them to start a nursery. The Cooleys bought land west of Silverton, opened a nursery and printed their first catalog in 1928 (figure 7.2). They established an extensive mail order business and became the primary source of new iris cultivars by America's foremost hybridizers, including Dr. Kleinsorge. Their nursery soon built a reputation for the excellence of its plants and its retail service. It became the world's largest supplier of iris cultivars in the 1980s after five decades of operation (figure 7.3).[22]

In 1931, the Cooleys asked Lord and Schryver, who had purchased plants from them, to prepare a plan for an iris display garden at their commercial site (figure 7.4). The area had been used for production. It was 390 feet long on an angular property, and its greatest width was 130 feet. Schryver's successful proposal was a naturalistic design with a curvilinear system of pathways winding through the iris beds.[23] As a central attraction, she placed two pools divided by a small waterfall, but to build it would have meant diverting a local stream, which required a government permit.[24] The Cooleys

7.2 Rholin Cooley, founding owner of Cooley's Gardens, Silverton, Oregon (1949). Courtesy Judy Ernst Nunn and the American Iris Society.

7.3 Inside the iris packing warehouse at Cooley's Gardens, Silverton, Oregon (1950). Courtesy Judy Ernst Nunn and the American Iris Society.

decided not to pursue the pool option. They groomed the new display area for many years. Its waves of color at the peak of bloom soon decorated the covers of their catalogs, and it became a showplace during Silverton's annual Iris Week celebrations (figure 7.5). The Cooleys wanted it to be at perfection by 1949 for the American Iris Society's annual meeting, and it was.[25]

In 1951, Schryver designed a second, more elaborate "exhibition garden" for the nursery with pathways, boxwood hedges, and iris beds that swirled across the ground in a pattern of scrolls. The new lot was larger, 300 feet long by 230 feet wide, a rectangle with a slight depression in the center—a shallow bowl of green lawn. Schryver defined the larger paths in grass and the smaller ones in flagstones, paying careful attention to the patterns and textures underfoot.[26] The new garden was featured on color postcards and in nursery catalogs with the iris in full bloom (plate 21).

Three generations of the Cooley family managed Cooley's Gardens for more than eight decades. The nursery finally closed in 2011. Many in the American Iris Society still remember the beauty of Cooley's exquisite plants, their display gardens, and the catalogs. The Northwest region remains a major center for the production and distribution of these ever-popular perennials and for numerous other specialty plants.

7.4 Edith Schryver
overseeing
construction of
Cooley's Gardens
iris exhibit, Silverton,
Oregon (1949).
Courtesy University
of Oregon Libraries,
Special Collections
and University
Archives, Coll 098,
Lord & Schryver
architectural records.

7.5 Special garden
exhibit designed by
Lord and Schryver
for Cooley's Gardens,
Silverton, Oregon
(1949). Courtesy Judy
Ernst Nunn and the
American Iris Society.

➤➤➤ The Mr. and Mrs. T. A. Peterman Garden, 1929

Lord and Schryver's expertise in planting design was evident in their work for Mr. and Mrs. T. A. Peterman of Tacoma, Washington. Mr. Peterman built a fortune by starting a company to manufacture wood products, such as plywood, and then transforming it to the mechanical manufacture of the Peterbilt truck.[27] In 1924, the Petermans had constructed a new Dutch Colonial style home in Tacoma, but they had never done much with the landscape. In January 1929, the month Lord and Schryver opened for business, Mrs. Ida Peterman learned of their work through the Portland Garden Club and contacted them for a plan. The Petermans would be their first clients in Tacoma.

Tacoma was a day's drive from Salem. Schryver traveled there alone to meet her client at the Winthrop Hotel and to spend the night. The following day, she completed a preliminary survey of the property. After returning home, Lord and Schryver prepared a conceptual design. Their sketch plan left an existing raspberry bed undisturbed at the owners' request. In her letter to the Petermans, Schryver explained her idea to have three terrace gardens "of different proportions which will give far more interest. . . . The small garden near the Swimming Pool is to be the more intimate and secluded spot, . . . the second little garden, or the transition garden (14 feet by 24 feet) for most of your Rock Plants. . . . The third garden is more of a Flower and Rose Garden."[28] The three gardens were on different levels stepping downhill with a spectacular view of Puget Sound.

Mrs. Peterman requested a planting plan for the terraces, which Lord designed in rich detail, after consultation with the client (figure 7.6). She sent it along with Schryver's construction drawings by November 1929.[29] The planting plan amply demonstrated Lord's expertise in horticultural composition and provided an arrangement of seasonally specific colors. Lord also considered plant height, form, and leaf texture to accentuate three-dimensional depth in each garden. Lord specified, in notes on the planting plan, "The gardens have been planted chiefly for effect between May thru September. . . . The first terrace is treated as an old-fashioned enclosed garden with columbines, Foxgloves, Canterbury bells, Lilies, Jap. [Japanese] Anemones etc."[30] This terrace had an outer hedge of boxwood to be kept less than two feet tall and an inner hedge of boxwood less than six inches tall. The color scheme of the second garden was yellow, lavender, and white, allowing spaces for creeping rock garden plants such as thyme and sedum. Hydrangeas and white phlox would give it interest all summer. The lowest terrace, or Rose Garden, "has a perennial border of pinks and blues to supplement the pink and yellow tea roses" and a groundcover of violas with a low border of ageratum. As an addition, Lord recommended that

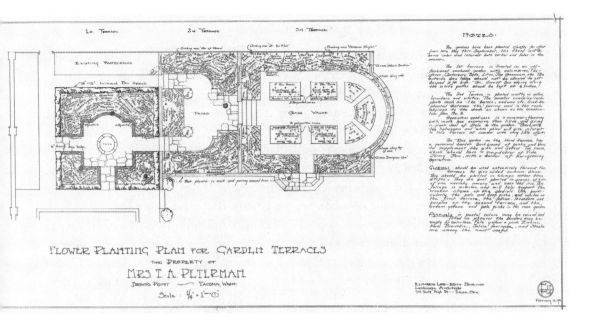

7.6 Lord and Schryver's planting plan for Mrs. T. A. Peterman, Tacoma, Washington (1930). Courtesy University of Oregon Libraries, Special Collections and University Archives, Coll 098, Lord & Schryver architectural records.

gladioli be used extensively throughout the terraces to give more summer bloom, and she specified planting them in "clumps rather than drifts" along with annuals of prescribed colors.

Lord's approach to planting design, including the use of seasonal color schemes and her manner of arranging plants in the beds, derived from the practices of the famous English artist and garden designer Gertrude Jekyll (1843–1932). Jekyll designed approximately four hundred gardens from the late Victorian period through the early twentieth century, working closely with the English architect Edwin L. Lutyens (1869–1944). Her approach to garden design as an art evolved from her early training as a painter in the Impressionist mode. When her eyesight began to fail, she turned her creativity to the landscape, where she emphasized the synergy between landscape design and art.[31]

Jekyll created a highly distinctive style of planting design by using numerous perennials planted in groups of a single type in elongated "drifts." She often ran the drifts diagonally across the width of a bed as she believed that this produced the visual effect of movement. Both Lord and Schryver had learned this style of planting design at Lowthorpe. Ellen Shipman had adopted a similar style, which Schryver had practiced in Shipman's office. In contrast to Jekyll, Lord's planting plans often used semicircular groups rather than long drifts.[32] The ultimate effect of her three-dimensional arrangement of plants in the garden was one of lushness, density, and abundance.

"To casually plant a tree without having any idea of its kind, habit, ultimate shape, durability and physical needs is a mistake," declared Lord and Schryver in their March 1932 article for the *Sunday Oregonian*.[33] Lord further expounded on this in a radio talk for Station KOAC in the 1940s. This lecture, titled "Flowering Trees for Your Garden," reveals how carefully Lord would evaluate particular landscape plants. She also described some of her favorite flowering trees and how to use them correctly in designs.

Lord began the lecture by discussing the cultural history of the cherry tree and the popularity of the Cherry Blossom Festival in Japan. She then turned to some very practical horticultural information. First, she described four distinct types of trees: the large tree, the pyramidal and slender variety, the weeping type, and the low, creeping shrub-like kinds.[34] She then explained the best use for each type and recommended that the tall slender form could be used in an old fashioned flower garden, but advised the home gardener, "to keep the planting low underneath, so the tree stands as an accent."[35] Lord elaborated on all the aspects one should consider for long-term beauty: correct placement, habit of growth, period of bloom, color of flowers, and the fruit.

Lord then listed the ornamental trees that she considered best for Oregon gardens, organized according to their sequence of bloom, beginning in the spring with the Japanese weeping cherry (*Prunus subhirtella* var. *pendula*). She ranked flowering crabapples as the most important and interesting group of small trees and highly recommended the Sargent crabapple, which was discovered in Asia and named for Professor Charles S. Sargent, the first director of the Arnold Arboretum. She noted, "*Malus sargentii*, to my mind, is one of the loveliest of all Crabs. A dwarf type, [with] low and creeping form, the branches are dark, twisted and spreading. Flowers purest white and very crowded with yellow stamens. The fruit is wine color and very showy in the Fall."[36] She went on to cover the hawthorns, another of her favorite small trees, describing "*Crataegus carrierei*," or the Carrier's thorn (Lavalle hawthorn), "a very striking tree in the Fall.[37] Its habit is pyramidal instead of outspreading and it is especially attractive planted in a grouping of small Trees. The leaf retains its vivid glossy texture until late in the Fall and the white flower, producing scarlet fruit, is very striking and very prolific until late in the season."[38] Lord and Schryver planted two of these hawthorns to frame the entrance gate at Gaiety Hollow, where they continue to grow today.

Two other flowering trees, both native to the southeastern United States, that Lord highly recommended were the fringetree (*Chionanthus virginicus*) and the Carolina silverbell (*Halesia tetraptera*). Both are still considered

PLATE 1   Garry oaks and spring camassia in Bush's Pasture Park (2019).
Courtesy Salem Art Association.

PLATE 2 Edith Schryver's senior thesis, Wynndie-Lea (1923). Courtesy University of Oregon Libraries, Special Collections and University Archives, Coll 098, Lord & Schryver architectural records.

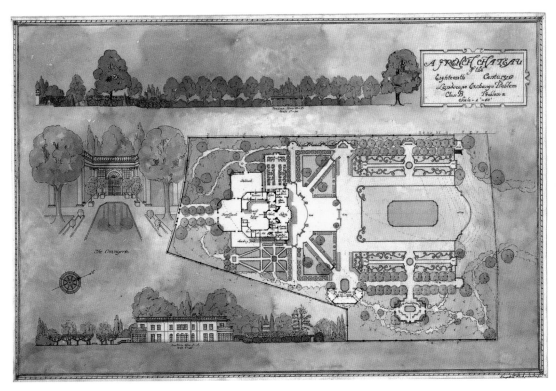

PLATE 3   Elizabeth Lord's class assignment, "A French Chateau" (c. 1927).
Courtesy University of Oregon Libraries, Special Collections and University
Archives, Coll 098, Lord & Schryver architectural records.

PLATE 4 Augustus Saint-Gauden's house, Aspet, Cornish, New Hampshire (2018). Courtesy the author.

PLATE 5 Use of wall to separate middle-ground scenery from background at Charles Platt's house, Cornish, New Hampshire (2000). Courtesy the Charles Platt family.

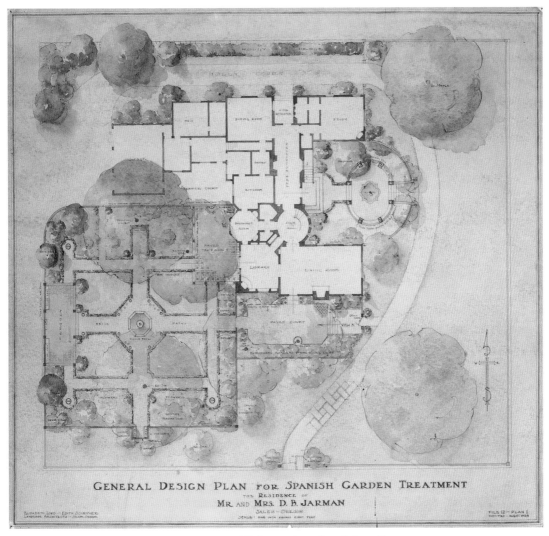

PLATE 6   Lord and Schryver's plan for Daniel B. Jarman's garden, Salem, Oregon
(1929). Courtesy University of Oregon Libraries, Special Collections and University
Archives, Coll 098, Lord & Schryver architectural records. Frank Miller photo.

PLATE 7   Central fountain in
Daniel B. Jarman's garden, Salem,
Oregon (c. 1930s). Courtesy University of
Oregon Libraries, Special Collections and
University Archives, Coll 098, Lord &
Schryver architectural records

PLATE 8   Wall fountain in Daniel B.
Jarman's garden (c. 1930s). Courtesy
University of Oregon Libraries,
Special Collections and University
Archives, Coll 098, Lord & Schryver
architectural records.

PLATE 9   Teahouse Garden gate at Deepwood (2018). Courtesy Mark Akimoff.

PLATE 10   Teahouse Garden at Deepwood (2019). Courtesy Mark Akimoff.

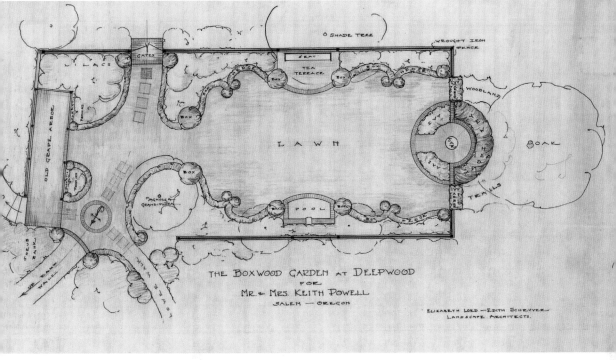

PLATE 11 Lord and Schryver's plan for the Scroll Garden at Deepwood (1945).
Courtesy Deepwood Museum & Gardens.

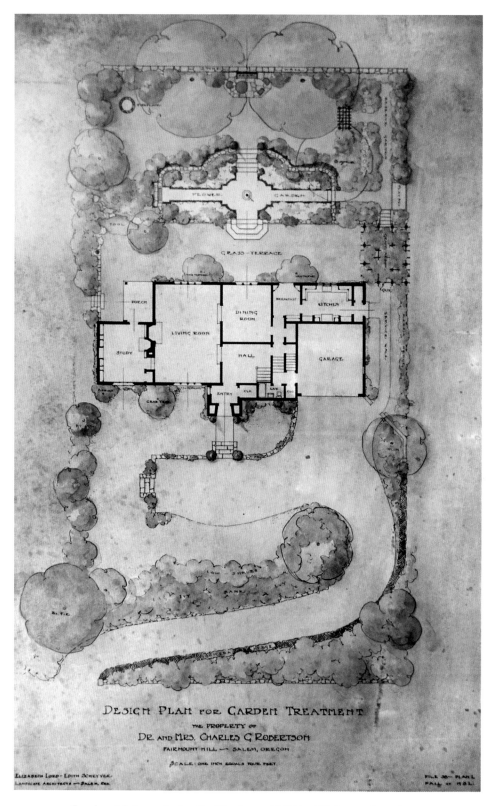

PLATE 12   Lord and Schryver's plan for Charles and Mildred Robertson's garden
(fall 1931). Courtesy Lord & Schryver Conservancy.

PLATE 13   View of the
Robertson's terrace, (2018).
Courtesy the author.

PLATE 14   Pergola with the fireplace, a later addition to the Robertson garden
(1988). Courtesy Lord & Schryver Conservancy, Anne M. Kingery Library.
Frances Duniway photo.

PLATE 15   The Crabapple Allee at Gerald Beebe's house, Lake Oswego, Oregon (2018). Courtesy the author.

PLATE 16   The walled flower garden at the Beebe house, Lake Oswego, Oregon (2014).
Courtesy Jay Raney.

PLATE 17   The flower garden gate at the Beebe house, Lake Oswego, Oregon (2018).
Courtesy the author.

PLATE 18   Heather bank in the Beebe's garden (2018). Courtesy the author.

PLATE 19 The Kingery flower garden (1990). Courtesy Lord & Schryver Conservancy, Anne M. Kingery Library. Frances Duniway photo.

PLATE 20 Flower garden terrace in Mr. and Mrs. R. E. Avison's garden, Portland, Oregon (2010). Courtesy Lord & Schryver Conservancy, Anne M. Kingery Library.

PLATE 21 Cooley's Gardens iris display beds (1950s). Courtesy Judy Ernst Nunn and American Iris Society.

PLATE 22   Portland Garden Club, rear entrance (2019). Courtesy the author.

PLATE 23   Garden view from the Portland Garden Club's library (2019). Courtesy the author.

PLATE 24   Bush House Museum in autumn (2020). Courtesy Jay Raney.

PLATE 25   Tartar Rose Garden with sundial, Bush's Pasture Park, Salem, Oregon (2008). Courtesy Gretchen Carnaby.

PLATE 26   Edith Schryver in the Flower Garden at Gaiety Hollow, Salem, Oregon (1980). ©USA TODAY NETWORK.

PLATE 27   Glass slide of the Flower Garden at Gaiety Hollow (c.1935). Courtesy University of Oregon Libraries, Special Collections and University Archives, Coll 098, Lord & Schryver architectural records.

PLATE 28   Axial view north through the arbor to the Flower Garden at Gaiety
Hollow (2018). Courtesy Susan Napack.

PLATE 29   West Allee with house at Gaiety Hollow (2018). Courtesy Didra Carter-Hendrix.

PLATE 30   The Evergreen Garden at Gaiety Hollow (2020). Courtesy Jay Raney.

PLATE 31   The Flower Garden at Gaiety Hollow (2020). Courtesy Mark Akimoff.

PLATE 32   View of the Flower Garden from second floor of Gaiety Hollow (2020).
Courtesy Mark Akimoff.

among the finest of our small flowering trees. She closed with a recommendation for the audience, that if they were interested in flowering trees, "and wish to see them in all their glory, there is in no place in this country where you may have a closer view . . . than that of the Arnold Arboretum near Boston."[39] The arboretum was, of course, where Lord and Schryver had studied the trees and shrubs firsthand.

Schryver also presented a talk for KOAC titled "Looking toward the Fall Garden." The show was broadcast in April 1944, and Schryver noted the irony of her timing, saying, "On a lovely spring day like this with flowering trees, shrubs and early bulbs in full bloom, it is only the true gardener who has the imagination and the foresight to look forward to the Fall garden and plan for a wealth of bloom at that time."[40] She began by discussing the transition from the pastel colors of summer, if one had chosen them, to the warm colors of fall, with "marigolds, chrysanthemums; red, orange and yellow zinnias; glads [gladiolas] and dahlias in one last burst of warmth before the cold rains of winter come."[41] In addition to color schemes, Schryver explained the importance of the form and shape of both the flowers and the whole plant. She also discussed using contrasting leaf shapes and textures. With these three criteria—color, form, and texture—she then delved into her preferred list of fall-flowering plants, placing autumn asters last, the natural flowers of season's end.

Lord and Schryver understood and appreciated the distinction between North American native plants and introduced ornamentals, but they did not demonstrate a preference for one over the other. They selected Northwestern natives where they were most appropriate for the site, as, for example, in the design for Breitenbush Hot Springs, a wilderness resort, and later, for Salem's Pringle Creek Park. They knew about the prominent movement in American garden design that celebrated the use of North American native plants and the making of so-called wild gardens, where such plants were grown naturalistically.[42] Many highly popular publications from early in the twentieth century promoted this concept. In fact, one of Lowthorpe's early graduates, Elsa Rehmann (1886–1946), contributed to this movement as coauthor of *American Plants for American Gardens*. Rehmann collaborated with Edith A. Roberts (1881–1977), a professor of botany at Vassar College, to produce this pioneering work on landscape ecology. Published in 1929, it is one of the very first works to study natural plant communities and describe their aesthetic value.[43] Lord and Schryver retained a sizeable horticultural library and may have owned this book as well as Rehmann's *The Small Place: Its Landscape Architecture* (1918). Schryver certainly knew of the latter and placed it on her reading list for landscape design students at Oregon State College.

In 1939, while Lord and Schryver were overseeing the planting for the McLoughlin historic house in Oregon City, they realized that Mrs. Cabell, an important patron of the project, preferred native plants. Lord invited her to see a planting she described as follows: "There is a very fine Beech tree in the corner of the steps and we thought the combination of Oregon Grape [*Mahonia aquifolium*] underneath would be good in leaf color and texture with the Beech and the yellow of the Azalea. With the Madrone [*Arbutus menziesii*] and dark glossy leaf of the Southern Oregon Myrtle [*Umbellularia californica*], this entire planting is composed of native material and all is evergreen except for the Azaleas."[44]

When, in 1946, Lord and Schryver outlined their vision for Bush's Pasture Park in Salem to the city's Long-Range Planning Commission, they recommended using Oregon's native plants in one section. The *Capital Journal* published their entire report in December 1946, which stated, "The Oak Grove section is a thing of beauty as it stands. . . . Our suggestion is to keep this area as natural as possible, retaining all trees possible, . . .whatever planting to be done, to use only native Oregon wild material. Here would be a great opportunity to display our own collection of Oregon shrubs at little cost and upkeep."[45]

➤➤➤ Elizabeth Lord's Garden Journals

Elizabeth Lord had learned a great deal from her mother, Juliet Montague Lord, who loved gardening and worked together with her daughter for many years.[46] Elizabeth's passion for hands-on gardening and the process of garden-making is evident in her garden journals for Gaiety Hollow. These handwritten notebooks, preserved in the archives of the University of Oregon, begin with the spring of 1936 and continue until summer 1939, when there is a break of almost twenty-four years. When the journals resume in the spring of 1963, they do not cover every year; they end in July 1976. The missing journals, if they ever existed, were not among the firm's professional papers when the collection was archived.

In her later years, Lord's garden journal became a personal diary, too, in which she admitted her pleasures and some frustrations—particularly her frustrations with the workmen they employed to do their projects. She was not always pleased with their work ethic or the way they pruned particular plants. Often, it had been difficult for Lord and Schryver to be on their job sites to direct the laborers because of the number of sites and the distances between. They found it hard to make the workmen carry out tasks in the precise manner that they wanted to have them done. During the Depression years when unemployed men from every background found it necessary to work as laborers under federal New Deal programs, Lord and Schryver's oversight on their public projects was important. In 1940, while working on an installation for Reed College in Portland, Lord became quite frustrated with the men scheduled to work on a day when there was heavy rain. She told Miss Gauld, the college representative, "When we arrived, we found the men did not like the idea of placing anything and it took a good deal of coaxing to put them in any kind of humor. It always irks me when men feel they cannot do work on account of rain when a woman can without weeping over the disaster. But they were very agreeable in the end."[47] And the job was accomplished.

The garden at Gaiety Hollow was Lord's haven (figure 7.7). She continually studied it, worked in it, improved it, and eventually felt overwhelmed by it when she recognized that she no longer had the strength to do all that she wanted to do. As she aged, Schryver did not spend as much time in the garden. Lord noted in September 1970, "Looking back over the summer—on the whole the garden was pretty nice, but had to do all the work. Nina [Edith] now, unable to do anything in the garden and Kurt [their gardener] attends only to the lawn, trimming & hedge cutting. Sometimes his pruning is pretty bad. . . . Very hard to get Nina interested in the garden. I seldom mention it to her."[48] These difficulties continued as they both aged.

Spring was Lord's favorite time in the garden as she recorded each type of flower when it appeared and disappeared, the sequence of bloom. In May of 1969, she noted, "Everyone speaks of the tulip season [as] the most beautiful, but I still like the bubbling of early spring. . . . It is a riot of bloom in the West gardens—The little Azalea garden all white varieties of Azalea and white, tho' a yellow tinge, dogwood, behind it a tall very pretty yellow Mollis Azalea. Orangy Salmon along the windows, sorry not same color as the yellow opposite side—but the gr. [great] Mistake is the Pink Rhododendron 'Bow Bells' so flourishing well right in the midst of the white and the [illegible] across—very bad—must be taken out."[49]

For the period 18 March to 1 April 1970 she writes, "Leave daffodils as they are—beautiful collection and placing around the edging of the Flower Garden only take out the yellow under the cherry. . . . Camellias still blooming are beautiful flowers, they keep coming—an awful mess—but guess worth the work." At the same time, she noted that her mother's lilac, planted in 1906, was in bloom.[50] This was probably the lilac she had named "Juliet."

On 1 April 1970, "The last week in Jan. and all thru Feb. and Mar. beautiful blooms of Camellias. Today, April 1st, the reds are lovely, especially those by the Oak tree and Prunus trees."[51]

In 1973, Lord wrote, "All these years passed, 10 in fact, and nothing written since 1964—our garden is almost the same. Material dies and more is bought. Some have to be taken out and forgotten, some replanted and we forget the glory of the past. But we enjoy it from year to year and in piecemeal. I'll try to tell of doing so" (figure 7.8).[52]

There is a sadness about Lord's entries in the garden journal the last few years of her life. She talks about the need to give up driving their car, the diminishing interest Schryver takes in the garden, and the necessary

7.7 Axial view east through the pergola to the Flower Garden
at Gaiety Hollow, Salem, Oregon (1935). Courtesy University of
Oregon Libraries, Special Collections and University Archives,
Coll 098, Lord & Schryver architectural records.

7.8 Gardener Carl Hendrickson prunes the espaliered pear tree at Gaiety Hollow, Salem, Oregon (1955). Courtesy University of Oregon Libraries, Special Collections and University Archives, Coll 098, Lord & Schryver architectural records.

scaling back of their lives. However, when in a positive mood, Lord continued to be interested in their gardens, as was Schryver, musing about their plants' performance from year to year, "In the late winter, early Feb—the Rhododendron 'Bric-à-brac' had an unusually graceful bloom and held well owing to the mild winter—too much rain hurt the flowers—finally, but what was especially lovely was the 'Bo-peep' pale yellow, dainty flowers. I made a bouquet of White Camellia 'Finlandia' (my favorite) for Mrs. M next door and she tho't combination lovely."[53] It reminds one of what Gertrude Jekyll wrote in 1899, a philosophy that Lord and Schryver would have understood: "I have learned most thoroughly. . . to never to say 'I know'—there is infinitely much to learn and the conditions of different gardens vary so greatly, even when soil and situation appear to be alike and they are in the same district. Nature is such a subtle chemist that one never knows what she is about, or what surprises she may have in store."[54]

8

Cultivating the Profession

> Landscape architecture is first of all an art, secondly a profession and
> last of all a business.
> —Edith Schryver, 1981

From their arrival in 1929 until late in their lives, Lord and Schryver played
a very important role in the development of the Northwest's professional
community, both by setting a high standard with their own work and by
imparting a greater knowledge of design and horticulture to the public.
They became founding members of the Northwest's first professional
organization for landscape architects, the Oregon Society of Landscape
Architects (OSLA). Providing a role model for young professionals, they
helped mentor Wallace K. Huntington and other students. They created a
thoughtful design and superb plant arrangement for the Portland Garden
Club's new headquarters, with a fully accessible teaching garden. They undertook numerous civic projects for the City of Salem and beyond, lending
their expertise wherever they believed they could be helpful. They were ac-
tively involved in the Salem Art Association and gave generously of their
time to volunteer efforts including the transformation of the Bush's Pasture
Park and its historic house museum (discussed in chapter 10).

The Oregon Society of Landscape Architects

In January 1937, a letter arrived from W. Dorr Legg, a landscape architect
and the newest faculty member at Oregon State College, asking if Lord
and Schryver would join the American Society of Landscape Architects
(ASLA).[1] Founded in New York in 1899, the ASLA was the first professional organization for American landscape architects. The panel of its
nine charter members included eight men and one woman, Beatrix Jones
(later Beatrix Farrand).[2] The founders modeled their organization on the

American Institute of Architects (AIA) founded in 1888. Like the AIA, the American Society of Landscape Architects' goal was to win professional recognition, establish contract standards, define requirements for a professional education, and influence legislation. In his letter to Lord, Professor Legg stated, "I wish that you . . . (and Miss Schryver) were members of the Society. There's so few members in this region that the general public is not even aware that there is such a thing as a profession of landscape architecture."[3]

Professor Legg was correct, for the most part. The public was not aware of the distinctions among landscape architects, landscape gardeners, contractors, and nurserymen. No regulating body in the Northwest (or in many states) defined the profession and its practice until 1961, when professional licensing became the law. To add to the confusion, it was possible to call oneself a landscape architect without having the appropriate education or expertise in spatial design and engineering.[4] In 1929, Lord and Schryver became the first landscape architects to list their firm in Polk's Directory for Salem, the classified Yellow Pages of its day. They continued to do so for the next four decades, until they closed their practice in 1969.[5]

The federal government added an incentive in 1940 for landscape architects to organize by requesting that they register in the event their services were needed for emergency work related to the war overseas. The American Society of Landscape Architects asked all known professionals to fill out and return a questionnaire to be kept on file. The organization also provided a series of pamphlets on how their services might benefit the government under the National Defense Program.[6] Professor Cuthbert at the University of Oregon forwarded the questionnaire to Lord and Schryver, who responded that they would consider assisting. Schryver, however, added, "It did not specify what type of work might be needed, and I did not think that any government projects would be much in our line, and whether it would mean that I might be called away from Salem. I would be perfectly willing to do any drafting at home, but could not afford to be called to go elsewhere."[7]

In November 1940, Professor Legg called the first meeting of Oregon's landscape architects at Oregon State College in Corvallis. The purpose was to discuss "problems common to the profession and the benefits derived from forming an association in the state."[8] Edith Schryver attended this meeting, as did Florence H. Gerke. The group formed an organizing committee and elected Arthur L. Peck, head of the joint program in landscape architecture at Oregon State College and the University of Oregon, to be the temporary chair.[9] Three of the topics covered at their first meeting were city planning, highway beautification and state and national parks. By the end of the day, they had formed a new organization—the Oregon Society of Landscape Architects, or OSLA. It became a chapter of the American Society of Landscape Architects in 1961, at which time it established licensing requirements for landscape architects in Oregon.[10]

Both Lord and Schryver participated in the Oregon Society of Landscape Architects, but Schryver took a more active role. On 24 April 1941, they hosted an organizational meeting at their home, Gaiety Hollow, where the group discussed a constitution. Florence and Walter Gerke attended this meeting and became part of the group's leadership.[11] Schryver was elected the OSLA's secretary-treasurer.[12] She presided over the November 1941 meeting in Arthur Peck's absence and gave the treasurer's report. They had exactly $9 in their account.[13]

The Oregon Society of Landscape Architects may have been off to a slow start, but Washington state still did not have any professional group. Professor Cuthbert proposed combining the two states into a Northwest Society of Landscape Architects, with two state chapters. In hopes of bringing this about, they invited landscape architects from Washington to attend the OSLA's second annual meeting on 6 December 1941 in Portland.[14] They wanted this to be a prestigious event and extended invitations to the president of the American Institute of Architects, Oregon's commissioner of public works, the state highway engineers, the nurserymen's association, and newspaper editors of the real estate and garden columns. The only woman speaker at the meeting was Edith Schryver. She gave an address titled, "The Landscape Architect in Private Practice."[15] Lord reported on her efforts to explain the importance of the OSLA to Governor Charles A. Sprague and the director of the Oregon Economic Council. Despite their best attempt, few of Seattle's landscape architects attended the Portland meeting. As a consequence, Florence Gerke announced, "it did not warrant further effort" to try to combine forces.[16]

As charter members of the OSLA, Lord and Schryver continued to support the organization, lending their time and energy when called on and hosting garden visits at Gaiety Hollow for students (figures 8.1, 8.2). At the annual meeting in 1948, Lord was elected vice president.[17] In 1955, the OSLA convinced the *Sunday Oregonian* to promote the profession with a column titled "You and Your Landscape Architect," with articles by and about different firms. On 17 July 1955, the newspaper column featured Lord and Schryver, demonstrating their continued prominence in the field. In the article they wrote, they described the challenge of designing a garden on a steeply sloping site, owned by Mr. and Mrs. Robert E. Avison of Dunthorpe.[18] Later in their lives, when the OSLA was well established, Lord and Schryver played less active roles.[19] They were members of the organization when it became a chapter of the American Society of Landscape Architects in 1961.

8.1 Edith Schryver at an Oregon Society of Landscape Architects exhibition (c. 1945). Courtesy University of Oregon Libraries, Special Collections and University Archives, Coll 098, Lord & Schryver architectural records.

8.2 Elizabeth Lord at an Oregon Society of Landscape Architects exhibition (c. 1945). Courtesy University of Oregon Libraries, Special Collections and University Archives, Coll 098, Lord & Schryver architectural records.

>>> A Role in Higher Education

Lord and Schryver always enjoyed having students of landscape architecture visit their Gaiety Hollow garden. In 1936 Professor Cuthbert of Oregon State College offered glowing praise of their garden following his class visit.[20] Professor L. S. Morris of Utah's Brigham Young University wrote to Lord after bringing his class to Gaiety Hollow in 1939: "I think the work that you are doing is particularly outstanding. There is a charm and unity about all your gardens which we visited. Of course, your own garden is one of the finest pieces of landscape design and composition that I have ever seen, ... not from the point of view of breath-taking expanses but from a point of view of design with a particular emphasis upon circulation and unity. I sincerely congratulate you on this fine piece of work."[21] This was gratifying praise from a professional educator.

With the formation of the OSLA, Lord and Schryver's contact with faculty and students increased. They welcomed frequent classes to their garden and accompanied college groups led by their professors on landscape tours. They were invited to participate in critiques of student projects on campus. When Professor Legg oversaw the national student design competition

"Modern City Home" in 1940–1941, sponsored by the American Society of Landscape Architects, he invited Lord and Schryver to be members of the jury.[22] In 1942, Professor Peck, the head of the department, asked Schryver to participate in the "criticisms" (critiques) for studio courses in landscape architecture and offered to pay her travel expenses to Corvallis.[23]

The United States' entry into World War II on 8 December 1941 radically changed life on the campus of Oregon State College, as it did for the rest of America. Many of the male students and faculty either enlisted or entered the ROTC. More women than men became undergraduates for the first time in the college's history, and they filled the void in leadership of campus activities (figure 8.3).[24] Fewer professional men outside the college were available to teach or to attend student critiques. This created an opening for Schryver, who became a part-time instructor and a valued member of the landscape architecture faculty. For three academic years, 1943 to 1946, she traveled from Salem to Corvallis several times a week

8.3 Chair Arthur Peck and students in front of the Memorial Union, at the thirtieth anniversary of the Landscape Architecture Program, Oregon State Agriculture College (now OSU), Corvallis, Oregon (1941). Courtesy Architecture and Landscape Architecture Department Photographs, Special Collections and Archives Research Center, Oregon State University Libraries, P099.079.

to teach her classes. Her courses included First Year Landscape Design, Third Year Landscape Design, Layout of Small Properties, and Planting Design. During the 1945–1946 academic year, she also taught a course for the Cooperative Extension in Salem, Home Ground Planning, in which many of the students were women. Fortunately, Schryver's class notebooks, reading lists, assignments, and studio projects have been preserved in the archives of the University of Oregon. They offer important insight into her educational approach during the 1940s.

>>> The Portland Garden Club Building and Garden, 1955–1957

Soon after Lord and Schryver had established their firm, they joined the Salem Garden Club and the Portland Garden Club. They offered lectures and garden tours to club members around the state, while Lord, in the early years, became chair of the Willamette Valley Division of the State Federation of Garden Clubs. Many of their most important commissions came through the connections they made with club members. In 1955, Lord and Schryver received a prestigious commission from the Portland Garden Club to landscape their new headquarters in downtown Portland.

The Portland Garden Club had begun fundraising in the 1930s to build a horticultural center for the city. They paused in their efforts during World War II, but resumed afterward. In 1943, the heirs of Mrs. C. E. S. Wood donated her property comprising half a city block (.65 acres) in an older residential neighborhood of southwest Portland. By 1952, the building committee, chaired by Mrs. Henry F. Cabell, had raised $50,000, and it was time to select an architect. Florence H. Gerke, a club member, recommended a young architect and World War II veteran, John W. Storrs (1920–2003).

John Storrs was new to the Northwest. With a degree in architecture from Yale University, he moved to Oregon in 1950 and rented office space in Mrs. Gerke's professional building. The Portland Garden Club was his first major architectural commission, and it became one of his most admired buildings. Storrs became widely known for his contribution to the development of Northwest Regional style. After his death, he was identified as "one of the stalwart regionalists who defined Oregon's most distinct phase of twentieth-century architecture."[25] Salishan Lodge (1965) in Gleneden Beach, Oregon, is considered Storrs' most iconic design, along with the World Forestry Center (1969) in Portland.

The site on which the new club headquarters would be built had been occupied by a grand family home. After the house had been removed, some mature plantings of unusual trees and shrubs remained within an encircling hedge of English holly (*Ilex aquifolium*). Utilizing less than half the lot, Storrs located the building close to SW Vista Avenue to the west

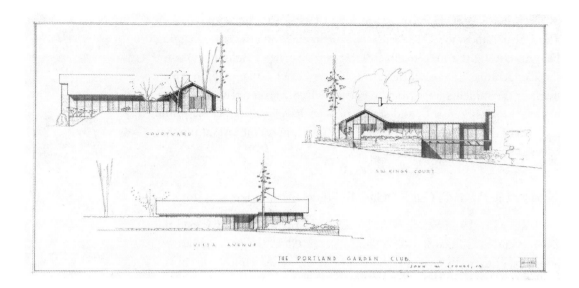

and Kings Court to the south. He designed the L-shaped building with a marked sensitivity to the landscape (figure 8.4). It had a long, low profile, a hipped roof, deep overhanging eaves, and a naturally finished wood exterior, features that exemplified Storrs' approach to the Northwest Regional style. The building "nestled comfortably into the generously wooded, yet tightly urban neighborhood of older homes" and opened to the outdoors in an appealing, Asian way.[26] It had large windows looking out on the garden under deep eaves like Japanese traditional architecture. After Storrs completed the building in 1955, it was considered so outstanding that he subsequently received dozens of commissions for private houses, and his career was launched.[27]

Schryver clearly articulated goals for the landscape design when she wrote about it for the club's newsletter in 1956: "What we hope to achieve is a beautiful garden with a subtle blending and combination of plant groupings so that we will be learning painlessly while we enjoy!"[28] Beyond a large terrace adjacent to the rear of the building, the garden would surround the new headquarters to the north and east. Since the garden was higher than the terrace, it needed very sensitive handling to avoid drainage problems. Storrs consulted with Schryver on the site's grading plan.[29] The result was a landscape divided into thirds: a small parking area, a seating area enclosed by informal plantings, and a lawn surrounded by naturalistic planting beds (figure 8.5).

One of the garden club's primary criteria was that the site have an educational display of plants similar to that of a botanical garden. In response, Lord and Schryver developed an oval pathway encircling the entire garden,

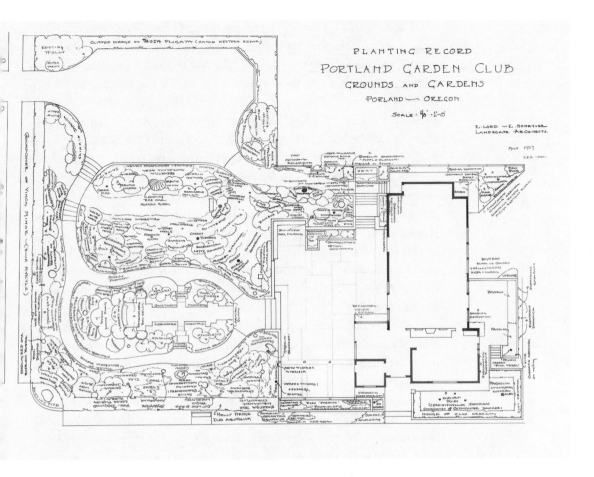

a central seating area, and a comprehensive planting plan organized around three distinct themes. Their themes not only provided a strong educational experience but visually unified the composition. They thought very carefully about every choice of plant as they worked on the garden's refinement over the next two years.

Lord and Schryver identified the existing holly hedge as the plant they would use to create the first theme within the garden. The hedge provided privacy and enclosure as well as a sound buffer from traffic noise. Its glossy, dark green foliage was an attractive backdrop for other plants, so they retained it.[30] By selecting shrubs with a similar appearance to English holly, they created visual continuity throughout the landscape. Their selections included other species of holly (*Ilex pernyi*), two cultivars of Japanese holly (*Ilex crenata*), "Dutch holly" (unidentifiable), and three species of *Osmanthus*, a closely related, broad-leaved evergreen. They called for the inside of the holly hedge to be clipped flat "like a wall" and the exterior facing the sidewalk to be left "loose" or more natural, an interesting treatment.[31]

8.5 Lord and Schryver's planting plan for the Portland Garden Club, Portland, Oregon (1957). Courtesy University of Oregon Libraries, Special Collections and University Archives, Coll 098, Lord & Schryver architectural records.

By adding small flowering trees "for spring beauty," Lord and Schryver created the second planting theme. They wove their design around several mature specimen trees that formed "the 'backbone' of the garden." They valued the trees because they created a setting for the building and gave, in Schryver's words, "a sense of age and character to the garden."[32] Among them were a beautiful cutleaf European beech (*Fagus sylvatica* 'Asplenifolia'), European white birch (*Betula pendula*), a sweet gum (*Liquidambar styraciflua*), a sassafras (*Sassafras albidum*), and Northern red oaks (*Quercus rubra*). Sizable trees, they also provided high overhead shade, a perfect environment in which to grow rhododendrons and other broad-leaved evergreens. The understory beneath their canopy also included Eastern pink dogwood (*Cornus florida* var. *rubra*), native Northwestern dogwood (*Cornus nuttallii*), several magnolias, including *Magnolia* × *soulangeana* 'Bronzzonii,' Lavalle hawthorn, and the native vine maple (*Acer circinatum*). This created a rich composition of Northwestern natives, Eastern natives, and exotic ornamentals (plate 22).

For the third theme, specifically for areas near the building, Lord and Schryver proposed what they called an "oriental" aspect that was "suitable to the architecture of the Clubhouse." They used several forms of Japanese maple (*Acer palmatum*), bamboo (held in bounds by concrete curbs), false bamboo (*Nandina domestica*), and dwarf Oregon grape holly (*Mahonia nervosa*). The plantings near the front entrance of the building also featured two unusual Asian tree species with seasonal characteristics of particular attractiveness: a golden raintree (*Koelreuteria paniculata*), with yellow lantern-like flowers in spring, and three katsura trees (*Cercidiphyllum japonicum*) planted together in a group. Schryver recalled from her studies at the Arnold Arboretum that the heart-shaped leaves of the katsura released a wonderful fragrance of burnt sugar in autumn.[33]

At the center of the garden, Lord and Schryver's final plan included a seating area dedicated to the memory of Rebecca Biddle (Mrs. C. E. S.) Wood, whose heirs had donated the property, the funds to build the garden, and the funds to provide the curved stone bench (plate 23).

The Portland Garden Club was successfully nominated to the National Register of Historic Places in 2005. The garden was an important contributing factor in the nomination, and its history was fully documented.[34] According to the nomination form, the biggest change to the landscape came in 1980–1981, when Lord and Schryver's design was altered by their protégé and friend, Portland landscape architect Wallace K. Huntington. Many of the mature plantings had become overgrown, and his idea was to allow more light into the garden, creating a more spacious feeling and improving views of the plantings. Two of the original birch trees, damaged by ice storms, were removed, as were other large, overgrown shrubs. He

8.6 Lord and Schryver on the terrace of the Portland Garden Club, Portland, Oregon (c. 1960). Courtesy Lord & Schryver Conservancy, Anne M. Kingery Library.

replaced the white Gumpo azaleas encircling the seating area with a lawn edged with clipped boxwood hedges. Huntington placed a Sargent crabapple, one of Lord's favorite trees, in the center of the southern section. The rhododendrons behind the memorial bench had grown so large that Huntington had them pruned into trees. Behind them, he planted three Japanese umbrella pines (*Sciadopitys verticillata*), a relatively unusual evergreen. Where necessary, he replaced overgrown hybrid rhododendrons and camellias with deciduous shrubs, native species, and hardy perennials. He reconfigured the parking lot with angled planting beds to improve its function.[35] Despite Huntington's deep respect for Lord and Schryver's work, the garden no longer resembled their original creation. It was, and still is, a lovely space. Lord and Schryver knew this would be the fate of their gardens as plants grew and aged and needed to be replaced. "A garden is never the same," Schryver explained to David Duniway in 1981, "but its characteristics should be preserved, even though the availability of plant material always changes" (figure 8.6).[36]

9

"Yard Architects" for Period Gardens

One of my Newberg friends said, "How can you restore a garden where there never was a garden?"
—Elizabeth Lord, 1969

During their long career as landscape architects, Lord and Schryver designed two fine period landscapes in Oregon, one for the McLoughlin and Barclay Houses in Oregon City, and the other for the Hoover-Minthorn House in Newberg. Since there were few, if any, surviving garden features on the properties, they could not create what we today would consider authentic historic restorations. However, with their knowledge of earlier American garden styles, in both the Northeast and the Northwest, they were able to create credible period garden settings for historic houses.

The McLoughlin and Barclay Houses, Oregon City, Oregon, 1938–1941

John McLoughlin (1784–1857) was once the most important man in the Oregon Country.[1] As chief factor of the Hudson's Bay Company–Columbia Department, McLoughlin administered the lands surrounding the Columbia River from the Rocky Mountains to the coast of North America.[2] In 1824–1825, he assumed his position as superintendent at Fort Vancouver on the Columbia River in what is now the state of Washington. McLoughlin had a keen interest in agriculture; he introduced new vegetable and fruit varieties and planted a large orchard at the fort to supply food. After two decades of service, McLoughlin retired in 1845. He built a grand, two-story wood frame house on property he held in Oregon City at the "Falls of the Willamette."[3] He reserved a plot of open land on the hilltop bluff overlooking the river, and in 1850, he donated this property to Oregon City to be a public park. McLoughlin, who was born in Canada, became a naturalized citizen in 1851 and died in 1857. He was buried in the churchyard

9.1 Moving the home of Dr. John McLoughlin up Singer Hill, Oregon City, Oregon (1909). Courtesy Clackamas County Historical Society.

9.2 McLoughlin Park, Oregon City, Oregon (c. 1925). Courtesy Elisabeth Walton Potter.

of St. John the Apostle in Oregon City. When his wife Marguerite died in 1860, she was buried beside him.[4]

By the early 1900s, the area around McLoughlin's fine home by the Willamette River was slated for industrial development. The Oregon City Woman's Lewis and Clark Club began efforts in 1903 to save it and attracted a group of enthusiastic citizens who formed the McLoughlin Memorial Association. In 1909, the Memorial Association employed contractors to use a horse-drawn winch to pull the house up the steep Singer Hill grade on log rollers (figure 9.1). They placed the house facing the river in McLoughlin's park on Center Street, where it was renovated and opened to the public in 1910–1911. They landscaped the park with walkways edged with roses, flower beds, a lawn area, and a fountain dedicated to the Oregon City Woman's Club (figure 9.2).

During the Depression, the house gained the attention of the Oregon chapter of the American Institute of Architects, then engaged in documenting fine examples of settlement-era architecture. This was a new phase of professionalism in the preservation of Oregon's historic buildings. The Oregon AIA chapter contributed expertise and urged the state government to authorize funds for historic preservation.[5] From 1933 to 1939, Glenn A. Stanton, the Portland architect who chaired the AIA's historical survey committee, directed the improvement of McLoughlin Memorial Park for the Memorial Association. They obtained funding for planning and comprehensive repair and restoration of the house from a variety of sources, including private donors, state and municipal appropriations, and patriotic and historical societies. They also received critical federal assistance from New Deal work relief agencies.[6]

Glenn Stanton contacted Florence H. Gerke in 1935 to provide an updated landscape plan. She envisioned using many native plants and some ornamentals appropriate to the nineteenth century. Her estimate of $650 for the entire project, including design and construction, may have been daunting.[7] It is unclear to what extent her plan was carried out.

In 1937, the Memorial Association received the donation of a second house, built in 1849 for Dr. Forbes Barclay, who had been the chief medical officer at Fort Vancouver (figure 9.3). The one-and-a-half-story wood-framed cottage was to be used as a caretaker's dwelling and to support visitor services. In the early years, this included perhaps operating a tearoom. They moved this house from the riverfront to McLoughlin Memorial Park with the intention that it would complement the representation of Oregon City's pioneer past.

In 1938, Stanton contacted Elizabeth Lord regarding the proposed placement of a bronze bust of McLoughlin in the park and the relocation of the Woman's Club memorial fountain.[8] Stanton sent the existing plan of the park to Lord and Schryver, who were not impressed with its unimaginative arrangement. The bust on a pedestal was shown offset from a long, straight gravel path that crossed the park on a diagonal. Steps to a high point overlooking the falls were placed in an awkward location, and the many existing trees seemed to be randomly dotted across the site, providing neither visual framing nor a background for the two houses. Lord agreed that they would advise on the path and the plantings at no charge. But when Stanton later assumed that Lord and Schryver would take charge of the entire landscape project as volunteers, Lord replied, "It certainly was not our intention to assume all the responsibility."[9]

Despite grumbling, Lord and Schryver did generate a new plan in November 1938 that created a more cohesive appearance for the park (figure 9.4). They did not, however, find a place for the bronze bust.[10] It was eventually located at the Willamette Falls observation point on Highway 99E. They grouped trees informally behind the two historic houses and laid steps going up to the overlook knoll on a curve following the natural topography. Open grassy areas behind the houses were identified as "tea lawns," and

9.3 The Barclay House, Oregon City, Oregon (c.1940). Courtesy University of Oregon Libraries, Special Collections and University Archives, Coll 098, Lord & Schryver architectural records.

they relocated the fountain to a central axis from the McLoughlin House. They used a privet hedge along the sidewalk on Center Street in front of the Barclay House but did not plant a hedge in front of the McLoughlin House. Their most elaborate detail was the stone paved entrance walk to the Barclay House, lined on both sides with a flower border and their signature dwarf boxwood hedge. The overall effect of Lord and Schryver's plan was more sensitive to both the site and the scale and composition of the historic buildings than the city's original plan.[11]

When Lord and Schryver submitted their plan for the grounds of the McLoughlin and Barclay houses, they accompanied it with a letter stating that they had made several sketches for the Barclay House but thought that the one submitted was the best as "this simple treatment suited the type of architecture better than any we had drawn up."[12] Comprehending the danger of constant changes to the design, Lord urged Mr. Harding, the mayor of Oregon City and chair of the Memorial Association, to approve a plan and stick to it. She further suggested anyone making last minute suggestions be told that they had come in too late. "It is really very trying to work interrupted by so many people having so many ideas and the only way we can see to avoid this is to turn it over to the committee." In Lord's typically straightforward manner, she closed by saying, "Please do not think you have to accept this plan, we have only given our idea of the treatment for a simple pioneer home—it may not coincide with those of you who have worked so diligently on this structure and it is much better to be frank about it before any of the work begins."[13]

Lord also sent a copy of the plan with her letter to another member of the Memorial Association's board, Mrs. A. E. Rockey, expressing some of the firm's frustration with the project. They were very busy with clients in the fall of 1938 and had not visited the site as often as they wanted. Lord

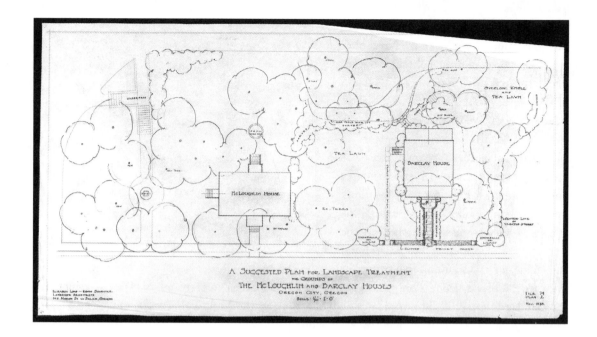

A SUGGESTED PLAN for LANDSCAPE TREATMENT
the GROUNDS of
THE McLOUGHLIN and BARCLAY HOUSES
OREGON CITY, OREGON
SCALE: 1/16": 1'-0"

9.4 Lord and
Schryver's landscape
plan for the
McLoughlin and
Barclay Houses,
Oregon City, Oregon
(1938). Courtesy
University of Oregon
Libraries, Special
Collections and
University Archives,
Coll 098, Lord &
Schryver architectural
records.

explained, "But when we gave suggestions to the man in charge, some were
carried out, some not, and to speak frankly, we became a bit discouraged
over the situation." There seemed to be too many people involved in the
project; Lord and Schryver were not able to be on-site often enough to take
control. Once again, Lord suggested that the association form a landscape
committee to oversee the work and appoint people who knew something
about garden plans for a historic home. "Then, if the plan is approved, we
would be pleased to see the plan carried out and we would like to be free of
all the suggestions from anyone outside of the Landscape committee. It is
really very difficult to work with too many suggestions."[14]

In February 1939, Lord contacted an influential friend from the firm's
garden club circle, Mrs. Henry F. (Margaret) Cabell of Portland, whom
Lord had earlier recommended to serve on the McLoughlin House landscape committee—if one were formed. Lord sent a "temporary planting
plan for the McLoughlin House," and discussed various attributes, including the use of low boxwood along the front walk leading to the Barclay
House, as shown on their 1938 plan. "I do not think you need to worry
about Box being too formal for these two houses. It was used here (and also
privit [privet]) in the early days a great deal, at least around Salem. The old
Patton house . . . had such a hedge planted when the house was built around
1860 [sic] and I have heard Court St. and State St. houses all had hedges in
the early days."[15] Both Lord and Schryver valued boxwood because of its
evergreen appearance.

The Memorial Association held an informal opening of the McLoughlin Memorial Park early in 1941, which neither Lord nor Schryver could attend. Afterward, Mr. Harding, the mayor of Oregon City, wrote to thank them for their contribution to the development of the grounds. He stated, "I quite agree with Miss Schryver and yourself that the simple plan you have furnished for the Park is most fitting. Your suggestion that all concerned agree upon a plan and then carry it through is the only satisfactory method of proceeding with the work."[16]

With one plan and one committee in charge, work proceeded on the park, and generous members of the Portland Garden Club donated a variety of plants. In October 1941, both Lord and Schryver spent a full day with Margaret Cabell on the grounds of the McLoughlin House, "replanting and adding to the roses down there. She [Mrs. Cabell] managed to get hold of 6 huge camellias and 24 large Rhodos [rhododendrons] from the Portland Park as a gift, enormous Boxes [boxwood] purchased reasonably and many other gifts of fine material—and to place it right with six inexperienced men was quite wearing. Edith took over the planting and it was a hard day. I hope now the McL[oughlin] Home is finished. I feel we have done our part on that charity and if that is scratched off—we do it with a sigh of relief" (figure 9.5).[17]

In 1941, the McLoughlin House, together with its grounds, was designated a National Historic Site after its preservation was promoted by retired lawyer and avid historian Burt Brown Barker of Portland. Dr. Barker spent his retirement years conducting groundbreaking research on the early history of Oregon Country and the Hudson's Bay Company. He was a major force behind Oregon's historic preservation projects for thirty years.[18] His scholarship and skillful advocacy to secure the McLoughlin House had been critical to its preservation.[19] It was the eleventh site in the United States to be so designated by the secretary of the interior. Today it is administered as a unit of Fort Vancouver National Historic Site.

Only fifteen years later, in 1956, the park was once again in need of restoration, and this time the Portland Garden Club employed a Portland landscape architect, Robert H. Ellis Jr., to develop the plan for the grounds. In her article for the *Sunday Oregonian*, the journalist Doris Holmes Bailey wrote that most of the plants donated to the park had been "planted with little thought to the future and flourished well—too well."[20] The

9.5 Lord and Schryver's Christmas card (1941). Courtesy Lord & Schryver Conservancy, Anne M. Kingery Library.

camellias that Lord and Schryver had placed near the McLoughlin House had grown too large and were moved to the edge of the cliff overlooking the river. To be historically more accurate, foundation plantings near the house were removed to show "the beauty of the structure." Thus, the need for "refurbishing."[21] Ellis placed the emphasis on using native evergreen plants such as wild ginger, salal, huckleberry, and Oregon grape holly. The author made no mention in her article of Lord and Schryver's hard work, and one can only wonder how they felt about this omission.

➤➤➤ "Yard Architect" for the Hoover-Minthorn House, Newberg, Oregon, 1952–1968

One April morning in 1952, Lord received a long-distance telephone call from Burt Brown Barker, who had been a childhood friend of former president Herbert Hoover. Dr. Barker knew Lord and Schryver from their work on McLoughlin Memorial Park. He asked if they would create a garden for the Minthorn House in Newberg, Oregon, as he was having it restored as a museum to honor Hoover. He assured Lord that her expertise would be much appreciated.[22] The nine-year-old orphaned Hoover had lived in the house with his aunt and his uncle, Dr. Henry J. Minthorn, superintendent of the Friends Pacific Academy, from 1885 to 1888, before the family moved to Salem. Lord was not sure that she and Schryver could fit this job in to their busy schedule. Lord was already serving on the Capitol Planning Commission and as president of the Salem Art Association. They were also working on an extensive residential design for the Avison property in Dunthorpe, a suburb of Portland. Nevertheless, Schryver enthusiastically agreed to accompany Lord to Newberg and look over the property.

They found a two-story, L-shaped house in good condition with weatherboard siding, a low hipped roof, and bracketed cornices (figure 9.6). It was a vernacular version of nineteenth-century Italianate architecture. During their visit, they both agreed to undertake the project and to design a landscape to complement the building's late Victorian style. Lord proposed that the garden should have a very simple plan, and the planting scheme should be composed of a selection of plants from the period of 1880 to 1900. As she had grown up in Salem during that era, Lord knew this period well. She phoned Dr. Barker to let him know she would accept his invitation and develop the garden plan at no charge.

The Minthorn house had been built in 1881 for Jesse Edwards, a Quaker who moved to Newberg to join the town's small Quaker community. He purchased an exhausted wheat farm and divided it into city lots for development, building his own house on three of the lots. Dr. Henry John Minthorn, from Canada, purchased the house in 1885 when he was

9.6 The Hoover-Minthorn House, Newberg, Oregon (c. 1955). Courtesy University of Oregon Libraries, Special Collections and University Archives, Coll 098, Lord & Schryver architectural records.

appointed the first superintendent of the Friends Pacific Academy. Dr. Minthorn was an educator, a businessman, and a medical doctor, as well as Herbert Hoover's uncle. Hoover had been born in Iowa. After his parents died, his uncle became his foster father and enrolled him in the new academy. Just three years later, Dr. Minthorn moved the family from Newberg to Salem. Herbert Hoover, after a difficult start, went on to graduate from Stanford University and become the thirty-first president of the United States, serving from 1929 until 1933, during the early years of the Great Depression. In 1947, Hoover's childhood friend Burt Brown Barker organized a foundation to purchase the neglected house and restore it. With work under way, and with the urging of his daughter Barbara Barker, he contacted Elizabeth Lord.[23]

The Oregon chapter of the National Society of the Colonial Dames of America endorsed the project with an initial contribution of $500 and an annual stipend of $50. Their members also donated many of the plants. It was Lord and Schryver's volunteer efforts that brought the landscape project to fruition. Lord acquired the correct plants, brought her own gardeners from Salem to work on the project, and even helped plant and weed the grounds over a period of sixteen years. As Lord told a journalist for Salem's *Oregon Statesman* newspaper, "I really have been doing this in memory of my mother, who admired Mr. Hoover greatly, who loved a garden more than anyone realized, and who was one of the charter members of the Colonial Dames."[24]

Since few of the original Victorian landscape features had survived at the Minthorn House, Lord and Schryver found little they could use to create a semblance of the original garden. They also confronted numerous problems in trying to create a new one. In March 1954, Lord wrote at length to Dr. Barker, providing him with their assessment of the property, "The Lawn is barely growing. This is due to the extremely poor soil over the entire area. It looks as if the top soil had been scooped off for we noted the two big Lilacs north of the house were well above the normal grade with roots exposed."[25] She recommended various soil amendments be purchased. She also was not pleased with the laurel hedge (*Prunus laurocerasus*) across the northern, rear boundary of the property. "I am not so sure that Laurel Hedges were used in the nineties [1890s]. I believe a high board fence would have been the proper solution at that time. I constantly go back to my memories of our old place here on Mission Street." Not mincing words, she continued, "Another thing I wish to mention is the deplorable condition of the existing fruit trees." They needed to be pruned in order to save them. Aware of the limited budget, Lord wondered if they should plant any flowers "for I know only too well there will be no upkeep and it would be a constant worry."[26] Meanwhile, she and Schryver had a plan under way for Dr. Barker to see when he returned to Oregon (figure 9.7).

Lord set to work with Schryver to determine how to develop the landscape and choose plants that would best represent the Victorian era. Dr. Barker had erected a low picket fence along two sides of the corner property that faced the street, to give a semblance of privacy and to introduce a feature that was commonplace in the historic period. The landscape architects retained the laurel hedge on the northern boundary and enhanced it with flowering shrubs: "highbush cranberry" (*Viburnum opulus*), "old-fashioned Snowball" (*Viburnum plicatum*), forsythia, and Oregon grape holly (*Mahonia aquifolium*). Lord worked with the Knight Pearcy Nursery of Salem to find the varieties of deciduous flowering shrubs appropriate to the Victorian period. She did not believe that many evergreen shrubs had been used then. Placing three native cedars (*Thuja plicata*) in the northwest corner, she tried to block out an unattractive view.

Wooden plank sidewalks led from the street to the front and side entrances of the house, and to the well and privy out back. Lord framed the front door with matching white lilacs and made two oval beds for roses close to the front walk.[27] Around the house she designed a narrow flower border for spring bulbs, perennials, and the old-fashioned red peony (*Paeonia officinalis*), the "Pinnie" she remembered from childhood. For the summer, she added phlox, Madonna lilies, dahlias, and hollyhocks. Fall asters completed the sequence of bloom. Lord later wrote, "In order to give an extra interest to this little garden, all the flower beds were edged by old bricks picked up

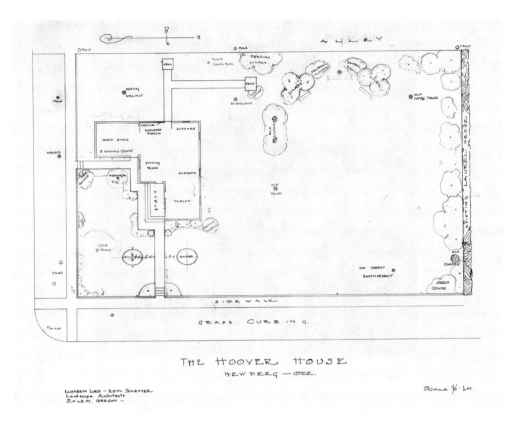

THE HOOVER HOUSE
NEWBERG — ORE.

from demolished buildings and brought down from Salem."[28] They planted a flowering crabapple in the small front lawn and, to the rear of the house, a limited selection of fruit trees to complement the one ancient pear tree, as every "pioneer" home had an orchard.[29]

To the west of the house, a fragrant honeysuckle vine would cover the well house, a "Privy Rose" would screen the outhouse, and a grapevine would grow across a latticework trellis on the woodshed. One shrub of the panicle hydrangea (*Hydrangea paniculata*) stood near the woodshed. A friend donated a plant of *Rosa wichuraiana*, a very special rose that had grown in Lord's mother's garden since 1910. Lord and Schryver grew it to climb over the fence at Gaiety Hollow and gave slips away to anyone who asked, just to assure that the rose remained in cultivation.[30]

In June 1954, the *Oregon Statesman* reported that there would be "a luncheon on Tuesday for which Mrs. Frank Spears, Mrs. Charles A. Sprague and Miss Elizabeth Lord will be hostesses. . . in compliment to the Oregon Members of the National Society of Colonial Dames of America. . . . Thirty are expected to drive to Salem from Portland. . . . En route they will stop in Newberg at the Hoover House, where Miss Lord is giving her time as 'yard architect' in cooperation with the Portland Society, which in turn

9.7 Elizabeth Lord's garden plan for the Hoover-Minthorn House, Newberg, Oregon (early 1950s). Courtesy University of Oregon Libraries, Special Collections and University Archives, Coll 098, Lord & Schryver architectural records.

9.8 Elizabeth Lord arriving at the Hoover-Minthorn House for the Colonial Dame's reception in her honor, Newberg, Oregon (1969). Courtesy University of Oregon Libraries, Special Collections and University Archives, Coll 098, Lord & Schryver architectural records.

gives the planting. . . . The three hostesses are the only Salem members of the Colonial Dames."[31]

Herbert Hoover came to Newberg for his eighty-first birthday on 10 August 1955 to dedicate the museum. Lord and Schryver were invited to the luncheon and convocation to be held in his honor. At the event, the former president reflected on his boyhood in the house: "This is a time and place of stimulated affections and recollections. In this cottage and orchard, with its cherries, its apples and its pears, I spent formative years of my boyhood. Here I roamed the primitive forests with their carpets of flowers, their ferns, their never forgettable fragrance. Here were no legal limits on the fish you could catch. No warden demanded to see your license."[32]

After eight years of work, Elizabeth Lord thought that Mr. Hoover would enjoy seeing some photos of the re-created garden of his childhood home, and she wrote to him in New York, explaining how she came to be in charge of replanting the grounds. She said how she tried to preserve all the existing plants and keep it as a garden of the 1890s, adding, "I have been very happy making this garden and hope to oversee the maintenance as long as I am able."[33] She was seventy-six years old.

By 1968, Lord had contributed all that she could to the project and agreed to turn it over to Mary Adams, whom the Colonial Dames had selected to carry on the work. Lord and Schryver were invited to do a final walk-through inspection of the property with Mrs. Adams. When they arrived at the house, they were surprised to see a number of cars parked around the area. The event was, in fact, a surprise party given in Lord's honor to thank her for all her hard work. During the party, she received a citation scroll, which meant a great deal to her. She remained their adviser for as long as she felt she could be helpful.[34] As Lord stated in 1961, "I feel we have made quite a showing and a colorful garden. . . . I hope from now on, the Minthorn House, where Herbert Hoover spent his boyhood, will be kept in good condition and be a credit to the generosity of the Colonial Dames" (figure 9.8).[35]

10

Salem Pride

> My mother was devoted to beautification projects, gardening and
> civic improvement. . . . My interests laid [lay] in the same direction
> and I continued that line of work all my life."
> —Elizabeth Lord, 1968

In January 1973, when Elizabeth Lord was eighty-six years old, the Mission
Mill Museum Association (now the Willamette Heritage Center) cited her
for "helping create the unique heritage of the Salem area." They asked her
to write an account of her life that they would publish in conjunction with
their annual "Panegyric."[1] The Panegyrics were formal community galas
and fundraisers to benefit the museum. They honored leaders, both past
and present, in business, the professions, and civic and cultural affairs and
were enthusiastically supported by Salem's citizens. In her short autobi-
ography, Lord explained that domestic garden design had not been her
primary concern during her long career. Her "main interest turned to civic
improvement, so much to do here and such a wealth of plant materials."[2]
She took on the challenge of public projects, because like her mother before
her, she believed that Salem had the necessary attributes to be one of the
most attractive small cities in America. "In fact, I am tempted to say the
most beautiful for its size. We hear that praise not only from our own citizens but from the traveling public and from our recent home seekers who
select our town for that very reason."[3]

The people of Salem had demonstrated a strong sense of civic engage-
ment and endeavored to build a culturally rich and equitable society. They
traditionally donated time, funds, and energy to support churches, frater-
nal orders, charitable organizations, educational institutions, and cultural
groups. Lord had carefully observed and, like her mother, participated in
some of the city's civic organizations.

As soon as their firm opened in 1929, Lord and Schryver began to receive requests for their service on public projects. Often the letters came to Lord, as her family had been deeply associated with community life in Salem.[4] One of the first inquiries came from Mr. H. S. Giles, president of Salem General Hospital. It read, "Dear Miss Lord: I am advised that you are interested in contributing your services to Salem General Hospital in the matter of laying out a landscape plan for the grounds belonging to the institution." He hoped Lord would work on this project, and he assured her, "I certainly am personally very appreciative of the fine spirit which you are showing in your desire to take this work over and carry it on along approved lines to beautify the splendid property which the Hospital owns."[5] Unfortunately, no plan for this project has been preserved in the archives, so we do not know whether it was ever carried out.

Requests for assistance came from a variety of institutions, including the Oregon State School for the Blind, located one block from their home; the Marion County Courthouse; and the United States Post Office building. Lord and Schryver's plans for public projects were always very practical regarding circulation, construction costs, and ongoing maintenance. The layouts may have appeared simplistic to more fashionable designers, but Lord and Schryver knew what maintenance departments could manage. They specified only the strongest foundation plants, ornamental shrubs, and street trees for each site. With an eye to sensible design and budgetary constraints, they satisfied many of the requests for assistance and made a lasting contribution to the public landscapes of Salem.

➤➤➤ The Marion County Courthouse

The Salem Garden Club often subsidized the improvement of the capital's public landscapes. In 1910, the club members paid to have shrubbery planted around the stately Second Empire-style Marion County Courthouse of 1873. By 1932, when the original plantings were looking tired and needed to be replaced, the club contracted Lord and Schryver to make a new plan. Their plan included replacing the shrubbery and adding street trees, but the old city judge Lord spoke to refused to pay, saying, "You planted it in the first place; why do you want to do it again? We have no money for such an extravagance."[6] Once again the garden club agreed to pay the bill. It was such a "tremendous building," according to Lord, that they decided the most suitable street tree would be the Eastern sycamore, or plane tree (*Platanus occidentalis*), which grew quickly, would achieve a great height, and tolerated urban conditions.[7] They had six trees planted to define the property edges along Court and State Streets and then planted hedges at the corners (figure 10.1). The Women's Veterans Society contributed another $10 to plant two southern magnolias (*Magnolia grandiflora*) in front of the building on High Street. It was a very simple plan that city workers would be able to maintain. In 1954, when Pietro Belluschi's modern courthouse building replaced the old courthouse, the original plane trees were retained and still shade the sidewalk.[8]

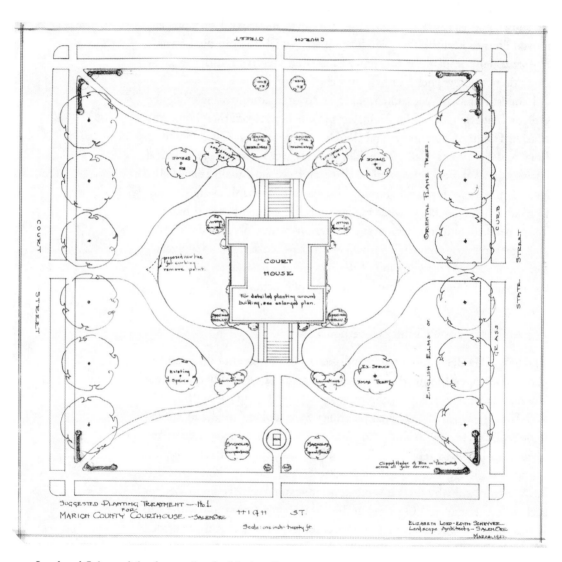

10.1 Lord and Schryver's landscape plan for Marion County Courthouse, Salem, Oregon (1932). Courtesy University of Oregon Libraries, Special Collections and University Archives, Coll 098, Lord & Schryver architectural records.

A remarkable number of public schools and regional institutions, primarily in Oregon, asked Lord and Schryver for assistance to improve their grounds. Bush Elementary School, Leslie Junior High School, Leslie High School, Salem Senior High School, and the Oregon State School for the Blind, all located in the capital, received their professional attention (figure 10.2). The College of Puget Sound in Tacoma, sororities at Willamette University in Salem, and Reed College in Portland requested plans from Lord and Schryver. They also carried out work for two churches in Salem: St. Paul's Episcopal Church and the United Brethren Church. The plans they provided were straightforward and planted with sturdy species because they knew through experience how little maintenance such landscapes might receive.

At the height of the Depression in 1937–1938, Salem was fortunate to have funding from the federal Works Progress Administration (WPA) to build a new, state-of-the-art high school, known today as North Salem High School. In fact, many of the public projects Lord and Schryver carried out during that difficult decade were partially funded by the WPA.[9] They were already engaged in designs for Bush Elementary School and

10.2 Lord and Schryver's landscape plan for Bush Elementary School, Salem, Oregon (1937). Courtesy University of Oregon Libraries, Special Collections and University Archives, Coll 098, Lord & Schryver architectural records.

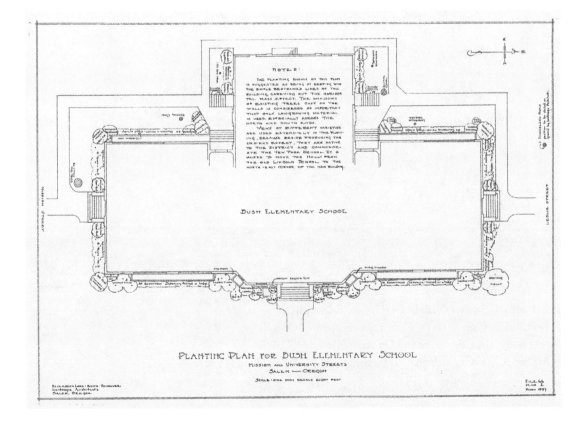

PLANTING PLAN FOR BUSH ELEMENTARY SCHOOL
MISSION AND UNIVERSITY STREETS
SALEM — OREGON
SCALE: ONE INCH EQUALS EIGHT FEET

Leslie Junior High School when the school board asked them to landscape the large, new high school building. They gladly accepted the project and successfully carried out the commission (figure 10.3).[10] Their bill for the planting plan and supervision came to $250, a very handsome sum at that time. The Salem school board subsequently hired them to conduct a survey of its nine public schools and report on the landscape conditions, seeking to improve the properties through their recommendations. It is not known how many of their recommendations were adopted (figures 10.4, 10.5).

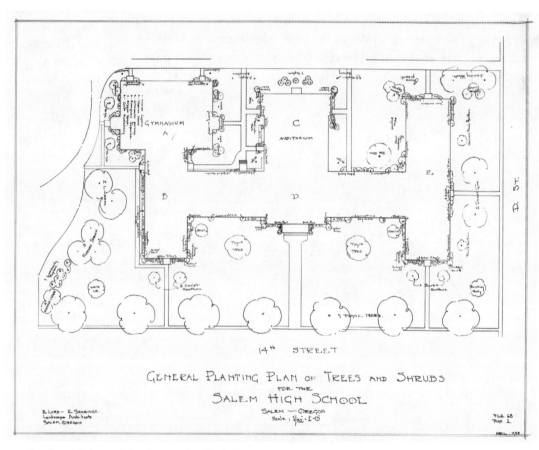

10.3 Lord and Schryver's landscape plan for Salem High School, Salem, Oregon (1938). Courtesy University of Oregon Libraries, Special Collections and University Archives, Coll 098, Lord & Schryver architectural records.

10.4 Salem High School, Salem, Oregon (1941). Courtesy Willamette Heritage Center.

10.5 North Salem High School, Salem, Oregon (2020). Courtesy Jay Raney.

As soon as Edith Schryver arrived in Oregon, she noticed the negative impact that increased automobile travel and commercial roadside advertising had on the natural beauty of landscapes along the highways. In June 1929, she shared her concern with their new client, Mrs. R. D. Merrill of Seattle, writing, "I am enclosing a picture we took on the Pacific Highway showing one of the worst offenses. The magnificent Dogwood [*Cornus nuttallii*] had been slashed and cut so that the billboards could be fitted in."[11] The state's concerned citizens had formed the Oregon Council for the Protection of Roadside Beauty in 1922 to keep billboard blight and tourist litter off the state's major roads. They considered roadside advertising not only detrimental to the scenic value but also to the public safety of Oregon's growing network of highways. Many garden clubs across the nation condemned billboard advertising and became active campaigners against it.

Lord and Schryver enthusiastically supported this cause. In 1938, they joined the newly renamed Oregon Roadside Council. Through the council's legislative efforts, Oregon passed the Outdoor Advertising Act in 1955, its first law to control commercial signage along highways. Many citizens, however, believed this law was too complicated to properly enforce. In 1959, Oregon's legislators returned to the issue to simplify and replace it with proposed Senate Bill 192 and House Bill 298. The members of the Roadside Council held a letter-writing campaign to persuade their politicians to support the new bills. After Lord and Schryver had reviewed both laws in draft form, Lord bluntly pressed Senator Anthony Yturri, chairman of the State Highway Commission, by saying, "Oregon Scenery is a great Tourist attraction. We spend vast sums of money advertising the wonders of Oregon. Both our Federal and State Highways are being ruined by unsightly Billboards."[12] But some of Oregon's legislators believed the income from advertising was more valuable to the state than its scenery, and when the bill was placed on the public ballot in 1960, it was defeated. Under pressure from the Roadside Council, outdoor advertisers considered a compromise solution. Senate Bill 233, the Scenic Area Law, was passed and adopted under Governor Mark Hatfield in 1961.[13] Ultimately, the council prevailed in protecting Oregon's scenic beauty. Lord and Schryver had played an active role in a cause that required almost forty years to come to fruition.

Mayor Robert Elfstrom appointed Elizabeth Lord to the Salem Park Board in 1937. She would serve until 1947, and her influence there became one of her most important contributions to the community.[14] As she later explained, "This was purely an honorary position with two very public-minded men: Mr. George Riches, quite a gardener himself, and Mr. Milton Meyers, who had been very active in civic affairs but who didn't know a plant from weed."[15] From her point of view, "there were so many, many problems to decide and progress to make."[16] Lord was interested in creating a park system for the entire city that would draw together resources for their improved care. From the beginning of her tenure, Lord believed that the parks were underfunded by the city council. In fact, the council budgeted only $6,000 that year for park improvements and maintenance.[17] The only parks in Salem whose landscapes she considered complete were Marion Square Park and Willson Park, and they were "nearly as old as the city."[18]

Lord was correct, Marion Square Park and Willson Park were as old as the city of Salem. Both parks had been created when the city was laid out by William H. Willson (1805–1856), a lay member of the Methodist Mission. He claimed the land that would become Salem in 1839 and platted the city in 1846, reserving three blocks at the center of the plat. He labeled these blocks "Willson Avenue" and marked the location for the capitol building at one end and the county courthouse at the other. In 1850, he laid out Marion Square Park on three-plus acres, close to the Willamette River on the city's west side. In 1853, Willson and his wife donated the east end of Willson Avenue for the Territorial Statehouse and the remainder for a public park.[19] By the 1930s, these two historic parks had well-established landscapes, although they still required seasonal attention and periodic improvement.[20]

By the summer of 1941, the park board had been trying unsuccessfully to convince the city council to apply for a grant from the Works Progress Administration to improve neighborhood parks. The board anticipated three-quarters of the necessary funding for the parks to come from the WPA and one-quarter from the city.[21] Schryver had already drawn up plans for all the parks, signed with her name alone, not with Lord and Schryver. Naturally, Lord did not expect to be paid for her service on the board.[22] But she did argue that Schryver, as landscape architect, should be paid a suitable fee of $200 to $250 for the park plans because of the amount of work entailed. Lord further stated, "I want it to be understood that Miss Schryver is not to be connected with me in this project and whatever sum decided upon by the committee shall be delivered to her."[23]

The park board members agreed that Lord, as chairman, should write two articles for Salem's major newspapers, the *Capital Journal* and the *Oregon Statesman*, to rally the public's support.[24] To introduce the desirability of improving Salem's parks, Lord explained in her article for the *Oregon Statesman*,

> Salem's attractiveness has much to do with its gaining population. The situation is ideal, the surrounding hills clothed with fruit trees and forest is breathtaking in its peacefulness. The city itself is fortunate in having wide streets well planned and a central park area—donated to us by a very generous pioneer [William H. Willson]. Added to all three qualifications, the natural scenic beauty around Salem is rare indeed for not many towns can claim a river, streams and wood areas. . . . Because we are so fortunate and have been given so much of nature's handiwork, we should not neglect foresightedness of adding to good fortune and extending parking [park] beautification while we can afford the property and while Salem is in the small city size.[25]

Lord's assessment of the opportunity for Salem was accurate, and it convinced some of the council members. The Salem Park Board did receive better funding, and one of their first efforts was to complete Kay (Englewood) Park in northeast Salem. In 1926, the city had purchased seven acres of land abutting Englewood School for $6,000. It was the first land acquired by the city government for park and recreation purposes.[26] More than 350 towering conifers and deciduous trees grew on the site in the center of a residential district. The stand of fir trees was so thick that the park board advised thinning them out. This caused some local residents to object, but as Lord later declared, "We carried our point with reason."[27] In 1941 they opened circular clearings in the woods, built paths, and added picnic tables and a wading pool to make it more enjoyable for families. The only additional planting consisted of twenty-four European mountain ash trees (*Sorbus aucuparia*) sited along the curbside. They were beautiful and short-lived. Lord later recounted, "On the first Halloween night of their existence, two carloads of boys drove down the curb, cutting every tree along the way. It was death to the poor trees and a hard loss to park finances. They were not replaced."[28] Decades later, many of the original forest trees continue to create an impressive, high canopy. Today, the public may enjoy walking trails, picnic tables, and a children's pool beneath their majestic forms, reminiscent of the original forest (figure 10.6).

The area surrounding Pringle Creek was a very important natural resource and scenic asset in downtown Salem. The waters of Pringle Creek, Shelton Stream, and Mill Stream all joined together under the Church Street bridge to flow into the Willamette Slough, a large, wetland branch of the river. "In former days, these streams, surrounded by lovely wooded banks were one of the beauty spots of the city," Lord wrote.[29] The development

of Pringle Creek Park began in 1923 when the city purchased acreage from the Joseph A. Albert estate. The site was at first used as an "auto park camp" (locally called the "Old City Camp Ground"), where people could park their vehicles and camp overnight.[30] The city ended this practice in 1940. Periodically, the three watercourses overflowed their banks and flooded the surrounding properties. Stone retaining walls to reduce the risk of flooding had been partially constructed, but never finished. Lord's park board was able to complete the walls and create an attractive picnic ground on level land between Pringle Creek and Shelton Stream. They also moved an older building that served as a youth center away from the center of the park to a less prominent site.[31] The Salem Park Board added parking, pathways, and amenities such as picnic tables and fireplaces. Because the native Garry oaks and maples along the waterways were so large and beautiful, Lord explained, "The plan for Pringle Creek is definitely naturalistic. Only appropriate native plant material of trees and shrubs are on the planting list."[32] The park board also considered the north end of Pringle Creek Park at Cottage Street to be a most desirable site for a future community hall and art center, connected by a footbridge across the Shelton Stream.[33]

10.6 A contemporary view of Kay (now Englewood) Park, Salem, Oregon (2020). Courtesy Jay Raney.

Among the various designs Schryver provided for the park was one for a log footbridge set on stone pilings to reach the entrance of the proposed community hall. Lord and Schryver's concept of a naturalistic park, planted with Northwest natives and featuring a rustic bridge recalled their use of naturalistic design for the Breitenbush Hot Springs Resort early in their career. Only this time the park would be in the heart of a city.

In 1946 the park board built Highland Park across the street from Highland School. The site was a vacant lot in a northern residential neighborhood where no park had previously existed (figure 10.7). Schryver created two designs for the park. In 1946 she replaced her more formal plan, drafted in 1940, with an informal design that featured a "grass dell" for young children and a colorful planting plan.[34] There were red maples (*Acer rubrum*) lining the street and "tulip trees [*Liriodendron*] and spring-flowering cherries and crabs [crabapples], a large azalea bed, red in color, and low Mugho pines." According to Lord's account, "the park . . . was a charming bit of landscape development merely meant for those who lived in this area of Salem. . . . I am sorry to relate that this little park had a short life." Within three years of its making, the city government was reorganized, and a city manager placed in charge had all the plantings removed to build a tennis court and a men's baseball field.[35]

The Salem Park Board, if not the city council, had a broad, farsighted vision of what the city could accomplish to create a green urban haven. Lord

10.7 Edith Schryver's landscape plan for Highland Park, Salem, Oregon (1946). Courtesy University of Oregon Libraries, Special Collections and University Archives, Coll 098, Lord & Schryver architectural records.

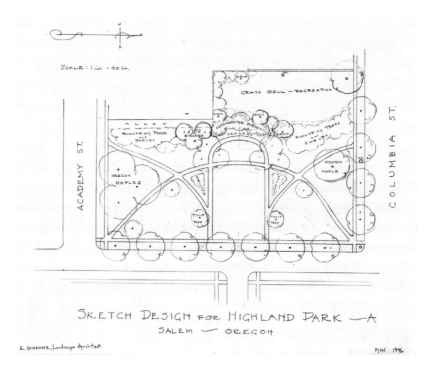

described this in 1941 when she wrote, "There are many vacant blocks that could be converted into City Squares, planted to shade trees, which would not require much up-keep, but the main thing is to acquire the property while the land is available and to select sites in different sections of the city so that everyone may benefit by the parking [park] system."[36] Lord's advice, however, was not followed. The City of Salem disbanded the park board in 1948 and created the Park Planning Committee with Elizabeth Lord still at the helm.[37]

Another matter soon arose regarding city beautification—street trees. Lord envisioned planting both sides of the city streets with a single species of tree, marching uniformly into the distance. "Such is the way of progressive towns wishing to create an impressive vista down a street, or an avenue."[38] Instead, Salem's existing law granted property owners the right to plant the area between the curb and the sidewalk with whatever plants they wanted, resulting in a hodgepodge of growth instead of an "impressive vista." Many property owners failed to maintain the plantings, but they could not remove them without permission from the city. This law nearly drove Lord to distraction. When she tried to have it overturned, to allow a tree commission to take over the planting and care of all street trees, the city attorney and the city manager claimed they "couldn't afford such extravagance. Just like a woman."[39]

10.8 Elizabeth Lord at Gaiety Hollow, Salem, Oregon (1969). Courtesy the *Oregonian*.

In 1950, however, Mayor Elfstrom appointed Lord to chair Salem's new Tree Commission, because he appreciated her commitment to Salem's urban beautification and her formidable knowledge of plants. The other members of the commission were Edith Schryver, Paul B. Wallace, Mark Taylor, and Milton Meyers. The mayor asked the Tree Commission to conduct a survey and make recommendations to the city attorney, who would prepare a street tree ordinance. Lord's voice on the matter did have its intended impact on city leaders, but not until many years later. Salem adopted a street tree ordinance in 1971. It was so successful that, in time, the city received thirty Tree City Awards from the National Arbor Day Foundation.[40]

Despite major hurdles and difficulties, Lord was able to make progress and see that new parks were built and improvements made to existing ones. Acting as an advocate for public landscape improvements and street trees was often a frustrating and thankless task, but she persevered, much to Salem's future benefit (figure 10.8).

Oregon's imposing capitol building of 1876, to which a dome was added in 1893, burned to the ground in 1935. A new, modern capitol building was erected between 1935 and 1938 (figure 10.9). Growth of the state's governmental functions in the decade following reconstruction indicated the need for planning an expanded Capitol Mall (figure 10.10). To accomplish this, state government established the Capitol Planning Commission in 1949.[41] It served as an advisory body of seven citizens from across Oregon. In 1952, Governor Douglas McKay appointed Elizabeth Lord to the new planning commission. She later admitted, "I hesitated taking this job as my loss of hearing was dominant and I realized I could never hear well enough to enter into discussions with a group of men—all architects, engineers and successful businessmen. . . . But Governor McKay would not take 'no' for an answer. He wanted a landscape architect to direct any layout around the Capitol area. He won his point."[42]

Lord had periodically been an outspoken critic of what she viewed as "eyesores" being placed on the Capitol Mall. In 1947, she had written to the editor of the *Capital Journal* to condemn a glasshouse the government proposed to erect in the grass-covered sunken forecourt at the north front of the capitol. "Our Capitol is a building of great dignity, beautiful workmanship of Vermont marble, and to place any kind of edifice, no matter how small, will not only detract from the surrounding buildings, but cheapen the entire assemblage."[43] The glasshouse was not built.

Lord was adamant about the design of the mall, and sprang into action again when a member of the legislature proposed an underground parking lot beneath Willson Park. "It seems to me that this very important addition to the Capitol should have more study and more

10.9 The Oregon State Capitol Building, Salem, Oregon, 1970s, Courtesy Lord & Schryver Conservancy; Anne M. Kingery Library.

people should take an interest in our lovely city—but we sit by and let 'the other fellow do the job.' Wake up Salem! It is time to act—so many drastic changes have been made in the last few years, but to my mind this [is] one of the most important presented to the public."[44] Lord's voice for citizen action was assured and respected. No underground parking garage was built beneath the mall at that time; however, one was constructed in 1991.[45]

The extension of the Capitol Mall in a northerly direction was the result of the "Capitol Expansion Plan 1935–1938."[46] Two city blocks were to be cleared and lined with new government buildings along the mall. The larger purpose of the commission, however, was to establish a long-range plan for

BIRDSEYE VIEW FROM STATE CAPITOL, SALEM, OREGON.

the development of the capitol area in Salem. First, the commission had to decide how large an area it would be. Next, they would advise on the acquisition of property, the construction of buildings, the layout of streets, and the landscaping of public areas. In 1956, arrangements were made for the architectural firm of Wilmsen and Endicott of Eugene, Oregon, to conduct a comprehensive study. After two years had passed and dozens of schemes had been reviewed and rejected, the commission approved a final masterplan in 1958. This plan was influential but would not be carried out in every detail.[47]

Lord was charged with advising the young landscape architect assigned to design the plantings for the new government buildings along the North Mall—the Transportation Building in 1951 and the Labor and Industries Building in 1958–1961.[48] She quite enjoyed the work and supported his choices, perhaps because he incorporated many of her favorite trees and shrubs.[49] When a major windstorm ravaged the city of Salem on Columbus Day, 1962, Lord immediately met with an arborist to assess the damage to the trees on the Capitol Mall, Willson Park, and Deepwood (figure 10.11). She strongly recommended that the city employ professional arborists to remove fallen trees and salvage those that could be saved. After some resistance from the commission over the expense of the work, they accepted her advice and the job was properly completed.[50] The damage was so extensive in Willson Park that the park had to be redesigned, rebuilt, and replanted by the firm of Lloyd Bond and Associates under a state contract.[51] Lord's strong voice and knowledgeable opinions continued to influence the commission until she retired in July 1963.

10.10 Willson Park, post office, and Marion County Courthouse looking west from the Oregon State Capitol Building (c. 1915). Courtesy Oregon Historical Society Research Library.

10.11 Damage at
Deepwood from
high winds after
the Columbus
Day Storm, Salem,
Oregon (1962).
Courtesy Willamette
Heritage Center,
2006.002.3527.005.

> > > Bush's Pasture Park

Bush's Pasture Park in Salem is a green jewel located several blocks south
of the city's central business district. Encompassing ninety and a half acres,
it is the former estate of Asahel Bush (1824–1913), pioneer businessman
and founding editor of the *Oregon Statesman*. The property included wide
meadows, mature stands of Garry oaks, and swaths of native wildflowers
and ferns, along with a wooded section of Pringle Creek. Bush and his wife
Eugenia purchased the land from Reverend David Leslie in 1860 and built
an Italianate mansion there in 1877. His son, Asahel Nesmith Bush (called
"A.N.") and daughter Sally Bush deeded the eastern fifty-seven acres to
the city as a municipal park in 1917 to honor their late father. The property
would not come to the city until all four of the Bush children had passed
away. They also retained a lifetime tenancy of the family house on the western portion of the estate.[52] After their deaths, the city would be able to
purchase the remaining forty-three acres, including the house, a barn, and a
separate conservatory, for a municipal bond of $175,000 (plate 24).[53]

Lord grew up a close friend of the Bush family, and Schryver later became Miss Sally's devoted friend, too. During their first years in business,
Lord and Schryver had assisted Miss Sally with the selection and layout
of a very fine collection of ornamental trees, mostly crabapples and cherries, for the northern slope of the property along Mission Street. Some of

the varieties they chose were very unusual and, by the 1950s, difficult to find at nurseries. One in particular, a cultivar of Japanese flowering cherry, *Prunus subhirtella* 'Whitcomb', is no longer available in the trade.[54] Lord and Schryver considered the property worthy of being treated as an arboretum within a public park because of its collection of trees.

In 1945, the city tried to pass a citizen-approved bond to purchase the remaining forty-three acres, not included in the original gift. When Willamette University offered to pay $25,000 for an athletic field of nine and a half acres in the lower pasture, the voters approved the deal.[55] Two years after Miss Sally died, her brother A. N. Bush moved into the house, putting some of the city's plans on hold. Upon his death in 1953, the remaining acreage and the mansion and outbuildings were secured for public use.

While negotiations for the park's purchase were ongoing, the debate began: How much of the land should be reserved for a naturalistic park and how much should be developed for recreational activities? Members of the Men's Garden Club of Salem grew concerned that the recreation advocates might take over the grounds. In 1946 they weighed in with a request that "the upper levels of the park be maintained for horticultural purposes."[56] Salem's Long-Range Planning Commission of the Chamber of Commerce assured residents that they would respect this request. Earlier that year, the Long-Range Planning Commission hired David E. Thompson, a landscape architect in Portland, to develop an initial comprehensive plan for the park. When she was asked, Edith Schryver agreed to serve as his local liaison and collaborate on the plan.[57] Several months later, Schryver communicated with Thompson that she had "done nothing further in designing any of the areas in which I was so vitally interested, as I have realized that the general policy for the development had already been well organized. . . and have come to the conclusion that, in as much as all of the work to date, including the designing, planning, contracting, consultation and expense has been yours, the full credit for the design, as well as the full fee should be yours alone; and I prefer that you present the final plan without my name attached."[58] She believed that there had been some confusion over the meaning of "collaboration." Thompson provided a plan, aspects of which influenced the final layout of the park; however, not all of his suggested areas were built (figure 10.12).

The situation became rather strained by the end of 1946, as Lord and Schryver sent a three-page report to the chamber's Long-Range Planning Commission outlining their vision for the ninety-acre site.[59] They were intimately familiar with the grounds of Bush's Pasture Park, and perhaps wanted to offer the city's officials and the public a compromise. They considered the lower, more level area the most appropriate space for recreation and athletic fields, parking, and playgrounds. The upper level around Bush

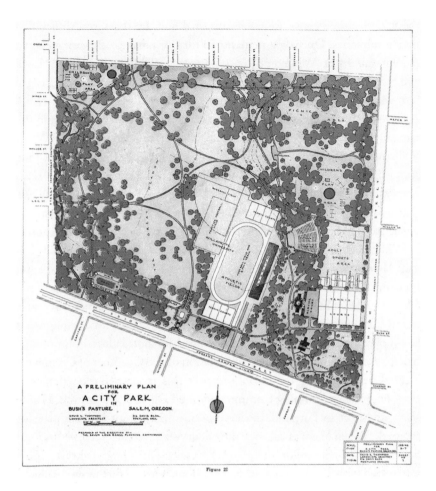

10.12 Landscape
Architect David
E. Thompson's
preliminary plan for
Bush's Pasture Park,
Salem, Oregon (1946).
Courtesy University
of Oregon Libraries,
Special Collections
and University
Archives, Coll 098,
Lord & Schryver
architectural records.

House had meadows suitable for planting and a grove of ancient Garry oaks to the south. The long-established gardens of Miss Sally Bush lay to the north along Mission and High Streets.

> This latter portion contains the remnants of the original Apple Orchard planted by Father [David] Leslie in the year of 1860.[60] In the past twenty years, Miss Bush added a large planting of Oriental Flowering Trees and rare shrubs of horticultural value, including the famous Dove Tree [*Davidia involucrata*], which has won national recognition and has brought many strangers to Salem to view its unusual beauty. This planting could be reorganized and could be expanded into the meadow land, making it a very fine horticultural collection which could be the center of attraction for the garden-minded of the Willamette Valley, as well as attracting many tourists when passing through Salem.[61]

Over time their proposal to commemorate Sally Bush changed to a proposal for an arboretum in memory of Salem's fallen veterans. Neither idea, however, was fully utilized as official policy.

The city had already promised the Salem Rose Society one acre on which to plant a municipal garden of hybrid tea roses. In 1955 they hired Arthur Erfeldt, a landscape architect in Portland, to design it. Lord and Schryver consulted with him and maintained their involvement with decision-making about the grounds. The rose garden was on a gentle slope to the west of the main house. In 1960, when Salem's noted rosarian, Mrs. Mae Tartar, offered to donate two hundred old-fashioned and period roses to the city, Schryver designed a second rose garden with a Victorian theme (figure 10.13).[62] The Tartars said these roses had been collected from early homesteads and historic cemeteries around Salem and represented varieties brought to the Northwest by the Anglo-American pioneers.[63] In midwinter, Schryver oversaw the labeling, moving, and transplanting of all the bushes. Lord could not assist her because she was in Manila at the time with her brother Montague, who was terminally ill. Schryver later informed her partner that it was "the hardest and coldest job she ever did."[64] Both rose gardens are still maintained for the

10.13 Edith Schryver's planting plan for the Tartar Collection of Old Roses in Bush's Pasture Park, Salem, Oregon (1965). Courtesy Lord & Schryver Conservancy, Anne M. Kingery Library.

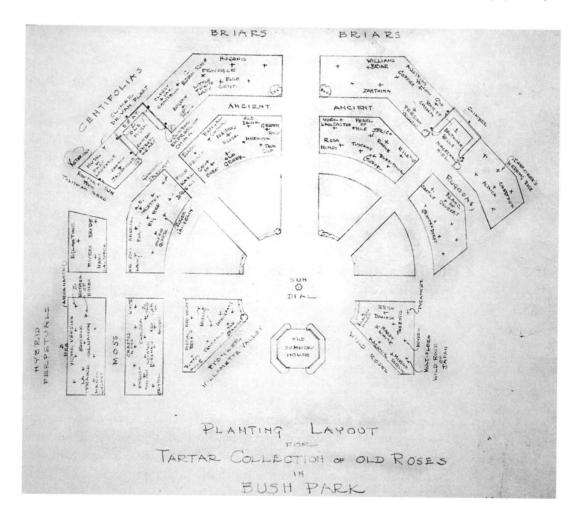

10.14 Aerial view of the Tartar Collection of Old Roses in Bush's Pasture Park, Salem, Oregon (2020). Courtesy Ron Cooper.

public's enjoyment by the City of Salem and the Mission Street Parks Conservancy (figure 10.14; plate 25).

The year after Sally Bush's death, a group of Salem residents worked to revitalize the Salem Art Association, which had languished during World War II. Although Lord at first considered the association's plans "a hopeless undertaking," both she and Schryver took great interest in the project and wanted to support it.[65] In 1948 Lord agreed to serve on the association's board. In 1951, while they were on a trip to the Far East, the Salem Art Association elected Lord their president. She was not entirely pleased and later declared, "I feel one reason the honor was bestowed on me was on account of collecting money from interested people, a job I dislike intensely. Another duty I dislike intensely is being president of an organization."[66]

Nevertheless, she accepted the responsibility and was twice reelected president. Lord helped the Salem Art Association make significant progress (figures 10.15, 10.16). In 1953, following A. N. Bush's death, the city council approved their use of the first floor of Bush House as a museum and the second floor as a venue for art exhibitions.[67] Schryver was appointed as their liaison officer to collaborate with the city on landscape improvements in the surrounding park. Many citizens came forward to assist with the work, offering both their time and skills. In the mid-1950s, the Salem Art Association began planning a new art center in the historic barn, conditional on the park department's ability to move to a new facility. The large barn caught fire in October 1963 and was partially gutted. This created more interest in the possibility of developing a Bush Barn Art Center and moving the galleries out of the mansion. The Salem Art Association commissioned Charles E. Hawkes, a Salem architect, to design a multipurpose art center with space for galleries, studios, and offices. He offered a plan for an effective solution that resulted in a handsome purpose-built space. The City of Salem assisted the Art Association with their fundraising by donating the settlement from the fire insurance company. Following a successful citywide fundraising campaign, the Bush Barn Art Center opened in April 1965. Lord and Schryver were able to add their special touch by designing the planting schemes for the main entrance to the art center and gardens near the house.

10.15 The Salem Art Fair and Festival in Bush's Pasture Park, Salem, Oregon (c. 1957). Courtesy Robert Melnick, FASLA.

10.16 Square dancing at the Salem Art Fair and Festival in Bush's Pasture Park, Salem, Oregon (c. 1957). Courtesy Robert Melnick, FASLA.

10.17 Elizabeth Lord and
Edith Schryver standing
at the entrance to Gaiety
Hollow (1970). ©USA TODAY
NETWORK Ron Cooper
photo.

In her senior years, Lord expressed regret that "Salem people have never seemed to realize the great privilege we possess to make this city one of the outstandingly beautiful, attractive cites in the country. With all the beautiful streams from the far northern Mill Creek (so alive with wild fowl and even salmon trying to wind their way upstream) to the extreme southern boundary of Bush Pasture Park, we have completely ignored their possibility of beautification."[68] Time has proven that this was not really true. The battles that Lord and Schryver waged to make Salem a more beautiful and cultivated city were successful (figure 10.17). The Salem Art Association, Bush House Museum, Deepwood Museum and Gardens, and many other sites continue to thrive and the natural streams crisscrossing the city are protected and preserved as part of an attractive and well-designed public park system in the very heart of Oregon's capital.

11

Final Years

Well, sometimes, you know, plants are like people, they just wear out.
　—Edith Schryver

Over the decades, Lord and Schryver's style of design had varied little, and it remained highly admired in the Northwest. Their gardens, however, did require the commitment of owners to a high standard of maintenance. Naturally, some of the landscapes they had designed were well maintained and some were not. Properties changed hands, and all the alterations, whether caused by time, nature, or new gardeners, were noticed by the two designers.

New property owners did, on occasion, turn to Lord and Schryver for advice on the renovation of an original design. Sometimes the firm made the initial contact. Such a case was the Robertson property, designed in 1931–1932, on Leffelle Street in Salem. In 1941 Lord and Schryver wrote to the new owners, Mr. and Mrs. Carl E. Nelson, and explained that they knew the landscape had been neglected and asked if they would like it restored. "[We are] most interested because, as you may know, the garden is one of our early creations and we have always considered it one of our best planned in Salem."[1] The Nelsons agreed to have them look at it, and Lord and Schryver went to see what they could do. They offered a full report on the proper revisions. Lord wrote, "I hope this resumé of work and plans will give you an idea of what we consider important in order to make this garden one of the outstanding gardens in Salem."[2] The work they suggested was extensive: rebuilding the terraces, adding a privacy fence, replacing much of the planting, shoring up the driveway border, and properly pruning all the shrubs and some of the trees. Schryver would be responsible for designing any new structures, such as an arbor, and two workmen Lord and Schryver recommended would carry out the tasks—under their supervision. The Nelsons had their recommendations completed in a timely fashion.

In 1952 the property changed hands again when Mr. and Mrs. Robert M. Gormsen, owners of the Miles Linen Mill, bought it. Nancy Gormsen was an interior decorator who greatly admired Lord and Schryver's work. The three became good friends and served on the Salem Art Association's board together. When Mrs. Gormsen asked Schryver to design an outdoor fireplace for them, Schryver literally set up her chair and little sketching table in the garden and drew it while the masons stood by with trowels ready Mrs. Gormsen had them incorporate an unusual decorative item in the garden—an iron balustrade from the old Marion County Courthouse, demolished in 1952.[3] The courthouse railing reminded Schryver of the balustrade used at Deepwood for the Scroll Garden. The care that the Nelsons and the Gormsens devoted to the property ensured that the Robertson house and garden were exceptionally well preserved. It was placed on the National Register in 1983. On the nomination form, the preservationists declared that the landscape was "a quintessential Lord and Schryver garden."[4]

In the 1960s, Lord began to express both acceptance of and frustration with her increasing limitations in the garden, as she was now in her seventies. She confided in her garden journal, which also served as a personal diary, "I wish I knew more about pruning small trees—never can learn now because I am too set in my ways & always let Nini [Edith] have her way."[5] She was also less inclined to tolerate those who could not really appreciate the special quality of the plants that she and Schryver had collected. On 15 April 1964 she wrote, "I had written to Lillian Madison [Lillie L. Madsen, garden editor for the *Statesman*] that she should see the beauty of [magnolia] Kobus and especially this variety was rare and said by Journal editor there were none in the Willamette Valley. She took my picture in front of the [magnolia] soulangeana and had a picture of the Kobus—labeled as the Prunus pissardii! Decided, then & there, it was hopeless and wouldn't bother her to see the garden again (nor anybody else, they can come if they want to, but I'm thru asking anyone—my friends look at me as tho' I asked them to visit the zoo)."[6]

Both had difficulty working with their gardener, Kurt Roesnick, whom they nonetheless employed for many years. Roesnick emigrated from Germany in the 1940s and took great pride in his work. He was a skilled gardener, but he found Schryver demanding and opinionated; she had the same complaint about him.[7] Nonetheless, they worked together into the late 1970s. In the 1960s, he also worked for the City of Salem at Bush's Pasture Park.

Through 1968, the ladies were still working for a few clients. They were replanting the landscape of the St. Paul's Episcopal Church in Salem when Lord was taken ill. She recorded the events in her garden journal,

"There was some subconscious reason why I was determined to complete this Church planting—the reason became very apparent by the middle of March [1969]. Illness struck me on the 15th and I was not on steady ground till June first. By May 1st an operation seemed to be a necessity—my first in all my 80 years of life—but I did not dread it and rallied wonderfully well."[8]

This may have precipitated Lord and Schryver's decision to close their firm in 1969. After forty years of design work for approximately two hundred clients, they would now focus on personal interests such as their own garden at Gaiety Hollow. In June of that year, while still recovering from the operation, Lord wrote, "As for the garden—work has been hard for me. Nina . . . has had a miserable year, in fact the last 5 years, and she cannot help me in the garden. It is now a bit much continual work for me, in spite of two men to help. The heavy debris from the shrubs by over burden bloom keeps me & Nelson [their assistant] continually busy."[9] Schryver's health was also failing. She suffered from an accidental fall in 1970 that required several months for her recovery.[10]

Both Lord and Schryver were very sociable, and the circle of friends that had provided them with encouragement and pleasure over the years remained very important to them as they aged (figure 11.1). Blanche and Charles A. Sprague lived one street away. Charles Sprague was the former governor of Oregon as well as the owner and editor of the *Statesman* newspaper. He had influenced public opinion in Oregon for decades. With them on the board of the Salem Art Association were Kathryn and James Walton, Alice Brown Powell of Deepwood, and Nancy Gormsen. Frances and David C. Duniway were their good friends as well. David Duniway's primary interest was historic preservation, and he served as Oregon's first state archivist as well as the first director of the Mission Mill Museum in Salem. Landscape architect and protege Wallace Kay Huntington was also one of their circle, as were numerous members of the garden clubs and civic organizations they had supported through the years. Members of the younger generation, their friends' children and grandchildren, frequently visited or called on "the girls." Schryver was particularly fond of entertaining young friends, such as her goddaughter Neena Kirsh, when she came to Salem to visit her grandmother, Mrs. Walter H. Smith. Lord and Schryver had created a small garden for Mrs. Smith, who lived just one block away, where they emphasized flowers in her favorite color, pink.[11]

Schryver also maintained a friendship with one of her most notable classmates from Lowthorpe—Joanna C. Diman (1901–1991). In the photograph with her class outside, circa 1920, Diman is seated next to Schryver with her arm resting on the other's lap. Their correspondence over the decades has not survived, but one notice in the *Statesman Journal* indicates that Diman was a lifelong friend who came to Salem to visit Schryver in April 1963.[12]

11.1 Lord and
Schryver in the
gardens at Gaiety
Hollow (1973).
Courtesy Lord &
Schryver Conservancy,
Anne M. Kingery
Library. Neena Kirsch
photo.

Diman was an extraordinary figure in the field of twentieth-century land-scape architecture, and her professional path was completely different from that of her friend in Oregon.

Diman had been Schryver's colleague in Ellen Shipman's office in New York from 1924 to 1926.[13] She went on to gain experience in the New York offices of Annette Hoyt Flanders and Louise Payson. In 1934, after two years of unemployment because of the Depression, Diman was hired by the New York City Department of Parks as their planning designer, and from then on her career soared. Her oversight encompassed large-scale urban projects and transportation plans for New York's most famous com-missioner of parks, Robert Moses. Under his lead, New York began an unsurpassed period of development with parks, parkways, housing, and infrastructure projects funded by the federal government. Diman left the parks department in 1939–1940 for a trip to the Philippines (where her brother was a missionary), China, and Japan. In 1944 she joined the architectural firm of Skidmore, Owings and Merrill (SOM), a world-famous architectural firm headquartered in Manhattan, and remained there until her retirement in 1967.[14] She became the head of the landscape architecture department of SOM at a time when few would anticipate such a challenging position be awarded to a woman. Known by her colleagues to be "cantankerous" and strong-minded, Diman was highly respected and effective in her role at SOM. The projects completed under her leadership included college campuses, corporate headquarters, national museums, and international developments. Her reunion with Edith Schryver in 1963, four years before she retired and exactly forty years after they had graduated from Lowthorpe, must have been exciting and gratifying for them both.

Their relatives, despite living far away, also provided Lord and Schryver with companionship and a strong sense of connection. Lord survived both of her brothers by many years. William P. Lord died in 1948 and Montague in 1960. Her closest remaining relative was her nephew Melvin S. Lord, Montague's adopted son, who stayed in touch with her throughout her lifetime. During military service in Spain, Melvin Lord met and married Carmen DePages. They returned to live in the United States and had three children: Marilee, Montague, and Carmen. The whole family frequently came to visit their aunt in Oregon. During the summer months, a favorite place for them to gather was the Lord cottage at Seal Rock (figure 11.2).

When Elizabeth Lord died on 9 October 1976, she was eighty-eight years old. In her will she left Edith Schryver a lifetime tenancy of Gaiety Hollow, a substantial sum of cash ($50,000), her club memberships, and the car. She left all her real property, including the house and furnishings at 545 Mission Street, worth $475,000, in trust with the US National Bank of Oregon. Their good friend David C. Duniway gave the eulogy at her memorial service in the garden at Gaiety Hollow. He began by saying, "Elizabeth Lord was our friend, and for each of us she had a very special meaning. The twinkle in her eye, her smile, her graciousness, and the ring of her voice, we all remember and can cherish. But it was her delight in gardening, in trees, in nature that enriches our lives today."[15] He went on to describe all of Lord's many contributions to the community and to the Northwest because of the ideas and inspiration she brought to the firm. Her ashes were buried next to those of her parents at Mount Crest Abbey Mausoleum in Salem. The epithet on her stone reads, "Her garden was her pleasure."

After Lord's death, Schryver continued to be involved with the Bush House Museum and the Salem Art Association. She made donations in her partner's name to organizations Lord had supported such as the Colonial Dames, the Mission Mill Museum, and the garden clubs. She particularly

11.2 Elizabeth Lord and Edith Schryver at their beach cottage, Seal Rock, Oregon (1973). Courtesy Lord & Schryver Conservancy, Anne M. Kingery Library.

enjoyed doing the floral arrangements for social events at the Bush House Museum. She was asked to advise the volunteer group that was energetically rejuvenating the gardens at Deepwood after the property was acquired in 1971 for a city park. After viewing their work, Schryver commented, "It's lovely, but it's all wrong." She went on to explain the design as she and Lord had envisioned it decades before (plate 26).

Edith Schryver died on 20 May 1984 at the age of eighty-three, having survived her lifetime partner by seven and a half years. She had also outlived her brother, Harry G. Schryver, who died in 1961. She had kept in touch with her cousin Kathyrn (Kay) Heavey and two nieces, Eileen Eleanor Mosher and Mary Louise Hyde, who lived in Pennsylvania and New York state, respectively. At settlement of her estate, each of her nieces received an inheritance. She directed that her body be returned to Kingston, New York, to be buried next to her parents in the Wiltwyck Cemetery.

At Schryver's memorial service in the garden at Gaiety Hollow, David C. Duniway fondly recalled her talent as well as the times when she could be "a terrible procrastinator. The removal of a tree was a matter of anguish extending over many seasons. On the other hand, the planting of a tree was also a difficult decision. There are many stories of how a tree once planted could be moved two hours later, and then again before a day was over. Even a few feet, or the relation of a branch to the vista made a difference to her."[16]

After Schryver's death, Melvin S. Lord, Elizabeth's nephew, inherited the house at Gaiety Hollow, the cottage at Seal Rock, and the furnishings of both, as well as his aunt's personal belongings and investments. Lord and Schryver's professional papers, plans, photographs, and books from their office at Gaiety Hill were donated to the University of Oregon's archives in Eugene, where they form Special Collection 098. Their personal papers were removed, although some of their photographs and notebooks were included in the collection (plate 27).

➤➤➤ The Lord & Schryver Conservancy

Appreciative buyers who had admired the design of both the house and garden purchased Gaiety Hollow in 1985. They took excellent care of both over the next twenty-eight years. They made improvements and repairs where necessary but did not alter its basic elements or composition. By the time they decided to sell the property in 2013, a growing movement in the community had developed to preserve the house and garden (figure 11.3). A

11.3 Lord and Schryver's home at Gaiety Hollow in winter, Salem, Oregon (1996). Courtesy Lord & Schryver Conservancy, Anne M. Kingery Library.

11.4 The West Allee at Gaiety Hollow in winter, Salem, Oregon (1996).
Courtesy Lord & Schryver Conservancy, Anne M. Kingery Library.

11.5 Restoration of the West Allee at Gaiety Hollow, Salem, Oregon
(2020). Courtesy Mark Akimoff.

third owner came forward to secure the property until a new organization, the Lord & Schryver Conservancy, a 501(c)(3), had raised sufficient funds to acquire it.

When the Gaiety Hill/Bush's Pasture Park National Historic District was created in 1986, the house at Gaiety Hollow was a contributing factor. In 2014, the house, outbuildings, and garden were accepted to the National Register of Historic Places for the excellence of their design and the professionals associated with it: Clarence L. Smith for the house, and Lord and Schryver for the garden. In 2004, the Lord & Schryver Conservancy invited two professional landscape historians, William Noble, then director of preservation for the Garden Conservancy, and David C. Streatfield, professor of landscape architecture at the University of Washington, to visit the property. Noble and Streatfield urged the organization to go forward with their plans, as neither could identify a garden of comparable stature on the West Coast. To foster awareness and credibility in the community, the Lord & Schryver Conservancy volunteers undertook a rehabilitation of the historic gardens at Deepwood Museum and Gardens, commissioned a cultural landscape report for Gaiety Hollow, assembled an archive of materials to supplement the holdings at the University of Oregon, and presented public programs. The Lord & Schryver Conservancy acquired Gaiety Hollow in June 2015, with the mission to "preserve, interpret and steward the legacy of Elizabeth Lord and Edith Schryver for public enrichment." Restoration of the garden to its period of significance began (figures 11.4, 11.5; plates 28 to 32).

Lord and Schryver's good friend Wallace Kay Huntington described the garden at Gaiety Hollow best in his essay in the comprehensive edited volume *Space, Style and Structure: Building in Northwest America*:

> Plant composition with them [Lord and Schryver] was an art form—albeit fragile and transient—and in the Salem garden of Elizabeth Lord we have, still surviving in the 1970s, a lost art. So subtle are the foliage colors and textures and so skillfully arranged is the succession of bloom, that, like an impressionist painting it may at first seem deceptively simple but upon closer examination the incredible command and knowledge of their media—plants instead of paint—is truly stunning. Here the geometry of the compartmented scheme is at its most effective and the quality of design in arbors and fences at its classic finest. Anyone who conceives of a formal garden as being static has only to study the calculated interplay of spatial relationships in this tour de force of garden design.[17]

Acknowledgments

The story of Elizabeth Lord and Edith Schryver is a transcontinental tale: two young women, one from the West and one from the East, meet on a European garden tour in 1927 and become friends, partners in a new business venture, and lifelong companions. The story behind this book is also a transcontinental one, as the Lord & Schryver Conservancy in Salem, Oregon, employed me, a landscape historian in Maine, to research and interpret their trajectory and accomplishments.

Many individuals and institutions have contributed to bringing the concept into reality. First of all, I would like to thank Judith Tankard for bringing the project to my attention and Bobbie Dolp, president of the Lord & Schryver Conservancy's board, for her confidence that this story was worth a place in history.

Over many years, a dedicated cadre of people has been integral to the evolution of the Lord & Schryver Conservancy and, in particular, to the production of this book. I am grateful for their sharing a range of talents critical to its realization:

Mark Akimoff
Gretchen Carnaby
Carmen Lord
Ron Cooper
Pat Deminna
Kenneth Helphand
Roger Hull
David Lichter
Valerie McIntosh
Gayle Meaders
Robert Melnick
Peter Miramon

Susan Napack
Bill Noble
Kylie Pine
Elisabeth Walton Potter
Elizabeth Powers
Jay Raney
Ruth Roberts
Derek and Julia Sadowski
Mary Anne Spradlin
David C. Streatfield
Ross Sutherland
Pam Wasson

The behind-the-scenes support staff at various organizations have been invaluable in searching out so many of the bits and pieces that contribute to the richness of the story. These resources include: Blue Hill Public Library, Willamette Heritage Center, Oregon Historical Society, Deepwood Museum and Gardens, Bush House

Museum, Cornell University Library, Dartmouth College Library, and Oregon State University Library. In particular we would like to thank the exceptional staff of the Special Collections and Archives at the University of Oregon, home of Lord and Schryver's professional papers.

Kudos as well to the professional staff at the Oregon State University Press, who have stayed the course for many years and provided endless support for the myriad details to translate the rough drafts to a stunning product: Tom Booth, Mary Braun, Kim Hogeland, and Micki Reaman, and copy editor Susan Campbell.

For their patience and constant encouragement, I am extremely grateful to my husband, Jay, and my good friend and editorial critic, Virginia Tuttle.

Notes

⇒ Notes to the Introduction

Epigraph from, Cynthia Reiner, "Landscaper Will Help Deepwood Bloom Again," *Statesman Journal*, 10 August 1980, p. 3E.

1   Ross Sutherland, "Early Influences, Early Expression," in Carnaby et al., *Influences Find Expression*, 1.

2   Both schools were located near Boston.

3   Interview with Jennifer Hagloch, 7 July 2010, LSC.

4   Ibid.

5   E. Schryver's travel diary, 1927, UO 098-17-1.

6   Interview with Jennifer Hagloch, 7 July 2010, LSC.

7   Duniway, "Lord-Schryver," 107.

8   Huntington, "Parks and Gardens of Western Oregon," in *Space, Style and Structure*, 562–563.

9   Yoch, "Florence Yoch and Lucille Council," in *Pioneers of American Landscape Design*, 470–474.

10 In 1929 the Jarman family moved from Southern California to a new house in Salem, Oregon.

11 With the end of the World War II, both architecture and landscape architecture changed dramatically with the advent of Modernism. Lord and Schryver continued to carry out principles for residential gardens that had worked well for their clients and were much admired.

12 The first treatment plan for a historic landscape was published by the US National Park Service (NPS) in the 1960s. The National Historic Preservation Act of 1966 created the National Register of Historic Places. The NPS authorized the Historic American Landscapes Survey (HALS) in 2000 (nps.gov).

13 Huntington, "Parks and Gardens of Western Oregon," in *Space, Style and Structure*, 576.

14 Huntington, "Lord and Schryver's Influence on the Evolving Northwest Style," in Carnaby et al., *Influences Find Expression*, 30.

Epigraph from, Fred Lockley, "Fred Lockley's Impressions," column in *Oregon Daily Journal*, 19 November 1944, Sec. 2, p. 1.

1   Charles Henry Carey, "William Paine Lord," 260–263.

2   Born Juliette Cooke Montague, as recorded on the 1850 and 1860 Massachusetts census, she had shortened her name to Juliet M. Lord by the Oregon census of 1900, and thereafter.

3   Lockley, "Impressions and Observations of the Journal Man," 8.

4   Comstock, "With Lincoln at the Ball," 11.

5   The neighborhood later became known as Gaiety Hill.

6   Elizabeth Lord, typescript of radio address for the DAR, 1944, OHS Mss. 2050-5-9.

7   Notes by Elizabeth Lord, OHS Mss. 2050-5-9.

8   Elizabeth Lord, typescript of radio address for the DAR, 1944, OHS Mss. 2050-5-9.

9   Letter, E. Lord to Frances "Fanny" Duniway, 16 January 1976, LSC.

10 E. Lord, remembrances of her family, binder titled "William Lord & predecessors…" OHS.

11 Buren, "Governor's Daughter Gives Girl's-Eye View of Politics."

12 Elizabeth Lord, typescript of radio address for the DAR, 1944, OHS Mss. 2050-5-9.

13 Notes by Elizabeth B. Lord, OHS Mss. 2050-5-9. Her brother Montague was at business college in San Francisco. Juliet Lord went there for medical treatment.

14 St. Helen's Hall became the Oregon Episcopal Academy.

15 Letter, E. Lord to Frances "Fanny" Duniway, 16 January 1976, LSC.

16 Ibid.

17 Charles Henry Carey, "William Paine Lord," 263.

18 Lockley, "Impressions and Observations of the Journal Man," 8.

19 Letter, E. Lord to David Duniway, 23 July 1973, LSC.

20 Ibid.

21 Eliz. Lord, typescript of radio address for the DAR, 1944, OHS Mss. 2050-5-9.

22 Interview by author with Elisabeth W. Potter, 25 January 2018.

23 Letter, E. Lord to Helen Mershon, 8 August 1968, vertical files, Biography, William P. Lord, OHS.

24 E. Lord's notes on her mother's life, nd, Carmen Lord's collection, box 319.

25 Letter, F. H. Gerke to E. Lord, 11 January 1929, UO 098-7-1.

26 Kingston had originally been named Wiltwyck by the Dutch in 1661 but was renamed by the English in 1669 after they took control of New Netherland.

27 Schryver's grandfather did not agree with the original church's practice of serving wine.

28 Interview with Kay Heavey, 17 May 2004, LSC.

29 Letter, E. Schryver to Kay Heavey, 18 June 1969, LSC.

30 Ibid.

31 Interview, Edith Schryver by J. Hagloch, 14 October 1982, LSC.

32 Material in E. Schryver Personal File, LSC.

33 E. Schryver's brother Harry did not approve of the marriage and avoided his father from then on. Interview with Kay Heavey 17 May 2004, LSC.

34 Ibid.

35 Ibid.

36 Scholarships were available for Lowthorpe, but it is unknown whether Schryver received one. Schneider, *A History of Lowthorpe*, 24.

⋙ Notes to Chapter 2: Lowthorpe School

Epigraph from, Richardson L. Wright, "Women in Landscaping," *House & Garden*, January 1926, p. 150. Wright was the very influential editor of *House & Garden* for thirty-five years.

1 Miss L. Louise Hetzer became the school's superintendent in 1911 and remained on the faculty for many years. Schneider, *A History of Lowthorpe*, 15.

2 Photograph of Edith Schryver, c. 1920, Melnick Collection, LSC.

3 Mrs. Low stated, "Lowthorpe was founded with a view to training women for taking an active and professional part in gardening, horticulture and landscape architecture." Schneider, *A History of Lowthorpe*, 9.

4 Schneider, *A History of Lowthorpe*, 7.

5 The school's name changed several times during its history. The legal name in 1909 was "The Lowthorpe School of Landscape Architecture, Gardening and Horticulture for Women." The school merged with the Rhode Island School of Design in 1945 as a department. Schneider, *A History of Lowthorpe*, 11.

6 Ibid., 8.

7 Ibid., 13.

8 Although Schryver remembered those three names as her friends, her graduating class included only Joanna C. Diman among them. The other four in the class of 1923 were Ada Beard, Marjorie Broadbent, Helen Russell, and Charlotte Lee. Schneider, *A History of Lowthorpe*, 75.

9 The typed notes contain typos such as "Landscape architecture . . . aims at . . . giving everything its proper place in relatin [relation] to the whole." Edith Schryver's notebook, UO 098-18-6.

10 Krall, "The Landscape Architect as Advocate," 19.

11 Strang, "Good Design Plus Good Personality," 283.

12 Not all the women who became landscape architects in the early 1900s joined ASLA, which was considered by some to be a male bastion.

13 Lowthorpe catalog, 1925–26, LSC.

14 Lowthorpe catalog, 1928–29, LSC.

15 Schneider, *A History of Lowthorpe*, 76.

16 Jesse A. Correy, "Flowers for Home and Garden," column, *Oregonian*, 3 March 1922. The first Illahee Country Club declined in the 1930s, to be replaced by the Illahee Hills Country Club.

17 Jesse A. Correy, "Flowers for Home and Garden," column, *Oregonian*, 18 March 1923, p. 66.

18 "Two Seasons in a Western Garden," 60.

19 Obituary, "Death Claims Mrs. W. P. Lord," in Mss. 2050-5-folder 12, and scrapbook labeled "In memoriam William P. Lord," OHS.

20 Cambridge and Lowthorpe School publications, UO 098-14-5.

21 Schryver designed an octagonal walled "Spanish garden" for Mrs. Henry D. Shelden of Gross Pointe, Michigan (nd) and "Garden in the Spanish Mood" for Evander B. Schley, Far Hills, New Jersey, 1926, both in UO 098-folder 89.

22 E. Lord's journal, 1927, UO 098-17-1.

23 E. Schryver's journal, 1927, UO 098-17-1.

24 Invitation card for "Exhibit of Garden Plans," dated 4 April 1929, LSC. UO Special Collection 098.

25 Richardson Wright, "Women in Landscaping," *House & Garden*, January 1926, p. 150.

Notes to Chapter 3: The Cornish Colony and Ellen Shipman

Epigraph from, Frances Duncan, "The Gardens of Cornish," *Century Magazine*, May 1906, p. 4.

1 Shipman always listed her business address as the more fashionable Cornish.

2 Van Buren, "Landscape Architecture and Gardens in the Cornish Colony," 383. Shipman supported the Mothers' and Daughters' Club of Plainfield, New Hampshire, founded in 1901, which met in a building designed by Charles A. Platt. The club established craft industries, such as rug-making, that provided local women with an opportunity to earn an income.

3 Duncan, "The Gardens of Cornish," 18.

4 Clayton, "Reminiscence and Revival," 894–905.

5 Tankard, "Shipman in Seattle," 30.

6 Tankard and Close, *The Gardens of Ellen Biddle Shipman*, 37.

7 Platt, *Italian Gardens*.

8 Van Buren, "Landscape Architecture and Gardens in the Cornish Colony," 373.

9 Tankard, "Ellen Biddle Shipman," *Pioneers of American Landscape Design*, 350.

10 Clayton, "Reminiscence and Revival," 894–905.

11 Gilbert and Tankard, *A Place of Beauty*, 51.

12 See Tankard, *Ellen Shipman and the American Garden*.

13 Ibid., 55.

14 Aspet is preserved as the Saint-Gaudens National Historic Site. Shipman prepared a planting plan for the Saint-Gaudens' Memorial in 1928. Edith Schryver may have worked on this project; however, we do not know whether she was involved, as her name is not on the plan.

15 The Arts and Crafts movement, popular in both Britain and America around 1900, advocated products made by hand, not machine, as the industrialization of both countries threatened traditional craft industries and rural life. Frances Duncan celebrated the fact that Cornish gardeners used local stone and wood to give walls, arbors, fences, steps, and seats a delightfully rustic appearance.

16 E. Schryver's notebook, entry dated 16 September 1922, UO 098-14-1.

17 "A House on Beekman Place, New York," 516.

18 Ellen Louise Payson (1894–1977) graduated from Lowthorpe in 1916 and was Shipman's office manager for several years. Tankard, *Ellen Shipman and the American Garden*, 109.

19 Ellen Louise Payson's papers are retained by the Folger Library, University of Maine, Orono.

20 Cynthia Reiner, "Landscaper Will Help Deepwood Bloom Again," *Statesman Journal*, 10 August 1980, p. 3E.

21 Tankard, *Ellen Shipman and the American Garden*, 109.

22 Ibid., 191–193.

23 Ibid., 126.

24 Plans for the Shelden and Schley projects from Shipman's office, UO 098-folder 89.

➤ Notes to Chapter 4: A Venture Launched

Epigraph from, Letter, E. Lord to Mr. Fry, 6 March 1929, UO 098-2-8.

1 Oral history with Edith Schryver, 12 May 1982, Bush House Museum; "Mrs. Schucking Joins Miss Lord," *Daily Capital Journal*, 13 December 1928, p. 7; "Elizabeth Lord Home from Boston," *Daily Capital Journal*, 20 December 1928, p. 5.

2 Rose, *A Natural History of Minto Brown Island Park*.

3 Interview with Edith Schryver, 12 May 1982, Bush House Museum.

4 Huntington, "Parks and Gardens of Western Oregon," in *Space, Style and Structure*, 557–558.

5 Ibid.

6 *Polk's Directory of Portland*, the directory for Oregon's largest city, listed businesses much like the Yellow Pages of today; it advertised only one landscape architect in 1910 and a few by 1911. In contrast, there were numerous landscape gardeners. *Polk's Directory for Salem* had no listings for landscape architects before 1929.

7 The state had no licensing requirements for landscape architects until 1961, so anyone who thought they had the appropriate skills and knowledge could use the title.

8 List, "Salem—Announcement cards," 4 January 1929, UO 098-2-10.

9 Letter, E. Lord to Mrs. Johnson, 1 January 1929, UO 098-7-1.

10 Exhibition announcement card, Monroe Gilbert Studio, 4 April 1929, folder "Material from Mary L. Schryver, 2000," LSC.

11 Olive Doak, society editor, *Oregon Statesman*, 7 April 1929, p. 6.

12 Letter, John Davis Hatch, Jr. to E. Schryver, 2 May 1929, UO 098-7-1.

13 "Bit of Old Spain to Top Hill," *Capital Journal*, 6 March 1929, pp. 1, 7, UO 098-2-8.

14 Records do not indicate whether the garden was ever constructed, but six drawings in the archives at the University of Oregon show Schryver's design process for this project. To create a complex formal garden centered on a Spanish fountain, she experimented with two basic forms—an ellipse and an

octagon—ultimately selecting the octagon to develop into a more detailed and color-rendered plan. It contained a total of twenty beds of five different shapes, each one outlined in boxwood, UO 098-folder 89.

15 Letter, E. Lord to Mr. D. B. Jarman, 6 March 1929, UO 098-2-8.

16 Letter, Mrs. Jarman to E. Lord, 11 March 1929, UO 098-2-8.

17 Lord-Schryver's plans for Jarman garden, UO 098-folder 37.

18 McAlister's most famous house was Jane Mansfield's "Pink Palace" in Beverly Hills, California.

19 When first planted, the boxwood read as a row of small balls, but in time they grew into a solid line of green and were trimmed into a rectilinear form.

20 See plans drafted by E. Schryver in UO 098-folder 89.

21 Invoice, Mt. View Floral Company, 11 October 1929, UO 098-2-8.

22 E. Schryver handwritten notes, "Color Schemes," Jarman folder, LSC.

23 Letter, E. Lord to Mrs. Jarman, 26 February 1930, UO 098-2-8.

24 Ibid.

25 Letter, E. Lord to Mr. Wyatt, 6 November 1929, UO 098-7-2.

26 Letter, E. Schryver to Mrs. R. D. Merrill, 1 January 1929, UO 098-3-2.

27 Tankard, "Shipman in Seattle," 33.

28 Ellen Shipman, "Design Plan for the property of R.D. Merrill," August 1915, UO 098-folder 88.

29 Perkins, "Quiet Gardens in the Northwest," 63–67.

30 Letter, E. Schryver to Ellen Shipman, 20 February 1930, UO 098-3-3; LSC.

31 Ibid.

32 Letter, H. Ernest Colwell to E. Schryver, 5 November 1929, UO 098-7-2; receipt J. J. Bonnell Nurseries to Mr. R. D. Merrill, 31 May 1929, UO 098-7-1.

33 Letter, E. Schryver to Ellen Shipman, 20 February 1930, UO 098-3-3; LSC.

34 Ibid.

35 Ibid.

36 Letter, Ellen Shipman to E. Schryver, 25 February 1930, UO 098-3-3.

37 Tankard, "Shipman in Seattle," 37.

38 Ruth Roberts, "A Practice Is Established," in Carnaby et al., *Influences Find Expression*, 9.

39 Cool, "From Hot Springs to Heritage," 55.

40 Stationary for Breitenbush Hot Springs, 12 August 1929, UO 098-4-7.

41 Letter, E. Lord to Mrs. McNary, 16 November 1929, UO 098-7-2.

42 Lord-Schryver, "Proposed Landscape Development Plan of Breitenbush Resort Tract," undated [1930], UO 098-folder 12.

43 Ibid. The great increase in automobile ownership in the 1920s and the American love of exploration fostered the development of "auto camps," where one could drive a vehicle up to a campsite.

44 Letter, E. Lord to Dr. Mark Skiff, 9 October 1929, UO 098-4-7.

45 Florence Holmes changed her name to Florence Holmes Gerke in 1922 when she married Walter Gerke.

46 Letter, F. H. Gerke to E. Lord, 11 January 1929, UO 098-7-1.

47 News article, "Federal Job Won: Miss Florence Holmes, Portland, Receives Call," nd, in clipping file, LSC.

48 Interview, by Ruth Roberts and David Lichter, with Marianne Gerke Ott, daughter, 11 March 2018.

49 "Obituary: Landscape Architect Florence Holmes Gerke," *Oregon Journal*, 24 August 1964; interview with Marianne Gerke Ott, daughter, 11 March 2018.

50 Interview with Marianne Gerke Ott, daughter, 11 March 2018.

51 Letter, F. H. Gerke to E. Lord, 7 March 1929, UO 098-7-3.

52 "To Judge Garden Contest," *Oregon Sunday Call*, 4 May 1929, UO 098-7-3.

53 Letter, E. Schryver to F. H. Gerke, undated [July 1929], UO 098-7-3.

54 Letter, Miss Lou Richardson to E. Lord, 11 January 1929, UO 098-7-1.

55 Letter, E. Lord to editor, *Sunset* magazine, 16 January 1929, UO 098-7-1.

56 Letter, E. Schryver to Henry Davies Hatch, 6 May 1929, UO 098-7-1.

57 Letter, E. Schryver to Henry Davies Hatch, 10 May 1929, UO 098-7-1.

58 Letter, E. Schryver to Edith Loomis, 18 September 1929, UO 098-7-2.

59 Letter, E. Lord to Edith Loomis, 22 October 1930, UO 098-7-3.

60 Edith Loomis was a friend of Dorothy May Anderson, who graduated from the Cambridge School and settled in Seattle. Anderson wrote and published *Women, Design and the Cambridge School* in 1987.

61 Letter, E. Lord to Mrs. McNary, 16 November 1929, UO 098-7-2.

❧ Notes to Chapter 5: Against All Odds

Epigraph from E. Schryver to Sue Polston in 1983, oral interview with Sue Polston, 11 June 2013, LSC.

1 McKay, *An Editor for Oregon*, 76.

2 Letter, E. Lord to Mr. Case, 31 March 1931, UO 098-6-2.

3 Letter, William Borsch to E. Lord, 15 October 1931, UO 098-6-1.

4 Letter, E. Lord to Mr. Case, 3 December 1935, UO 098-6-2.

5 Letter, E. Lord to Mrs. Edna Hubbard McNary, 16 November 1929, UO 098-7-2.

6 Letter, Mrs. Edna Hubbard McNary to E. Lord, 16 December 1929, UO 098-7-2.

7 Letter, E. Lord to Pendleton Park Commission, 31 October 1930, UO 098-3-8.

8 Lord-Schryver plan for Pendleton Pioneer Memorial Park, UO 098-folder 54.

9 Letter, Mrs. Edna Hubbard McNary to E. Lord, 12 November 1930, UO 098-3-8.

10 After 1935, Lord and Schryver believed Sally Bush had decided she had sufficient plantings to keep her workers busy.

11 Designed by architect William C. Knighton; Melnick, Deepwood—Historic Landscape Report, II-3; *Oregon Statesman*, 29 August 1894.

12 Albert Bigelow Paine, *In the Deep Woods* (New York: R. H. Russell, 1899).

13 Interview with Plum Snow (aka Vivienne Brown), 12 February 2007, LSC.

14 Interview with Phil Webb, 20 March 2013, LSC.

15 William Brown, Alice Brown Powell's grandson, to author, 28 September 2018.

16 William Brown to author, 28 September 2018: "While on a hunting and fishing trip to Alaska, the boat Clifford Brown was in overturned and his body was swept away. It was not recovered. He was forty-two."

17 William Brown to author, 28 September 2018.

18 Letter, E. Lord to Alice [Brown], 8 December 1930, UO 098-7-3.

19 Letter, Alice Brown to E. Lord & E. Schryver, [1931] UO 098-1-7.

20 David C. Duniway, "Notes on telephone calls to Edith Schryver," 2–3 February 1983, LSC Archive.

21 Interview with Plum Snow (Vivienne Brown), 12 February 2007, LSC.

22 William Brown to author, 28 September 2018.

23 Interview with Wallace K. Huntington, 2 May 2006, LSC.

24 Letter, Louise Leland to E. Schryver, 3 September 1931, UO 098-7-4.

25 Letter, Henry A. Frost to E. Lord, 14 October 1931, UO 098-7-4.

26 Letter, E. Lord to Mrs. Robertson, 14 September 1931, UO 098-4-1.

27 David C. Duniway, "National Register of Historic Places Inventory— Registration Form, Dr. & Mrs. Charles G. Robertson House and Garden" (Salem OR: State Historic Preservation Office, 24 August 1982), Section 8, p. 1.

28 Ibid.

29 Lord-Schryver, garden and construction plans Mr. & Mrs. Raymond Brown, UO 098-folder 14.

30 Letter, E. Lord to Mrs. Brown, 14 April 1931, UO 098-1-7.

31 David C. Duniway, "Notes on on a dinner with Edith Schryver," 25 July 1981, LSC.

32 Letter, E. Lord to Edward M. Miller, 10 February 1932, UO 098-9-1.

33 Ibid.

34 Letter, Edward M. Miller to Lord-Schryver, 23 February 1932, UO 098-9-1.

35 Lord and Schryver, "Essentials of Landscape Architecture for Average-Sized City Dwelling Given," 6 March 1932.

36 Lord and Schryver, "Garden's Charm Heightened by Appropriate Features," 1 May 1932.

37 The final property size of Gaiety Hollow was .40 acres.

38 The architecture is described as "Colonial Revival" on the National Register Registration form and "English cottage" in other documents.

39 Lord-Schryver, poster for *House Beautiful* contest, UO 098-PH146-box 6.

40 Plan of Gaiety Hollow, National Register of Historic Places- Registration form, 2014, 65.

41 Plan "Bulb Planting—1938-39, Gaiety Hollow, 545 Mission St. Salem Ore.," UO 098-folder 42.

42 Identified as the "North Lawn" in Matthews et al., Gaiety Hollow—Cultural Landscape Report (2012), it has a bow shape.

43 Lord and Schryver called this area the Flower Garden. Lord often capitalized words in her writings that she wanted to emphasize. It was capitalized in Matthews et al., Gaiety Hollow—Cultural Landscape Report (2012).

44 Lord and Schryver, "Wide Perennial Border with Background of Hedge One of Simplest Garden Plans," in Peterson, *Essentials of Landscape Architecture*, 20.

45 Ibid.

46 Huntington, "The Motor Age," in *Space, Style and Architecture*, 557.

Notes to Chapter 6: Onward

Epigraph from, Letter, Dr. W. W. Baum to E. Schryver, 6 April 1937, UO 098-1-2. Their landscape design was for a Clarence Smith–designed house in Salem.

1 Clients in Oregon: Salem, Portland, Pendleton, Seal Rock, Breitenbush, Silverton, and Lake Oswego; in Washington: Seattle, Tacoma, and Walla Walla.

2 Letter, E. Schryver to Kay Heavey, 17 September 1934, folder "Edith Schryver Personal," LSC.

3 Misc. photographs, UO 098-Ph146-box 9.

4 See "Suggested Planting Plan," dated June 1937, UO 098-folder 25.

5 "Southern Hemisphere Is Miss Schryver's Topic for Lecture," *Capital Journal* (March 1936), UO 098-9-1.

6 Gerald Beebe ran the Beebe Company in Portland, a family business founded in 1884 to build boats. It evolved into a major producer of marine and outing supplies for various industries in the Northwest.

7 Letter, Mary L. Beebe to Miss Lord & Miss Schryver, 13 October 1934, LSC.

8 Letter, E. Schryver to Mrs. Gerald Beebe, 16 October 1934, UO 098-1-4.

9 Tucker was a partner of George Wallman in Tucker and Wallman from 1936–1946; they joined with H. Abbott to form Lawrence, Tucker and Wallman in 1946.

10 Lord-Schryver plan, "Preliminary Grading, the estate of Mr. and Mrs. Gerald Beebe," UO 098-folder 7. Letter, Mary Beebe to Elizabeth and Edith, 4 June 1936, LSC.

11 In the 1950s, Schryver modified the patio with a paving of slate tile and brick edging.

12 An allee was traditionally an avenue or walk with a row of trees arranged symmetrically on each side. All the trees would be of the same type.

13 Multiple plans by Lord-Schryver for the Gerald Beebe garden, UO 098-folder 7.

14 Schryver may have intentionally framed the view with woodlands but they are not shown on the existing archival plans.

15 Aymar Embury, "Charles A. Platt: His Works," *Architecture* 26 (August 1912), p. 142, as quoted in Keith N. Morgan, "The Formal Garden Revival in Italian Gardens," in Platt, *Italian Gardens*, 124.

16 Letter, Gerald Beebe to E. Schryver, 3 April 1936, Beebe file, LSC.

17 Letter, E. Lord to Mary Beebe, 17 October 1941, UO 098-1-4/5.

18 Interview with Edith Schryver by David Duniway, 25 July 1981, LSC.

19 Letter, E. Lord to Mrs. Gerke, 27 August 1931, UO 098-7-4.

20 Oregon State University changed names several times through its history. In

1888 it was informally called Oregon Agricultural College, the name adopted in 1907. In 1927 it was formally named Oregon State Agricultural College. In 1937 it became Oregon State College, and finally, in 1961, it was named Oregon State University.

21 Croman, Broadcasting Public, 30.

22 Ibid., 30.

23 Ibid., 11.

24 Ibid., 3.

25 The federation had a sizable membership in thirty clubs based throughout the state.

26 Croman, Broadcasting Public, 13.

27 Station KOAC pamphlet, "About Gardens and Gardening," nd, UO 098-8-11.

28 Ibid.

29 KOAC Lectures, UO 098-8-12; Mike Dicianna, Reference Department, OSU Library and Archives, to author, email, 6 September 2018.

30 Schryver considered the Kingery garden to be her finest design.

31 Letter, E. Schryver to Mrs. Kingery, 11 December 1938, UO 098-2-9.

32 Letter, Dr. Kingery to E. Schryver, 13 December 1938, UO 098-2-9.

33 Letter, Dr. Kingery to E. Schryver, 16 June 1939, UO 098-2-9.

34 Letter, E. Schryver to Dr. Kingery, 18 July 1939, UO 098-2-9.

35 Letter, E. Schryver to Dr. Kingery, 7 December 1939, UO 098-2-9.

36 Letter, E. Schryver to Dr. Kingery, 9 January 1940, UO 098-2-9.

37 Letter, E. Schryver to Dr. Kingery, 16 January 1940, UO 098-2-9.

38 The Kingerys' property overlooked Tryon Creek State Park, with six-hundred-plus acres of natural land.

39 Lord-Schryver plan, "Sketch Plan for the Garden Treatment, the Country Place of Dr. and Mrs. Lyle B. Kingery," 15 July 1939, UO 098-folder 39.

40 Letter, E. Schryver to E. Tucker, 24 July 1939, UO 098-2-9.

41 Letter, E. Lord to Mr. Walsh of Walsh & Rainwater, 16 January 1940, UO 098-6-11.

42 Ibid.

43 Letter, E. Schryver to Mrs. Kingery, 5 May 1943, UO 098-2-9.

44 Lord-Schryver, "Design Plan for Garden Development, the Residence of Mr. & Mrs. R. E. Avison," 1955, UO 098-folder 3.

45 Ruth Roberts, "Avison Garden Notes," 2010, LSC.

46 "Montague Lord Interned in Philippines by Japs," *Capital Journal*, 15 April 1943.

47 Misc. notes by Elizabeth Lord, OHS Mss. 2050-5-9.

▶ Notes to Chapter 7: Plantswomen

Epigraph from, Letter, E. Lord to Mrs. Paul, 21 September 1945, UO 098-3-8.

1 Shipman quoted in Petersen, "Women Take the Lead in Landscape Art," 83.

2 Letter, H. Ernest Conwell of Boxwood Nurseries, Milton, Delaware, to E. Schryver, 5 November 1929, UO 098-7-2.

3 Renamed the Oregon Association of Nurseries.

4   Arthur L. Peck, "Landscape Architecture in the Pacific Northwest," 31–33.

5   Oregon Association of Nurseries website, copyright 2018, p. 95 (accessed 20 April 2019).

6   Letter, E. Schryver to Mr. Rea, 2 May 1929, UO 098-7-1.

7   Letter, E. Lord to Mr. Walsh, 10 February 1938, UO 098-6-11.

8   Letter, E. Lord to Mrs. Case of B.O. Case & Sons Nursery, Vancouver, Washington, 27 October 1937, UO 098-6-2.

9   Letter, E. Lord to Mr. Barclay, 14 November 1941, UO 098-6-1.

10 Letter, E. Lord to Mary Beebe, 17 October 1941, UO 098-1-4/5.

11 Letter, E. Lord to Mr. Case, 3 December 1935, UO 098-6-2.

12 Ibid.

13 Letter, E. Lord to Mrs. Case, 18 May 1938, UO 098-6-2.

14 Letter, Mr. Lambert to Lord-Schryver, 10 March 1941, UO 098-6-7.

15 Letter, E. Lord to Mr. Lambert, 19 March 1941, UO 098-6-7.

16 Letter, E. Lord to Mrs. Goode, 17 February 1930, UO 098-6-5.

17 Letter, E. Lord to Mr. Goode, 2 December 1930, UO 098-6-5.

18 Letter, Mr. Goode to E. Lord, 12 February 1936, UO 098-6-5.

19 Letter, E. Lord to Mrs. A. Scott Bullitt, 29 October 1929, UO 098-1-8.

20 Letter, E. Lord to Mrs. A. Scott Bullitt, 27 September 1929, UO 098-1-8.

21 The American Iris Society was founded in 1920.

22 Miriam Cooley Ernst, "Starting a Backyard Business," *Tall Talk*, March 1999, pp. 7–8.

23 Lord-Schryver plan, "Layout Plan for Display Grounds at Cooleys' Gardens," September 1931, UO 098-folder 20.

24 Judy Ernst Nunn, the Cooleys' granddaughter, to author, email, 18 November 2018.

25 Ibid.

26 Lord-Schryver plan, "Preliminary Study for Exhibition Garden Layout Cooley Iris Gardens," dated 18 October 1951, UO 098-folder 20.

27 Mrs. Ida Peterman sold the Peterbilt firm in 1960.

28 Letter, E. Schryver to Mrs. Peterman, 2 August 1929, UO 098-3-9.

29 Lord-Schryver, "Flower Planting Plan for Garden Terraces," UO 098-folder 54.

30 Notes included with "Flower Planting Plan for Garden Terraces," UO 098-folder 54.

31 See Gertrude Jekyll, *Colour Schemes for the Flower Garden*.

32 See plan for Merriman Holtz, "Flower Planting Plant for South Garden," October 1943, UO 098-folder 35.

33 Lord and Schryver, "Trees Important Setting for Home on Medium Lot," 20 March 1932.

34 E. Lord, KOAC radio script, "Flowering Trees for Your Garden," nd, UO 098-8-12, p. 2.

35 Ibid., 2.

36 Ibid., 7.

37 The correct botanical name is *Crataegus × lavallei*, Lavalle hawthorn, USDA, NRCS. 2018 Plants Database, plants@usda.gov.

38 E. Lord, KOAC radio script, "Flowering Trees for Your Garden," nd, UO 098-8-12, p. 8.

39 Ibid., 9.

40 E. Schryver, KOAC program script, "Looking Forward to the Fall Garden," 27 April 1944, UO 098-8-12.

41 Ibid., 2.

42 William Robinson, a prominent British horticulturist and editor, had promoted this idea many years earlier with his book *The Wild Garden* (1870).

43 Roberts and Rehmann, *American Plants for American Gardens*. Rehmann left Lowthorpe in 1911 to teach and to practice landscape architecture.

44 Letter, E. Lord to Mrs. Cabell, 16 February 1939, UO 098-3-1.

45 "Bush Park Plan Offered by Landscape Architects," *Capital Journal*, 19 December 1946, pp. 1, 5, in UO 098-10-11.

46 Mrs. Lord died on 5 July 1924.

47 Letter, E. Lord to Miss Gauld, Reed College, 17 February 1940, UO 098-4-1.

48 E. Lord's garden journal, 3–17 September 1970, LSC Archive, 149.

49 Ibid., 112, 107.

50 Ibid., 144.

51 Ibid., 133.

52 Ibid., 173. This statement by Lord was not accurate, as there are journals from spring 1963 to 1976, but not for every year.

53 Lord's journal, spring 1970, p. 136.

54 Gertrude Jekyll, *Wood and Garden*, 17.

➤ Notes to Chapter 8: Cultivating the Profession

Epigraph from, Notes by David C. Duniway from a dinner with E. Schryver, 25 July 1981, LSC.

1 Oregon State College was renamed Oregon State University; letter, W. Dorr Legg to E. Lord, 8 January 1937, UO 098-7-5.

2 Frederick Law Olmsted Sr. was among the eight founders. Ellen Shipman never joined the ASLA. Some practitioners regarded it as a white male eastern bastion. The ASLA incorporated in Massachusetts in 1916.

3 Letter, W. Dorr Legg to E. Lord, 8 January 1937, UO 098-7-5.

4 In Portland the first listing for a "landscape architect" was Hugh Bryan in 1910. His name appeared in *Polk's Directory for Portland*. Over the next twenty years, *Polk's Directory for Portland* listed between five and seven names for "landscape architect," whereas more than three times that number identified their businesses as landscape gardeners. No landscape architect had listed their firm in Salem's *Directory* before Lord and Schryver.

5 Papers of the Oregon Society of Landscape Architects (OSLA), UO 098-10-6.

6 Letter, F. A. Cuthbert to Misses Lord and Schryver, 19 August 1940, UO 098-7-7.

7 Letter, E. Schryver to Mr. Cuthbert, 23 August 1940, UO 098-7-7.

8 Ibid.

9   Oregon State College (OSC) developed a program in landscape gardening in 1911, the first one west of the Mississippi River. In 1928 they instituted a degree in landscape architecture, the first in the Pacific Northwest. Frederick A. Cuthbert joined the faculty at OSC in 1929. In 1932, the degree program transferred to the University of Oregon with the appointment of Arthur L. Peck as department head. Alternating years of the program were still taught at OSC.

10 www.wasla.org/our-history (accessed 9 January 2019).

11 Other women to join OSLA were Eunice C. Brandt, Josephine Lumm, and Virginia Harrison Small.

12 Meeting minutes, OSLA, 24 April 1941; 13 November 1941; both from UO 098-10-6.

13 Meeting minutes, OSLA, 13 November 1941, UO 098-10-6.

14 The day before the Pearl Harbor attack, launching the United States into World War II.

15 Meeting minutes, OSLA, 6 December 1941, UO 098-10-6.

16 Ibid.

17 Meeting minutes OSLA, 23 August 1948, UO 098-10-6.

18 Lord and Schryver, "Home, Garden Development," *Sunday Oregonian*, 17 July 1955, p. 3.
    This was one of the few articles published about Lord and Schryver as landscape architects.

19 They were not without critics in later years, however, as some of the younger generation of landscape architects complained that Lord and Schryver did not charge enough for their services and that they volunteered too many hours to nonprofits. Notes by David Duniway from a dinner with Edith Schryver on 25 July 1981, LSC.

20 Letter, Fred A. Cuthbert to Lord-Schryver, 25 April 1936, UO 098-7-4.

21 Letter, L. S. Morris to E. Lord and E. Schryver, 29 June 1939, UO 098-7-6.

22 Letter, W. Dorr Legg to Lord-Schryver, 25 November 1940, UO 098-7-7. Problem statement, "The Landscape Exchange Problem 1940-41," UO 098-7-7.

23 Letter, Arthur L. Peck to E. Schryver, 7 March 1942, UO 098-7-9.

24 Tom Bennett, "World War II and OSU," 7-11.

25 Randy Gragg, "Remembering John Storrs." Storrs collaborated closely with the landscape architect Barbara Fealy, whom he called "Auntie Babs."

26 Ibid.

27 Ibid.

28 Edith E. Schryver, "Introduction to the Seven Areas of Our Garden," *Gardener's Magazine*, March 1956 (Portland Garden Club), UO 098-3-10.

29 Letter, John Storrs to E. Schryver, 5 February 1945 [1955], UO 098-3-10.

30 The architect had preserved the hedge when developing the building except for a section removed to allow trucks to enter. This portion was replaced with native red cedar.

31 Edith E. Schryver, "Introduction to the Seven Areas of Our Garden," *Gardener's Magazine*, March 1956 (Portland Garden Club), UO 098-3-10.

32 Ibid.

33 Ibid.
34 John M. Tess, National Register of Historic Places—Registration Form, Portland Garden Club. 24 August 2005. Salem, OR: State Historic Preservation Office.
35 Ibid.
36 David C. Duniway, quoting E. Schryver, "Memorial Service for Edith Schryver," 24 May 1984, LSC.

➤ Notes to Chapter 9: "Yard Architects" for Period Gardens

Epigraph from, Transcript of Elizabeth Lord's report for the Minthorn House, 1969, UO 098-2-7.

1 In 1907 the Oregon Historical Society bestowed the honorary title of "Father of Oregon" on McLoughlin posthumously for his role in the early development of Oregon Country and his assistance to overland settlers. The state legislature made the title official in 1957. Cassandra Tate, essay 10617, HistoryLink.org, 24 September 2013.
2 The Hudson's Bay Company was the powerful English fur trading enterprise that dominated the Pacific Northwest in the early 1800s.
3 Oregon City had been surveyed and named in 1842. McLoughlin filed the plat for his land in 1850.
4 To bury Marguerite in the churchyard required a special dispensation because she was half Native American. See Cassandra Tate, essay 10617, HistoryLink.org, 24 September 2013. They were reburied side by side on the grounds of the McLoughlin Memorial Park, Oregon City, as part of the park's development.
5 In a letter addressed to Governor-elect Charles H. Martin on 8 January 1935, Jamieson Parker, president of the Oregon chapter of the AIA, concluded, "We believe the State should include in its public works program due attention to the matter of historic buildings, of which there is probably none so significant as the McLoughlin house." Letter, Jamison Parker to Governor Elect Charles H. Martin, 8 January 1935, Papers of Glenn A. Stanton, OHS.
6 The agencies were the Civil Works Administration, the Public Works Administration, and the Works Progress Administration. Elisabeth Walton Potter to author, 11 May 2020.
7 Letter, Florence H. Gerke to Glenn Stanton, 13 July 1935, papers of Glenn A. Stanton, OHS.
8 Letter, Glenn Stanton to E. Lord, 6 May 1938, UO 098-10-4.
9 Letter, E. Lord to Glenn Stanton, 18 May 1938, UO 098-10-4.
10 The McLoughlin bust was acquired from the sculptor, Andrien Voisin, with funds raised from schoolchildren and the public. It was placed as a commemorative centerpiece of the turnout for the Willamette Falls observation point on Highway 99E. This section of highway was renamed McLoughlin Boulevard.
11 Lord-Schryver, "A Suggested Plan for Landscape Treatment, the grounds of The McLoughlin and Barclay Houses," [1938], UO 098-folder 48.

12 Letter, E. Lord to Mr. Harding, 19 November 1938, UO 098-3-1.

13 Ibid.

14 Letter, E. Lord to Mrs. A. E. Rockey, 21 November 1938, UO 098-3-1.

15 Letter, E. Lord to Mrs. Henry F. Cabell, 16 February 1939, UO 098-3-1. Lord probably refers to the Cooke-Patton House built in 1869–1872 in Salem. It was among the houses removed to make way for the Capitol Mall redevelopment project of 1935–1938.

16 Letter, L. O. Harding to E. Lord, nd, UO 098-3-1.

17 Letter, E. Lord to Mrs. Mary Beebe, 17 October 1941, UO 098-1-4.

18 Stephen Dow Beckham, "Burt Brown Barker—Profile," *Oregon Historical Society Spectator* 4 (Winter 2001): 20–21. Dr. Barker was recognized with an honorary title as early as 1935 by the Oregon Historical Society.

19 Ibid.

20 Doris Holmes Bailey, "Landscaping McLoughlin House."

21 Ibid.

22 E. Lord, "Planting the Garden of the Minthorne [*sic*] Home," April 1952 [1954], UO 098-2-5.

23 Interview with Mrs. Henry (Ruth) Richmond, 28 April 2006, LSC. Barbara Barker (later Mrs. John Sprouse) joined her father in leading preservation efforts in Oregon. Upon his death in 1969, she became the president of Oregon's Herbert Hoover Foundation.

24 Lillie L. Madsen, "Hoover House Garden Recalls Taste of Era," 20.

25 Letter, E. Lord to Dr. Barker, 9 March 1954, UO 098-2-5.

26 Ibid.

27 These rose cultivars selected never thrived, and by 1961 they were replaced with red floribunda roses.

28 E. Lord, report on the Minthorn Garden, dated 17 June 1969, UO 098-2-7. Garden writers of the early twentieth century promoted using old brick to add charm to old-fashioned gardens.

29 E. Lord, report on the Minthorn Garden, dated 17 June 1969, UO 098-2-7.

30 Ibid.

31 Society column, *Oregon Statesman*, 7 June 1954, p. 7.

32 Hoover-Minthorn House Museum website (accessed 10 November 2018).

33 Letter, E. Schryver to the Honorable Herbert Hoover, 1 July 1963, folder HHMH Garden E. Lord Letters, LSC.

34 The Hoover-Minthorn House is listed on the National Register of Historic Places. Since 1981, it has been owned and managed by the National Society of the Colonial Dames of America in the State of Oregon.

35 E. Lord, "Report on the Minthorn House, Newberg, Oregon," 9 June 1961, UO 098-2-7.

➤ Notes to Chapter 10: Salem Pride

Epigraph from, Elizabeth B. Lord's handwritten obituary, 1968, UO 098-1-2.

1 Four Panegyrics were given between 1972 and 1975, WHC.

2 E. Lord's account, 1973, in Duniway, "Lord-Schryver," 107.

3   "Park Board Reveals Programs; Projects Await City Funds," *Oregon Statesman*, 25 July 1941, p. 2, UO 098-10-11.

4   Requests would continue to arrive until their last years, even after they retired in 1969.

5   Letter, Mr. H. S. Giles to E. Lord, 2 May 1929, UO 098-7-1.

6   E. Lord's account, 1973, in Duniway, "Lord-Schryver," 107.

7   Ibid., 107.

8   Ibid., 107.

9   The WPA was an agency of the New Deal to employ underemployed workers on public projects from 1935 to 1939. The name was changed to Works Projects Administration in 1939 and operated until 1943.

10   Lord-Schryver, "Preliminary Plan for Salem High School," April 1938, UO 098-folder 64.

11   Letter, E. Schryver to Mrs. Merrill, 4 June 1929, UO 098-3-2. The Pacific Highway was built from Northern California to Vancouver, Washington, and completed in 1926. At the time, it was the longest paved road in the United States and part of a new auto trail system for travelers. Later it was extended from Vancouver, BC, to San Diego, California. Wikipedia.org (accessed 25 June 2020).

12   Letter, E. Lord to Anthony Yturri, 30 January 1959, UO 098-10-5.

13   In 1958 Congress passed the first outdoor advertising control legislation, commonly known as the "Bonus Act," PL 85-381. It was repealed and replaced by the Highway Beautification Act of 1965, strongly supported by Lady Bird Johnson. It is now found in the United States Code at 23 U.S.C. 131. Wikipedia.org (accessed 19 June 2020).

14   Salem's city charter created the park board in 1904 and stipulated that "no member of said board shall be discriminated against by reason of sex." Charter of City of Salem, Section 25, 1904, UO 098-4-5.

15   E. Lord's account, 1973, in Duniway, "Lord-Schryver," 107.

16   Ibid., 107.

17   This amount included the salaries for a superintendent and two gardeners for one year.

18   "Park Board Reveals Programs, Projects Await City Funds," *Oregon Statesman*, 25 July 1941, p. 2, UO 098-10-11.

19   www.oregonlink.com/salem_parks.html (accessed 20 December 2018).

20   Schryver's plan for Marion Square Park called for curving walkways and a new bandstand. See Schryver, "Proposed Treatment for Marion Square Park," nd, UO 098-folder 63A.

21   "Park Board Reveals Programs; Projects Await City Funds," *Oregon Statesman*, 25 July 1941, p. 2, UO 098-10-11.

22   Letter, E. Lord to J. H. Davis, city engineer, 3 January 1940, UO 098-4-3.

23   Ibid.

24   Letter, E. Lord to Harry Crane, editor of the *Capital Journal*, 22 July 1941, LSC.

25   "Park Board Reveals Programs; Projects Await City Funds," *Oregon Statesman*, 25 July 1941, p. 2, UO 098-10-11.

26 www.oregonlink.com/salem_parks.html (accessed 20 December 2018).

27 E. Lord's account, 1973, in Duniway, "Lord-Schryver," 107.

28 Ibid., 107.

29 "Park Board Reveals Programs; Projects Await City Funds," *Oregon Statesman*, 25 July 1941, p. 2, UO 098-10-11.

30 Letter, E. Lord to Mr. Thoma of the WPA, 19 February 1940, UO 098-7-6.

31 Letter, E. Lord to C. K. DeWitt, 3 October 1939, UO 098-4-2.

32 "Park Board Reveals Programs; Projects Await City Funds," *Oregon Statesman*, 25 July 1941, p. 2, UO 098-10-11.

33 [Elizabeth Lord] article, "Proposed Parks for Salem," enclosed with letter to Harry Crane, 22 July 1941, LSC.

34 E. Schryver plans for Highland Park, 1940 and 1946, UO 098-folder 63A.

35 E. Lord's account, 1973, in Duniway, "Lord-Schryver," 109.

36 [Elizabeth Lord] article, "Proposed Parks for Salem," enclosed with letter to Harry Crane, 22 July 1941, LSC.

37 Ross Sutherland, unpublished paper, "Lord & Schryver: The Salem Art Association and the Bush House Museum," LSC, March 2019.

38 E. Lord's account, 1973, in Duniway, "Lord-Schryver," 109.

39 Ibid., 109.

40 Ruth Roberts, "The Mature Practice," in Carnaby et al., *Influences Find Expression*, 17.

41 The Capitol Planning Commission was a continuation of the Reconstruction Commission.

42 E. Lord's account, 1973, in Duniway, "Lord-Schryver," 110.

43 Letter, E. Lord to editor of the *Capital Journal*, 4 February [1947], UO 098-10-11.

44 E. Lord, "The Willson Park Discussion Needs More Study," nd, UO 098-4-5.

45 Kathy Schutt, "State Capitol State Park, General Park Plan 2010," 16.

46 The first two capitol buildings had faced the river to the west. Both were destroyed by fire.

47 Brian Brown, "Capitol Planning Commission History," 2005, Oregon State Archives.

48 The name of the landscape architect is not clear in reports. It may have been George Otten, landscape engineer for the State Highway Department, Schutt, "State Capitol State Park, General Park Plan 2010," 13.

49 E. Lord's account, 1973, in Duniway, "Lord-Schryver," 110.

50 Ibid., 110.

51 "History of the Park Site," 2010, www.oregongov/oprd/PLANS/docs/state captiol (accessed 20 December 2018).

52 The eastern part was left in its existing state to the delight of many, including the Boy Scouts.

53 Roberts, "Bush's Pasture Park," 1–4. www.cityofsalem.net/bushs-pasture-park.

54 Information received from Michael K. Slater, past president of the board of the Mission Street Parks Conservancy, Salem, Oregon, February 2020.

55 Roberts, "Bush's Pasture Park," 1–4.

56   Letter, Men's Garden Club of Salem to David E. Thompson, 16 April 1946, UO 098-10-11.

57   Letter, David E. Thompson to Mr. C. B. McCullough, 15 February 1946, UO 098-10-11.

58   Letter, E. Schryver to David Thompson, 17 June 1946, UO 098-10-11.

59   Letter, E. Lord to the Salem Planning Commission, 5 December 1946, UO 098-10-11.

60   Reverend David Leslie, a Methodist missionary to the Northwest, probably planted the orchard in the 1840s–1850s, not in 1860. Elisabeth W. Potter to author, April 2020.

61   "Bush Park Plan Offered by Landscape Architects," *Capital Journal*, 19 December 1946, UO 098-10.

62   [Schryver] plan, "Planting Layout for Tartar Old Rose Collection," nd, UO 098-folder 63.

63   Ross Sutherland and Gretchen Carnaby, to author, 20 June 2020.

64   Letter, E. Lord to Elisabeth Walton Potter, January 1970, personal collection.

65   Elizabeth Lord's handwritten obituary, UO 098-1-2.

66   E. Lord's account, 1973, in Duniway, "Lord-Schryver," 110.

67   The Salem Art Association began as the Salem Arts League in 1919. It later became the Salem Federal Art Center and was housed in the basement of the Salem High School on High Street. It was one of a national network of art centers created during the Depression to provide work for unemployed artists. Ross Sutherland and www.salemart.org/history (accessed 1 July 2020).

68   E. Lord's account, 1973, in Duniway, "Lord-Schryver," 108.

➤   Notes to Chapter 11: Final Years

     Epigraph from, E. Schryver to Nancy Gormsen, from interview with Nancy Gormsen, 1 December 2003, LSC.

1   Letter, Lord-Schryver to Mr. Carl Nelson, 9 September 1941, UO 098-3-5.

2   Ibid.

3   David C. Duniway and Elisabeth Walton Potter, National Register of Historic Places—Registration Form, Charles G. Robertson House and Garden. (Salem OR: State Historic Preservation Office), 1 April 1983.

4   Ibid.

5   E. Lord's garden journal, 6 May 1963, p. 76, LSC.

6   E. Lord's garden journal, 15 April 1964, p. 77, LSC; Lillie L. Madsen, "Salem Could Be Called Magnolia City," *Statesman Journal*, 5 April 1964.

7   Interview with Shannon Maddox, December 2007, LSC.

8   E. Lord's garden journal, 1 May 1969, p. 95, LSC. Lord had uterine cancer.

9   E. Lord's garden journal, 23 June 1969, pp. 116–117, LSC.

10   E. Lord's garden journal, fall [1970], pp. 158–159, LSC.

11   Neena Kirsh to author, April 2019.

12   Jeryme English, "Around Town…" column, *Statesman Journal*, 23 April 1963, p. 7.

13   Nicholas Adams, "Joanna C. Diman (1901–91)," *Journal of Society of Architectural Historians* 77, no. 3 (September 2018): 339–348.

14   Some of Diman's better known projects include the landscapes for the LBJ Library and Museum in Austin, Texas (1971); corporate headquarters for the Ford Motor Company in Michigan (1944–1957); Connecticut General in Connecticut (1957) and Union Carbide in New Jersey (1960); and campus additions at Smith and Connecticut Colleges.

15   David C. Duniway, "In Remembrance [of] Elizabeth B. Lord," LSC.

16   David C. Duniway, "Memorial Service for Edith E. Schryver," 24 May 1984, LSC.

17   Huntington, "Parks and Gardens of Western Oregon," in *Space, Style and Structure*, 576.

Bibliography

➤ Archival Collections

Bush House Museum, Salem, OR (BHM)
Clackamas Co. Historical Society, Oregon City, OR (CCHS)
Lord & Schryver Architectural Records, Collection 098, Special Collections,
    Knight Library, University of Oregon, Eugene, OR (UO)
Lord & Schryver Conservancy Archive, Salem, OR (LSC)
Marion County Historical Society, Salem, OR (MCHS)
Oregon Historical Society, Salem, OR (OHS)
Oregon State University Library and Archives, Corvallis, OR (OSU)
Willamette Heritage Center, Salem, OR (WHC)

➤ Lord and Schryver's Published Articles (chronological order)

"Essentials of Landscape Architecture for Average-Sized City Dwelling Given."
    Sunday Oregonian, 6 March 1932.
"Making of a Garden Plan Step by Step Described." *Sunday Oregonian*, 13 March
    1932.
"Trees Important Setting for Home on Medium Lot." *Sunday Oregonian*, 20
    March 1932.
"Rose Bed Located in Lawn Lovely during Bloom Season." *Sunday Oregonian*, 27
    March 1932.
"Wide Perennial Border with Background of Hedge." *Sunday Oregonian*, 3 April
    1932.
"Uneven Ground Adds Charm and Interest to Gardens." *Sunday Oregonian*, 10
    April 1932.
"Hillside Garden May Be Developed as Rock Garden or Series of Terraces."
    Sunday Oregonian, 17 April 1932.
"Careful Planning Needed for Creation of Rural Garden as Thing of Beauty."
    Sunday Oregonian, 24 April 1932.
"Garden's Charm Heightened by Appropriate Features." *Sunday Oregonian*, 1 May
    1932.

➤ Books

Anderson, Dorothy May. *Women, Design, and the Cambridge School*. Boston: John Wiley, 1987.

Begg, Virginia Lopez. "Frances Duncan." In *Pioneers of American Landscape Design: An Annotated Bibliography*, edited by Charles A. Birnbaum and Robin Karson, 103–104. New York: McGraw-Hill, 2000.

Carey, Charles Henry. "William Paine Lord." In *History of Oregon*, vol. 3. Portland, OR: Pioneer Historical Publishing Co., 1922.

Carnaby, Gretchen, Wallace Kay Huntington, Ruth Roberts, and Ross Sutherland. *Influences Find Expression: Elizabeth Lord and Edith Schryver, Landscape Architects*. Salem, OR: Lord & Schryver Conservancy, 2010.

Clayton, Virginia Tuttle. *The Once and Future Gardener: Garden Writing from the Golden Age of Magazines, 1900–1940*. Jaffrey, NH: David R. Godine, 2000.

Gilbert, Alma M., and Judith B. Tankard. *A Place of Beauty: The Artists and Gardens of Cornish Colony*. Berkeley, CA: Ten Speed Press, 2000.

Griswold, Mac, and Eleanor Weller. *The Golden Age of American Gardens: Proud Owners, Private Estates, 1890–1940*. New York: Abrams/Garden Club of America, 1991.

Helphand, Kenneth I. "Elizabeth Lord" and "Edith Schryver." In *Pioneers of American Landscape Design: An Annotated Bibliography*, edited by Charles A. Birnbaum and Robin Karson, 227–230. New York: McGraw-Hill, 2000.

Huntington, Wallace Kay. "Parks and Gardens of Western Oregon." In *Space, Style, and Structure*, vol. 2, edited by Thomas Vaughn and Virginia Ferriday. Portland: Oregon Historical Society, 1974.

Jekyll, Gertrude. *Colour Schemes for the Flower Garden*. 8th ed. London: Country Life, 1936.

Jekyll, Gertrude. *Wood and Garden*. London: Longmans, Green and Co., 1899.

Libby, Valencia. "Cultivating Mind, Body and Spirit: Educating the 'New Woman' for Careers in Landscape Architecture." In *Women in Landscape Architecture: Essays on History and Practice*, edited by Louise A. Mozingo and Linda Jewell, 69–75. Jefferson, NC: McFarland and Company, 2012.

Libby, Valencia. "Marian Cruger Coffin." In *Pioneers of American Landscape Design: An Annotated Bibliography*, edited by Charles A. Birnbaum and Robin Karson, 64–68. New York: McGraw-Hill, 2000.

Lowell, Guy. *American Gardens*. Boston: Bates and Guild, 1902.

McKay, Floyd J. *An Editor for Oregon: Charles A. Sprague and the Politics of Change*. Corvallis, OR: Oregon State University Press, 1998.

Morgan, Keith N. "Charles A. Platt." In *Pioneers of American Landscape Design: An Annotated Bibliography*, edited by Charles A. Birnbaum and Robin Karson, 297–300. New York: McGraw-Hill, 2000.

Morgan, Keith N. *Charles Platt: The Artist as Architect*. New York: Architectural History Foundation / Cambridge: MIT Press, 1985.

Peterson, Sue, ed. *Essentials of Landscape Architecture: Elizabeth Lord and Edith Schryver, Landscape Architects*. Salem, OR: Lord & Schryver Conservancy, 2003.

Platt, Charles A. *Italian Gardens*. Reprint. New York: Sagapress/Timber Press, 1994 [1894].

Polk, R. L., and Company. *Polk's Salem City and Marion County Directory*. Annual. Seattle: R. L. Polk & Co..

Rehmann, Elsa. *The Small Place: Its Landscape Architecture*. New York: G. P. Putnam, 1918.

Roberts, Edith A., and Elsa Rehmann. *American Plants for American Gardens*. Reprint, with a foreword by Darrel G. Morrison. Athens: University of Georgia Press, 1996 [1929].

Robinson, William. *The Wild Garden*. 4th ed. Reprint. London: Scolar Press, 1977 [1894].

Rose, Sharon L. *A Natural History of Minto Brown Island Park*. Salem, OR: Author, 1999.

Tankard, Judith B. "Ellen Biddle Shipman." In *Pioneers of American Landscape Design: An Annotated Bibliography*, edited by Charles A. Birnbaum and Robin Karson, 346–351. New York: McGraw-Hill, 2000.

Tankard, Judith B. *Ellen Shipman and the American Garden*. Athens: University of Georgia Press, 2018.

Tankard, Judith B., and Leslie Rose Close. *The Gardens of Ellen Biddle Shipman*. New York: Sagapress/Abrams, 1996.

Vaughn, Thomas, and Virginia Guest Ferriday, eds. *Space, Style, and Structure: Building in Northwest America*. Vol. 2. Portland: Oregon Historical Society, 1974.

Way, Thaisa. *Unbounded Practice: Women in Landscape Architecture in the Early 20th Century*. Charlottesville: University of Virginia Press, 2009.

Yoch, James J. "Florence Yoch and Lucille Council." In *Pioneers of American Landscape Design: An Annotated Bibliography*, edited by Charles A. Birnbaum and Robin Karson, 470–474. New York: McGraw-Hill, 2000.

Zaitzevsky, Cynthia. *Long Island Landscapes and the Women Who Designed Them*. New York: Society for the Preservation of Long Island Antiquities, 2009.

➤ Articles

Apley, Kay. "An Oregon First Lady: Biography by Her Salem Daughter." *Oregon Statesman*, 26 July 1976.

Bailey, Dorris Holmes. "Landscaping McLoughlin House." *Sunday Oregonian*, 23 December 1956.

Begg, Virginia Lopez. "Frances Duncan: The New 'Woman' in the Garden." *Journal of New England Garden History* (Fall 1992): 28–35.

Bennett, Tom. "World War II and OSU." *Oregon Stater*, February 1991, pp. 7–11.

"Bit of Old Spain to Top Hill." *Capital Journal*, 6 March 1929, pp. 1 and 7.

Buren, Maxine. "Governor's Daughter Gives Girl's-Eye View of Politics." *Oregon Statesman*, 14 August 1964.

Clayton, Virginia Tuttle. "Reminiscence and Revival: The Old-Fashioned Garden, 1890–1910." *Antiques* 137 (April 1990): 894–905.

Comstock, Sarah. "With Lincoln at the Ball." *San Francisco Call*, 13 March 1903, p. 11.

Cool, Travis J. "From Hot Springs to Heritage: A Cultural History of Breitenbush Hot Springs." *Willamette Valley Voices*, Willamette Historical Society, 2013, p. 55.

Correy, Jesse A. "Flowers for Home and Garden." *Oregonian*, 18 March 1923, p. 66.

Duncan, Frances. "The Gardens of Cornish." *Century Magazine*, May 1906, pp. 3–19.

Duniway, David C. "Lord-Schryver: Landscape Architects." *Marion County History: Schooldays II*, vol. 14 (1983–84): 107–120.

Duniway, David C. "Notes on a Dinner with Edith Schryver, 25 July 1981." Salem, OR: Lord & Schryver Conservancy.

Gragg, Randy. "Remembering John Storrs." *Oregonian*, 3 September 2003.

Helphand, Kenneth I., and Nancy D. Rottle. "Cultivating Charm." *Garden Design* 7, no. 3 (Autumn 1988): 27–32.

Hill, May Brawley. "Grandmother's Garden." *Antiques* 142 (November 1992): 727–735.

"A House on Beekman Place, New York." *House Beautiful*, November 1927, p. 516.

Krall, Daniel W. "The Landscape Architect as Advocate: The Writings of Elizabeth Leonard Strang." *Journal of the New England Garden History Society* 2 (Fall 2003): 19.

Libby, Valencia. "Jane B. Haines' Vision: The Pennsylvania School of Horticulture for Women, 1910–1959." *Journal of New England Garden History* 10 (Fall 2002): 44–52.

Lockley, Fred. "Impressions and Observations of the Journal Man." *Oregon Daily Journal*, 24 October 1922, p. 8.

Madsen, Lillie L. "Hoover House Garden Recalls Taste of Era." *Statesman Journal*, 7 August 1955, p. 20.

Matthews, Laurie. "Gaiety Hollow: A Pacific Northwest Version of Beaux Arts Style." *Washington Park Arboretum Bulletin* (Summer 2013): 3–6, 29.

"Maxfield Parrish as Mechanic." *Literary Digest*, 12 May 1923, p. 40.

Noble, William. "Northcote: An Artist's New Hampshire Garden." *Journal of the New England Garden History Society* 2 (1992): 1–9.

"Park Board Reveals Programs; Projects Await City Funds." *Statesman Journal*, 25 July 1941, p. 2.

Peck, Arthur L. "Landscape Architecture in the Pacific Northwest." *Pacific Northwest* 1, no. 8 (1929): 31–33.

Perkins, Mrs. John Carroll. "Quiet Gardens in the Northwest." *House & Garden*, June 1927, pp. 63–67.

Petersen, Anne. "Women Take the Lead in Landscape Art." *New York Times*, 13 March 1938, p. 83.

Roberts, Don A. "Bush's Pasture Park, The History of Its Acquisition by the City of Salem." *Historic Marion* 37, no. 2 (Summer 1999): 1–4.

Roberts, Ruth, Gretchen Carnaby, and Bobbie Dolp. "Careless Grace: The Gardens of Lord-Schryver." *Washington Park Arboretum Bulletin* (Spring 2009).

Schryver, Edith E. "Introduction to the Seven Areas of Our Garden." Portland Garden Club. *Gardener's Magazine*, March 1956.

Strang, Elizabeth Leonard. "Good Design Plus Good Personality." *House Beautiful*, March 1930, p. 283.

Tankard, Judith B. "Ellen Biddle Shipman's New England Gardens." *Arnoldia* 57, no. 1 (Winter 1997).

Tankard, Judith B. "Shipman in Seattle." *Pacific Horticulture* (Summer 1997): 30.

"Two Seasons in a Western Garden: The Garden of Mrs. William P. Lord at Salem, Oregon." *House & Garden*, July 1924, p. 60.

Van Buren, Deborah E. "Landscape Architecture and Gardens in the Cornish Colony." *Women's Studies* (1988): 383.

➤ Theses, Unpublished Papers, and Government Documents

Brown, Brian. Capitol Planning Commission History. Oregon State Archives, 2005.

Croman, Thea. Broadcasting Public: Radio Station KOAC and the Making of Modern Citizens, 1923–1958. Master's thesis, University of Oregon, 2015.

Deck, Liz. Interpreting Classic Signature Elements for Garden Design: Rediscovering Pacific Northwest Landscape Architects Lord-Schryver. Master's thesis, University of Oregon, 2005.

Duniway, David C. In Remembrance of Elizabeth B. Lord. Memorial service address, October 1976.

Duniway, David C. National Register of Historic Places—Registration Form, Daniel B. Jarman, House and Garden. 30 April 1979. Salem, OR: State Historic Preservation Office.

Duniway, David C., and Elisabeth Walton Potter. National Register of Historic Places—Registration Form, Charles G. Robertson House and Garden. 1 April 1983. Salem, OR: State Historic Preservation Office.

Hartwig, Paul. National Register of Historic Places—Registration Form, Luke A. Port House (Deepwood). August 1973. Salem, OR: State Historic Preservation Office.

Laurnen, Leslie A., and J. David Riley. Lord and Schryver's Northwest Design Practice, The Robertson Garden. Unpublished report. 28 February 1989. University of Oregon, Lord & Schryver Conservancy.

Matthews, Laurie. Gaiety Hollow, Historic American Landscapes Survey (HALS) No. OR-5. 2013. www.nps.gov.

Matthews, Laurie, Robert Melnick, Rachel Edmonds, and Christina Frank. Gaiety Hollow—Cultural Landscape Report. Portland, OR: MIG, 2012.

Mausolf, Lisa. National Register of Historic Places—Nomination Form for Cornish Arts Colony in Cornish and Plainfield NH 1885–1930. November 1989. www. crjc.org.

Melnick, Robert Z. Deepwood—Historic Landscape Report, July 1990. Salem, OR: Deepwood Museum and Gardens.

Millegan, James W., and Dwight A. Smith. National Register of Historic Places—Registration Form for Gaiety Hill/Bush's Pasture Park Historic District. January 1986. Salem, OR: State Historic Preservation Office.

Schneider, Richard A. *A History of Lowthorpe*. Providence, RI: Rhode Island School of Design, Department of Alumni Relations, 1988.

Schutt, Kathy. "State Capitol Park, General Park Plan 2010." Salem: Oregon Parks and Recreation Department.

Sutherland, Ross. "Lord & Schryver: The Salem Art Association and the Bush House Museum." Unpublished report. March 2019. Lord & Schryver Conservancy.

Sutherland, Ross, and Diana Painter. National Register of Historic Places—Registration Form, Gaiety Hollow. 16 December 2014. Salem, OR: State Historic Preservation Office.

Tess, John M. National Register of Historic Places—Registration Form, Portland Garden Club. 24 August 2005. Salem, OR: State Historic Preservation Office.

White, Laura. Transplanted Traditions: The Pacific Northwest Gardens of Elizabeth Lord and Edith Schryver. Master's thesis, University of Oregon, 1992.

Index

Abelia × *grandiflora* 'Sherwoodii,' 116
Acer (maple), 161
   circinatum (vine maple), 138
   palmatum (Japanese maple), 138
   rubrum (red maple), 162
Adams, Mary, 150–51
ageratum, 122
AIA (American Institute of Architects),
   131, 142, 196nn5,6
Albert, Joseph A., 161
American Iris Society, 119, 193n21
American Plants for American Gardens
   (Rehmann and Roberts), 125
American Society of Landscape
   Architects (ASLA), 23, 130–31, 132,
   134, 185n12, 194n2
SS *Andania II* (cruise ship), 1, 28
Anderson, Dorothy May, 189n60
Anne Arundel Academy (Maryland), 12
aralia, 53
arbors, 70, 100, 105, plates 28,31
Arbutus menziesii (madrone), 126
architectural features
   aim/purpose of, 5, 83
   arbors, 70, 100, 105, plates 28,31
   benches, 51, *52*, 90, 138, plate 18
   in Cornish gardens, 35–36, 38–39, *40*,
      186n15, plates 4,5
   fences, 70, *71*, 87, 148, plate 9
   fountains, 41, 49, 51, *52*, 142, 143,
      187–88n14, plates 7,8
   gates, *71*, 87, 100, *101*, plates 9,17,
      27,32
   gazebos, 73–74, *74*, 77–78, *79*, plate 10

Lord and Schryver's use of, 5, 83
   pergola, 51, *52*, 89, *89*, 92, *128*, plate 14
   in Platt's gardens, *33, 34*, 35–36, plate 5
   in Shipman's Merrill garden, 54–55, *55*
   in Strang's landscape plans, 38
   See also ornamental features; terraces;
      walls
Arnold Arboretum (Boston), 22, 68, 114,
   124, 125, 138
Art Institute of Seattle, 49, 63, 64
Arts and Crafts movement, 186n15
Ascutney, Mount (NH), 32, 35
ASLA (American Society of Landscape
   Architects), 23, 130–31, 132, 134, 185n12,
   194n2
Aspet (Cornish, NH), 38, 186n14
aster, 148
auto camps, 57, 161, 188n43
Avison, Margaret, 108
Avison, Robert E., 108
   Avison garden (Portland), 108, *109*,
      110, *110*, *111*, 132, plate 20
azalea, 73, 87, *88*, 126, 162
   Gumpo, 139
   Mollis, 127

Bailey, Doris Holmes, 145–46
Barclay, Forbes, 142
Barclay, Hugh B., 116
Barclay House (Oregon City), 6, 142,
   143, *143*
   See also McLoughlin House and
      Memorial Park
Barker, Barbara, 147, 197n23

Barker, Burt Brown, 145, 146, 147, 148,
   197n18
Beard, Ada, 185n8
Beaux-Arts, 35, 47
Beebe, Gerald, 96–97, 191n6
Beebe, Mary, 96–97, 103, 116
Beebe garden (Lake Oswego, OR),
   96–97, *98, 99, 100*, 100–102, *101*,
   191nn11,12,14, plates 15–18
beech, 126
   European (*Fagus sylvatica* 'Asplenifolia'),
      138
Belluschi, Pietro, 154
benches, 51, *52*, 90, 138, plate 18
Betula pendula (European white birch),
   138
billboard advertising, 158, 198n13
Bingham, George C., 69, 70
Bingham, Mrs. George C., 69
"The Birdcage" gazebo, 73–74, *74*
Bloedel, Virginia, 56
Bloedel Reserve (Bainbridge Island,
   WA), 56
Blossom, Harold Hill, 22
Bonnell Nursery (Seattle), 55
boxwood
   availability of, in nurseries, 117–18
   background on use of, 5, 92, 144
   in Cornish gardens, 36
   cost of shipping, 55
   to define borders, 51, 87, *87*, 90, 92, 122,
      188n19, plates 7,16
   for exhibition garden, 120
   Lord's praise of, 118

to mark entrances, 70, *71*, 97, plate 15

in scrolls, at Deepwood, 72–73, *73*, plate 11

Brandt, Eunice C., 195n11

Breitenbush Hot Springs Resort (OR), 57, *58*, *59*, 60, 66, 125, 162, 188n43

Bremerton Air Force Base (WA), 61

Bretherton, Vivien, 72

Broadbent, Marjorie, 185n8

Brook Place (Plainfield, NH), 24, 33–34, 186n1

Brown, Alice. *See* Powell, Alice Brown

Brown, Clifford, 69, 70, 190n16

Brown, Mrs. Raymond, 77

Brown, Raymond, 77

Brown garden plan (Schryver), 77–78, *78*, *79*

Bryan, Hugh, 194n4

Bullitt, Mrs A. Scott, 118

Burroughs, Elizabeth, 16

Burroughs, John, 16

Bush, Asahel, 9, 166

Bush, Asahel Nesmith (A. N.), 166, 167

Bush, Eugenia, 166

Bush, Sally
estate inheritance of, 166, 199n52
friendship with, 47
ornamental trees of, 68, 116, 166–67, 168, 189n10
photography of, 9, *11*

Bush Barn Art Center (Salem), 171

Bush Elementary School (Salem), *155*, 155–56

Bush House (Salem), 9–10, 47, 166, 167

Bush House Museum (Salem), 170, 177–78, plate 24

Bush's Pasture Park (Salem), 6
Art Center in, 170
competing public plans for, 167–68
estate background of, 166, 199n52
Garry oaks in, 5, 9, 10, 126, 166, 168, plate 1
origin of name, 9
ornamental trees of, 68, 166–67, 168
plant recommendation for, 126
Tartar Rose Garden in, 169–70, *170*, plate 25

Buxus sempervirens 'Suffruticosa' (English boxwood), 118
See also boxwood

Cabell, Mrs. Henry F. (Margaret), 125–26, 135, 144, 197n15

camassia, 5, plate 1

Cambridge School of Architecture and Landscape Architecture for Women, 61
European tour program of, 1–2, 28–29
exhibits sponsored by, 75–76
location of, 183n2

camellia, 127, 139, 145, 146
'Finlandia,' 129

Canterbury bell, 122

Cape Town (South Africa), 94

Capital Journal (newspaper), 49, 126, 160, 164

Capitol Mall (Salem), 164–65, *165*, 199n46

Capitol Planning Commission (Salem), 164–65, 199n41

Carolina silverbell *(Halesia tetraptera)*, 124–25

Carrier's thorn *(Crataegus carrierei)*, 124, 193n37
See also hawthorn, Lavalle

Case, Alice, 115–17

Case, Burton O., 115–17

cedar
Port Orford, 108
Western *(Thuja plicata)*, 148, 195n30

Century Magazine, 33

Cercidiphyllum japonicum (katsura), 138

cherry, See *Prunus*

Chinese tea jar, 72, *72*

Chionanthus virginicus (fringetree), 124–25

Choisya ternata (Mexican orange), 51

chrysanthemum, 125

Church, Thomas, 56

churches, 155, 174–75

city parks
in historic settings, 140–46, *141*, *143*
in Pendleton, 66–68, *67*
in Salem, 159–63, 167–70

city schools, *155*, 155–56, *156*, *157*

Clapp, Channing, 16

Coffin, Marian Cruger, 3, 5, 65

College of Puget Sound (Tacoma), 155

Colonial Dames of America (Oregon chapter), 12, 147, 149–51, 177, 197n34

Colonial Revival gardens, 34, 36, *37*, 92, 110

"Color Schemes in Late Spring Gardens" (lecture, E. Lord), 104

columbine, 122

Columbus Day Storm (1962), 74, 165, *166*

Conwell's Nursery (Milton, DE), 114

Cooley, Pauline, 119–20

Cooley, Rholin, *119*, 119–20

Cooley's Gardens (Silverton, OR), 118–20, *119*, *120*, *121*, plate 21

Cornell University (Ithaca, NY), 18, 22

Cornish Colony (NH)
community members of, 32–33
craft tradition at, 38–39, 186n15
houses and gardens of, *33*, *34*, *36*, *37*, *40*, plates 4,5
Platt's influence at, 35–36
Schryver's visits to, 38–39, *39*
Shipman's practice at, 33–34, 36–37, 186n1

Cornus
florida var. *rubra* (Eastern pink dogwood), 138
nuttallii (Northwestern dogwood), 138, 158

Correy, Jesse A., 24

Council, Lucille, 3

"A Country Estate" (Schryver), 22

Country Place Era (1890–1930), 34–35

Court of the Oranges (Seville), 29

crabapple (flowering crab), 149, 162
in Bush's ornamental tree collection, 68, 166–67
in Park Commission project, 68
Sargent *(Malus sargentii)*, 124, 139

Crataegus
carrierei (Carrier's thorn), 124, 193n37
× *lavallei* (Lavalle hawthorn), 87, *87*, 124, 138

Croman, Thea, 103–4

Cuthbert, Frederick A., 63, 131, 132, 133, 195n9

Cydonia sinensis (quince), 53, 70

Cypripedium (lady's slipper), 10

daffodil, 127

dahlia, 125, 148

Davidia involucrata (Dove tree), 168

Davis Building (Portland, OR), 72

Deepwood (Salem)
"The Birdcage" at, 73–74, *74*

in Columbus Day Storm, 74, *166*

garden rooms of, 70, *71*, 72–74, *73*,
plates 9,10

private ownership of, 68–69, *69*

in public realm, 6, 74, 178

Scroll Garden plan for, plate 11

Diman, Joanna C., 21–22, 40, 175–77,
185n8, 201n14

dogwood

Eastern pink *(Cornus florida* var.
rubra), 138

Northwestern *(Cornus nuttallii)*, 138,
158

Dove tree *(Davidia involucrata)*, 168

Duncan, Frances, 33, 186n15

Duniway, David, 139, 175, 177, 178–79

Duniway, Frances, 175

DuPuy, A. L., 77

dwarf Oregon grape *(Mahonia nervosa)*,
138

Edwards, Jesse, 146

Elfstrom, Robert, 159, 163

Elliot, Charles W., 20

Ellis, Robert H., 145–46

Englewood (formerly Kay) Park, 160, *161*

English boxwood *(Buxus sempervirens*
'Suffruticosa'), 118

See also boxwood

Erfeldt, Arthur, 169

Ertz, Charles W., 77

Erythronium oregonum (lamb's tongue), 10

"Essentials of Landscape Architecture
for Average-Sized City Dwelling"
(article, Lord and Schryver), 82–83

European Travel Course (Lowthorpe
School, 1927), 1–2, 28–29

Fagus sylvatica 'Asplenifolia' (European
beech), 138

Fairchild, Mrs. G., 94, *96*

Fairmount neighborhood (Salem), 77

Farr, Bertrand, 117

Farrand, Beatrix, 3, 18, 130

Fealy, Barbara, 195n25

fences

at Deepwood, 70, *71*, plate 9

at Gaiety Hollow, 87

in historic settings, 148

fir, 160

Flanders, Annette Hoyt, 3, 176

flax farming, 13

flowering crab. *See* crabapple

flowering trees. *See* ornamental trees

"Flowering Trees for Your Garden"
(lecture, E. Lord), 124–25

Forget-me-not, 27

forsythia, 148

Fort Vancouver (WA), 140, 145

fountains

in McLoughlin Memorial Park,
142, 143

for Spanish gardens, 41, 49, 51, *52*,
187–88n14, plates 7,8

foxglove, 122

"A French Chateau" (design, E. Lord),
plate 3

Friends Pacific Academy (Newbery,
OR), 146, *147*

fringetree *(Chionanthus virginicus)*,
124–25

Frost, Henry Atherton, 28, 75–76

fruit tree industry, 114

Gaiety Hill/Bush's Pasture Park
National Historic District, 181

Gaiety Hill neighborhood (Salem), 49,
77, 83

Gaiety Hollow (Salem), ix, x, 6

architectural style of house, 83–84, *84*,
85, *87*, *179*, 190n38

boxwood at, 87, *87*, 90, 92

Conservancy's acquisition of, 179,
181

as display garden, 115

espaliered pear tree at, *129*

garden plans for, 86, *86*, *91*

garden rooms of, 86–87, *88*, *89*, 89–90,
92, *128*, *180*, 190nn42,43

Garry oaks at, ix, 90, *90*, 127, *180*

location and size of, 83, 190n37

Lord's journal on, 126–27, *129*, 174–75,
194n52

mementos of Juliet Lord at, 87, 89,
89, 149

memorial services at, 177, 178–79

on National Register of Historic
Places, 181

OSLA meetings at, 132

in period of significance, plate 27

professional praise of, 133, 181

restored gardens of, *180*, plates 28–32

Garden Club of America, 56

garden clubs

client commissions from, 96–97, 135

competitions sponsored by, 62–63

first, in Oregon, 12

Lord's commendation from, 24

photographic exhibitions at, 75–76

public landscape interests of, 145, 153,
158, 167

use of radio by, 103–4, 192n25

See also Portland Garden Club

garden lectures, 48–49, 53, 94

on ornamental trees, 124–25

radio broadcast of, 103–4

gardens

"charm" quality of, 23, 83

in Colonial Revival style, 34, 36, *37*,
92, 110

at Cornish Colony, *33*, 33–35, *34*, *36*,
37, 38–39, *40*, 186n15

of Country Place Era, 34–35

European and world tours of, 1–2,
28–29, 93–94

for exhibition, 115, 119–20, *121*, plate 21

in historic settings, 125–26, 142–45,
144, 146–51, *149*, 197nn27,28

as individual rooms, 70, *71*, 72–74, *73*,
86–87, *88*, *89*, 89–90, 92

of Jekyll, 123

lectures on, 48–49, 53, 94, 103–4,
|124–25

of native plant movement, 125, 194n42

with naturalistic theme, 57, *58*, 101, 108,
160–62, 191n14

newspaper articles on, 62, 82–83, 132,
195n18

of Platt, *33*, *34*, 35–36, 100, plate 5

radio programs on, 103–4, 124–25

with seasonal color schemes, 122–23

of Shipman, 33–34, 36–37, 54–55, *55*, 92

in sponsored competitions, 62–63,
133–34

with terraced designs, 35, 38–39, 79, *80*,
81, 82, 107–8, *109*, 110, 122–23

thematic plantings of, for garden club,
136–38, *137*, 195n30

See also architectural features; Lord
and Schryver projects

"Garden's Charm Heightened by
Appropriate Features" (article, Lord
and Schryver), 83
Garry oak *(Quercus garryana)*, 7
in Bush's Pasture Park, 5, 9, 10, 126,
166, 168, plate 1
at Gaiety Hollow, ix, 90, *90*, 127, *180*
in Pringle Creek Park, 161
gates
in Beebe garden, 100, *101*, plate 17
at Deepwood, *71*, plate 9
at Gaiety Hollow, 87, *87*, plates 27,32
Gattie, Mrs. (Lord and Schryver client),
117
Gauld, Miss (college representative),
127
gazebos
for Brown garden, 77–78, *79*
at Deepwood, 73–74, *74*, plate 10
"General Design Plan for Spanish
Garden Treatment" (Schryver), 50,
plate 6
Gerke, Florence Holmes
background and education of, 60–61,
188n45
landscape practice of, 4, 48, 61–62
Lord's association with, 14, 60, 102
McLoughlin Park plan of, 142
as OSLA member, 131–32
and Portland garden competition,
62–63
and John Storrs, 135
Gerke, Walter H., 48, 61, 132, 188n45
Gilbert, Mrs. A. N., 46
Giles, H. S., 153
ginger, 146
gladiola, 123, 125
golden raintree *(Koelreuteria paniculata)*,
138
Goode, Mrs. V. A., 117–18
Goode, V. A., 117–18
Gormsen, Nancy, 174, 175
Gormsen, Robert M., 174
grape
dwarf Oregon *(Mahonia nervosa)*,
138
Oregon *(Mahonia aquifolium)*, 51, 126,
146, 148
Great Depression, 65–66, 126–27, 155
Greenough, Mrs. Henry V., 41

Greenough estate plan (Schryver), 41,
42–43
groundcover, 116

Halesia tetraptera (Carolina silverbell),
124–25
Harding, L. O., 143, 145
Harvard University, 18
Hatfield, Mark, 158
Hawkes, Charles E., 171
hawthorn
Carrier's thorn *(Crataegus carrierei)*,
124, 193n37
Lavalle *(Crataegus × lavallei)*, 87, *87*,
124, 138
in Park Commission project, 68
heather, 102, plate 18
heavenly bamboo *(Nandina domestica)*, 138
Heavey, Kathryn (cousin of ES), 14, 178
hemlock, 34, 115
Hendrickson, Carl, *129*
Hetzer, L. Louise, 18, 185n1
Hidcote Manor (England), 28
High Court (Cornish, NH), *33*, 35, 100
Highland Park (Salem), 162, *162*
History of Oregon (Carey), 12
holly
"Dutch holly," 137
English *(Ilex aquifolium)*, 135
Ilex pernyi, 137
Japanese *(Ilex crenata)*, 137
at Portland Garden Club, 195n30
as sound screen, 110
hollyhock, 148
Home Garden Hour (radio program),
103–4
honeysuckle, 149
Hood, Mount (OR), 97, 101
Hoover, Herbert, 146, 147, 150
SS *Hoover* (cruise ship), 93
Hoover-Minthorn House (Newberg,
OR), 6, 146–51, *147*, *151*, 197nn27,
28,34
horticulture
evolution of, in Northwest, 114–16
hybridization component of, 115,
118–19
Lord's expertise in, 24, 66, 68
at Lowthorpe, 20, 113–14
radio programs on, 103–4, 124–25

Shipman's expertise in, 36–37
value of, at Bush Park, 167–70
See also gardens
"House and Garden for Miss Elizabeth
Lord at 545 Mission St. Salem Ore"
(design, Schryver), 86, *86*
House Beautiful (magazine), 84, *85*
House & Garden (magazine), 24, 26, *27*,
31, 54
huckleberry, 146
Hudson's Bay Company, 140, 196n2
Huntington, Wallace Kay, 75, 175
Deepwood project of, 74
on Lord and Schryver's style, 6, 181
on Northwest landscape architecture, 3
Portland Garden Club project of,
138–39
hybridization, 115, 118–19
Hyde, Mary Louise (cousin of ES), 178
Hydrangea, 122
paniculata, 149

Ilex
aquifolium (English holly), 135
crenata (Japanese holly), 137
pernyi, 137
Illahee Country Club (Salem), 24, 185n16
iris, 70, 117, 118–20, *119*, *120*, *121*, plate 21
Italianate design, 35, 36
Italian Gardens (Platt), 35
Italian Villas and Their Gardens
(Wharton), 35

Japanese anemone, 122
Jarman, Daniel B., 5, 49–50, 183n10
Jarman, Edith M., 53
Jarman garden (Salem), 29, 41, 49–51, *52*,
53, plates 6–8
jasmine, 53
Jekyll, Gertrude, 123
Johnston, Lawrence, 28

Kalapuya, 47
katsura *(Cercidiphyllum japonicum)*, 138
Kay (now Englewood) Park, 160, *161*
KFDJ (radio station), 103
Kingery, Anne, 105, 108
Kingery, Lyle B., 105
Kingery garden (Portland), 105, *106*, *107*,
107–8, 192nn30,38, plate 19

Kingston, NY, 14, 184n26

Kirsh, Neena, 175

Kleinsorge, R. E., 119

KOAC (radio station), 103–4, 124

Koelreuteria paniculata (golden raintree), 138

Ladd & Bush Bank (Salem), 9, 12

lady's slipper *(Cypripedium),* 10

Lakewold Gardens (Tacoma, WA), 56

Lambert Gardens (Portland), 117

lamb's tongue *(Erythronium oregonum),* 10

"The Landscape Architect in Private Practice" (speech, Schryver), 132

landscape architecture
　Depression's impact on, 65–66
　licensing requirements in, 131, 132
　listings for, in Polk's Directory, 48, 187n6, 194n4
　Lord and Schryver's principles of, x–xi, 5–6, 183n11
　nursery component of, 114–16
　in Pacific Northwest, 3, 47–48, 131, 187n7
　professionalization of, in Oregon, 131–32
　programs for women in, 18–20, 185n3
　See also women landscape architects

laurel hedge *(Prunus laurocerasus),* 148

Lawrence, Mary, 22, 185n8

Lazarus, Annie, 34

Lee, Charlotte, 185n8

Legg, W. Dorr, 104, 130–31, 133–34

Leland, Louise, 75

Leslie, David, 166, 168, 200n60

Lewis and Clark Exposition (1905), 73

lilac, 53, 67, 116–17, 127, 148

lily, 122
　Madonna, 148

Lincoln, Abraham, 8

Lindbergh, Charles, 1

Liquidambar styraciflua (sweet gum), 138

Liriodendron tulipifera (tulip tree), 162

Lloyd Bond and Associates, 165

"Looking toward the Fall Garden" (lecture, Schryver), 104, 125

Loomis, Edith, 63, 189n60

Lord, Carmen (grand niece of EL), 177

Lord, Carmen DePages (Mrs. Melvin S.), 177

Lord, Elizabeth (EL)
　birth and family background of, 7–8, *8, 11*
　on boxwood, 117–18, 144
　civic role of, x, 6, 102–3, 130, 152–53; as Bush Park advocate, 167–68; as Capitol Planning Commissioner, 164–65, 199n48; with landscape architecture students, 133–34; as Park Board chair, 159, 160–63; as Salem Art Association president, 170–71; as Tree Commission chair, 163; in World War I, 12
　commendations for, 24, *150,* 151, 152
　correspondence of: on billboard advertising, 158; on Capitol Mall "eyesores," 164; with clients, 49–50, 53, 64, 76, 96–97, 116, 118, 173; on fees, 60, 76, 159; with Henry Frost, 75–76; on garden competition, 62; on garden design articles, 82; with Herbert Hoover, 150; on Hoover-Minthorn House, 148; with Dorr Legg (ASLA), 130–31; on McLoughlin Memorial Park, 143, 144, 145; as mentor, 63; with nurseries, 65–66, 115–18; with Pendleton Park Commission, 66–67; from Alice Powell, 70, 72; from Salem General Hospital, 153
　deafness of, 12, 66, 164
　death, and eulogy to, 177
　declining years of, 127, 129, 174–75, *176,* 177, 200n8
　education of, 10, 12, 14, 24, 184n14, plate 3
　European and world tours of, 1–2, *2, 3, 12, 13,* 28–29, 93–94, *94, 95, 96*
　family home of, 8–9, *9,* 83, 184n5
　Gaiety Hollow home of, 83–84, *84, 85, 87,* 190n37
　as garden competition judge, 62–63, 133–34
　garden lectures by, 103–4, 124–25
　and Florence Gerke, 14, 60, 62, 102
　horticultural expertise of, 24, 66, 68, 122–23
　journal entries of, 126–27, 129, 174–75, 194n52

and Montague Lord, 12, *13,* 93–94, *94*
　on mother's interests, 9–10, 13–14, *15,* 147
　as OSLA member, 131–32, *133*
　planting plans of: awards for, 24; for Hoover-Minthorn House, 147–50, *149,* 197nn27,28; for McLoughlin Memorial Park, 125–26, 144, 197n15; for Peterman garden, 122–23, *123;* style of, 123
　plant standards of, 108, 115–16, 118, 124–25
　on road trip to Salem, 46–47
　on Salem's beauty, 152, 160, 172
　with Schryver, *115, 139, 145, 172, 176, 178*
　Schryver's partnership with, 1–2, 7
　at Seal Rock resort, 10, 74, 112, *178*
　See also Lord and Schryver, Landscape Architects; Lord and Schryver projects

Lord, Juliet Montague (mother of EL)
　background and marriage of, 7, 8, 184n2
　civic pursuits of, 12–14
　death of, 24, 194n46
　gardening interests of, *15*
　and Herbert Hoover, 147
　lilac named for, 117, 127
　mementos of, at Gaiety Hollow, 87, 89, *89,* 149
　nature and gardening interests of, 9–10, 24, *27*
　travels of, to Phillipines, 12, *13*

Lord, Marilee (grand niece of EL), 177

Lord, Melvin S. (nephew of EL), 177, 179

Lord, Montague (brother of EL), 10, *11*
　birth of, 8
　and Chinese tea jar, 72
　death of, 169, 177
　sister's visits with, 12, *13,* 93–94, *94*
　wartime internment of, 112

Lord, Montague (grand nephew of EL), 177

Lord, William P., Jr. (brother of EL), 8, *11,* 12, 14, 83

Lord, William P., Sr. (father of EL), 7–8, *9,* 10, 12

Lord and Schryver, Landscape
  Architects (firm)
  archived records of, 179
  civic/education commitment of, x, 6,
    103, 130, 133–35, 152–53
  closing of firm, 175
  Depression's impact on, 65–66
  with difficult clients, 55–56, 142,
    143–44
  division of labor at, 66
  employed workers of, 126–27, 174
  in fee negotiations, 60, 76, 105, 159
  in friendships with clients, x, 68, 70,
    72, 74–75, 101–2, 108, 174
  as garden competition judges, 62–63,
    133–34
  garden design articles by, 62, 82–83, 132
  garden lectures by, 103–4, 124–25
  historic preservation role of, 6, 183n12
  launching of firm, 2–3, 31, 63–64
  legacy of, in Pacific Northwest, x–xi,
    3–6
  nursery orders of, 55, 115–16, 117–18
  as OSLA members, 131–32, 133, 195n19
  in Polk's Directory, 48, 131, 187n6,
    194n4
  promotional tools of, 4–5, 31, 48,
    48–49
  See also Lord, Elizabeth; Lord and
    Schryver projects; Schryver, Edith
Lord and Schryver Conservancy, ix,
  179, 181
Lord and Schryver projects
  Avison garden, 108, 109, 110, 110, 111,
    132, plate 20
  Beebe garden, 96–97, 98, 99, 100,
    100–102, 101, 191nn11,12,14, plates
    15–18
  boxwood signature plant of, 5, 117–18
  Breitenbush Resort, 57, 58, 59, 60, 125
  "charm" theme of, 23, 83
  for city parks, 66–68, 67, 159–63,
    198n20
  Cooley's Gardens, 118–20, 121, plate 21
  Deepwood, 70, 71, 72–74, 73, plates
    9–11
  distinctive garden style of, x–xi, 5–6,
    133, 181, 183n11
  Hoover-Minthorn House, 146–51, 149,
    197nn27,28,34

Jarman garden, 29, 41, 49–51, 52, 53,
  plates 6–8
Kingery garden, 105, 106, 107, 107–8,
  192nn30,38, plate 19
McLoughlin Memorial Park, 125–26,
  142–45, 144, 197n15
Merrill garden, 54–56, 114, 115
number of, 5, 93, 191n1
Peterman garden, 122–23, 123
Portland Garden Club, 136–38, 137,
  139, 195n30
with problematic sites, 77–79, 82, 108,
  110
for public buildings and schools,
  153–56, 154, 164–65, 198n4, 199n46
renovation of originals, 173–74
Robertson garden, 77–79, 80, 81, 82,
  173–74, plates 12–14
Tartar Rose Garden, 169, 169–70, 170,
  plate 25
See also Gaiety Hollow (Salem)
"The Lost Battalion" (speech, Schryver),
  16
Low, Judith Eleanor Motley, 19–20,
  185n3
Lowthorpe School of Landscape
  Architecture for Women (Groton,
  MA)
  and Cambridge School exhibitions,
    75–76
  Cornish Colony tours of, 38–39, 39
  European Travel Course of, 1–2, 28–29
  founding of, 19–20, 185nn3,5
  horticultural focus of, 20, 68, 113–14
  location and setting of, 20, 21, 183n2
  Lord's attendance at, 14, 24
  planting style at, 123
  Schryver's attendance at, 17–18, 19, 23
  Schryver's designs at, 22, 24, 25, 26,
    plate 2
  Schryver's friends from, 21–22, 40,
    175–77, 185n8, 187n18, 201n14
  Shipman's ties to, 37
  Strang's role at, 22–23
  tuition at, 17, 185n36
Lumm, Josephine, 195n11
Lutyens, Edwin L., 123

madrone (Arbutus menziesii), 126
Madsen, Lillie L., 174

Magnolia
  grandiflora (Southern magnolia), 51,
    154
  Kobus, 174
  × soulangeana (saucer magnolia), 51
  × soulangeana 'Bronzzonii,' 138
Mahonia
  aquifolium (Oregon grape), 51, 126,
    146, 148
  nervosa (dwarf Oregon grape), 138
Malus sargentii (Sargent crabapple),
  124, 139
maple, See Acer
Maria Luisa Park (Seville), 29, 30
marigold, 125
Marion County Courthouse (Salem),
  153–54
Marion Square Park (Salem), 159,
  198n20
Martin, Charles H., 196n5
Massachusetts Institute of Technology
  (MIT), 18
McAlister, Glen C., 50–51, 188n18
McKay, Douglas, 164
McKinley, William, 10
McLoughlin, John, 140–41, 196nn1,3,4
  bronze bust of, 142, 143, 196n10
McLoughlin, Marguerite, 141, 196n4
McLoughlin House and Memorial Park
  (Oregon City), 6
  AIA's interest in, 142, 196nn5,6
  and Barclay House, 6, 142, 143, 143
  historic background of, 140–41, 141,
    196nn1–5
  as National Historic Site, 145
  planting plan for, 125–26, 144 , 144–45,
    197n15
  restoration of, by Ellis, 145–46
McLoughlin Memorial Association,
  141–42, 143, 145
Men's Garden Club of Salem, 167
mentorship, 3–4, 37, 63, 133–34
Merrill, Eula, 54, 55, 56, 158
Merrill, Richard D., 54
Merrill garden, 54, 54–56, 55, 114, 115
Metcalf, Joel H., 28
Mexican orange (Choisya ternata), 51
Meyers, Milton, 159, 163
Miller, Edward M., 82
Mill Stream (Salem), 160

Minthorn, Henry J., 146–47

Mission Mill Museum (now Willamette Heritage Center), 152, 175, 177

Mission Street Parks Conservancy (Salem), 170

MIT (Massachusetts Institute of Technology), 18

Monroe Gilbert Studio (Salem), 31, 49, 64

Moody, Bertha M., 20

Moorish gardens. *See* Spanish gardens

Morris, L. S., 133

Moses, Robert, 176

Mosher, Eileen Eleanor (cousin of ES), 178

Mothers' and Daughters' Club (Plainfield, NH), 186n2

mountain ash *(Sorbus aucuparia)*, 160

Mount Crest Abbey Mausoleum (Salem), 177

Nandina domestica (heavenly bamboo), 138

National Historic Preservation Act (1966), 183n12

National Register of Historic Places creation of, 183n12
  Gaiety Hollow on, 181, 190n38
  Hoover-Minthorn House on, 197n34
  McLoughlin House and Memorial Park on, 145
  Portland Garden Club on, 138
  Robertson house and garden on, 77, 174

National Society of the Colonial Dames of America. *See* Colonial Dames of America

native plants
  American movement for, 125, 194n42
  at Bush's Pasture Park, 5, 126, plate 1
  at Hoover-Minthorn House, 148
  at McLoughlin Memorial Park, 125–26, 142, 146
  at Portland Garden Club, 138
  at Pringle Creek Park, 161–62
  wildflowers, 5, 10, 70

Nelson, Carl E., 173

Nelson, Mrs. Carl E., 173

Nichols, Rose Standish, 32

Noble, William, 181

Nolen, John, 22–23

Northcote (Cornish, NH), 36, *37*

North Salem High School, *157*

Northwest Regional style, 135–36

nurseries
  Depression's impact on, 66
  expansion of, in Northwest, 114–15
  of iris cultivars, 118–20, *119, 120, 121*
  Lord's correspondence with, 65–66, 115–18
  Oregon association of, 114, 192n3
  plant availability in, 115–16, 117–18
  rail freight charges of, 55

OAC. *See* Oregon Agricultural College

The Oaks (Cornish, NH), 38–39, *40*

Olmsted, Frederick Law, 5, 194n2

Oregon Agricultural College (OAC, now Oregon State University), 60–61, 63
  name changes of, 191–92n20
  and nursery industry, 114
  public radio station of, 103–4
  See also Oregon State College

Oregon Federation of Garden Clubs, 103–4, 192n25

Oregon Floral Club, 24

Oregon grape *(Mahonia aquifolium)*, 51, 126, 146, 148

Oregon Nurserymen's Association, 114, 192n3

Oregon Roadside Council (formerly Oregon Council for the Protection of Roadside Beauty), 158

Oregon Society of Landscape Architects (OSLA). *See* OSLA

Oregon State Capitol Building, *164, 165,* 199n46

Oregon State College (OSC, now Oregon State University), 131, *134,* 134–35, 191–92n20, 195n9
  See also Oregon Agricultural College

Oregon State Land Board, 8

Oregon State School for the Blind (Salem), 155

Oregon Statesman (newspaper), 49, 147, 149–50, 160, 166

Oregon State University (OSU) former names of, 191–92n20, 194n1
  See also Oregon Agricultural College; Oregon State College

Oregon Sunday Call (newspaper), 62

Oregon Supreme Court, 7, 8

ornamental features
  balustrades, 72–73, *73,* 174
  birdbaths, plate 28
  bust of McLoughlin, 142, *143,* 196n10
  cherub statuary, 87, *88, 89,* plate 30
  Chinese tea jar, 72, *72*
  sundial, in rose garden, plate 25
  See also architectural features

ornamental trees
  in Beebe garden, 97, *99*
  on Bush family's property, 68, 116, 166–67, *168*
  expanded production of, 114–15
  Lord's lecture on, 124–25
  at Portland Garden Club, 138

OSLA (Oregon Society of Landscape Architects), 61–62, 130, 131–32, *133,* 133–34, 195nn11,14

Osmanthus, 137

Otten, George, 199n48

Outdoor Advertising Act (1955), 158, 198n13

Pachysandra, 116

Pacific Highway, 158, 198n11

Pacific Northwest
  boxwood supply in, 117–18
  horticultural evolution in, 114–16
  landscape architecture profession in, 3, 47–48, 131, 187n7, 194n4
  Lord and Schryver's legacy in, x–xi, 3–6

Palladio, Andrea, 35

Panegyrics (Salem fundraiser), 152, 197n1

Parker, Jamieson, 196n5

Parrish, Maxfield, 32, 35, 38–39, *40*

Parrish, Stephen, 32, 36, *37*

patios. *See* terraces

Pattee, Elizabeth Greenleaf, 22

Patton house (Salem), 144, 197n15

Payson, Louise Ellen, 40, 176, 187n18

Peck, Arthur L., 114, 131, 134, *134,* 195n9

Pendleton, Ellen F., 20

Pendleton Park Commission, 66–67, 68

Pendleton Pioneer Memorial Park, 66–68, *67*

Pennsylvania School of Horticulture for Women (Ambler, PA), 18–19

peony *(Paeonia officinalisi)*, 70, 117, 148
pergola, 51, *52*, 89, *89*, 92, *128*, plate 14
Peterbilt truck firm, 122, 193n27
Peterman, Ida, 122, 193n27
Peterman, T. A., 122
Peterman garden, 122–23, *123*
Philippines, 12, *13*, 93–94, *94, 95, 96*, 112
phlox, 115, 122, 148
pine
    Japanese umbrella *(Sciadopitys
        verticillata)*, 139
    Mugho [Mugo], 162
    white, 35–36
plane tree *(Platanus occidentalis)*, 153, 154
"Planning and Planting the Home
    Grounds" (KOAC program), 104
Platt, Charles A., 32, 186n2
    home and gardens of, *33, 34*, 35–36, *36*,
        100, plate 5
    on ideal landscape, 101
    Merrill project of, 54
    Shipman's work with, 34, 54
Polk's Directory, 48, 131, 187n6, 194n4
poppy, 70
Port, Luke A., 68–69
Portland Garden Club, 130
    architectural style of, 135–36, *136*
    garden views of, *139*, plates 22,23
    and McLoughlin Memorial Park,
        145–46
    memorial bench at, 138
    planting plan for, 136–38, *137*, 195n30
Powell, Alice Brown, 175
    boxwood order for, 118
    Deepwood home of, 68–69, *69*
    ornamental garden features of, 72, *73*,
        73–74, *74*
    Schryver on, 75
    written gratitude of, 70, 72
Powell, Keith, 73
Pringle Creek (Salem), 69, 70, 160–61,
    166
Pringle Creek Park (Salem), 125, 160–62
privet, 143
Prunus (cherry), 124, 162
    in Bush's ornamental tree collection,
        68, 166–67
    laurocerasus (cherry laurel), 148
    subhirtella var. *pendula* (Japanese
        weeping), 124

    subhirtella 'Whitcomb' (Japanese
        flowering), 167
public projects
    for city parks, 66–68, *67*
    for city parks, in Salem, 159–63,
        167–70, 198n20
    firm's commitment to, 6, 152–53
    of Gerke, 62
    for government buildings, 153–54, *154*,
        164–65, 199n46
    for period landscapes, 125–26, 140–46,
        141, 143, 147–49, 197nn27,28
    practical approach to, 153
    for schools, *155*, 155–56, *156*

Quercus
    garryana (*See* Garry oak)
    rubra (Northern red oak), 138
quince *(Cydonia sinensis)*, 53, 70

radio clubs, 104
radio programs, 103–4, 124–25
Reed College (Portland), 126–27, 155
Rehmann, Elsa, 125
rhododendron, 138, 139, 145
    'Bo-peep,' 129
    'Bow Bells,' 127
    'Bric-à-brac,' 129
Richardson, Lou, 63
Riches, George, 159
Roberts, Edith A., 125
Roberts, Ruth, 56
Robertson, Charles G., 76
Robertson, Mildred, 76
Robertson garden (Salem, OR)
    challenging site of, 77, 78
    fee negotiations on, 76
    renovation of, 173–74
    terraced design of, 79, *80, 81*, 82, plates
        12–14
Robinson, William, 194n42
Rockey, Mrs. A. E., 143–44
Roesnick, Kurt, 127, 174
Rosa wichuraiana, 149
roses
    in beds of single color, 110, *111*
    at Gaiety Hollow, 89
    at Hoover-Minthorn House, 148, 149,
        197n27
    at McLoughlin House, 145

    in Merrill garden, 56
    Tartar Collection of, 169–70, *170*,
        plate 25
    in terraced garden, 122
Russell, Marjorie, 185n8

Saint-Gaudens, Augusta, 32
Saint-Gaudens, Augustus, 32, 38, 186n14,
    plate 4
St. Helen's Hall (Portland, OR), 12,
    184n14
St. Paul's Episcopal Church (Salem),
    155, 174–75
salal, 146
Salem, OR
    acquisition of Bush property by,
        166–70, 199n52
    Art Fair in, *171*
    Capitol Mall expansion in, 164–65,
        165, 199nn41,46
    civic-minded citizenry of, 152, 158, 170
    in Columbus Day Storm, 74, 165, *166*
    County Courthouse project in, 153–54,
        154
    economy and topography of, 47
    as firm's destination, 2, 31
    Lord's family home in, 8–9, *9*, 184n5
    natural beauty of, 152, 160, 172
    public park improvements in, 159–63
    road trip to, from San Francisco,
        46–47
    "silver teas" of, 12–13
Salem Art Association, 6, 130, 170–71,
    174, 175, 200n67
Salem Chamber of Commerce, 167
Salem Garden Club (formerly Salem
    Floral Society), 12, 102, 153
Salem General Hospital, 153
Salem High School, 155, *156, 157*, 200n67
Salem Park Board, 159–60, 198nn14,17
Salem Tree Commission, 163
Salishan Lodge (Gleneden Beach, OR),
    135
Santiam National Forest (now
    Willamette National Forest), 57
Sargent, Charles Sprague, 20, 124
sassafras *(Sassafras albidum)*, 138
Scenic Area Law (1961), 158, 198n13
Schley, Evander B., estate, 41, 51, 186n21
schools, *155*, 155–56, *156, 157*

Schryver, Edith (ES)

background and childhood of, 14–16, *15, 16, 17,* 184n27

on Sally Bush, 47

as Bush Park advocate, 167–68, 169–70

civic and teaching role of, x, 6, 103, 130, 133–35, 158, 163

at Cornish Colony, 32, 33, 36, 38–39, *39*

correspondence of: on billboard advertising, 158; on Bush Park design, 167; with clients, 96–97, 101–2, 105, 108, 122, 158; on display garden, 115; on garden competition, 62–63; as mentor, 63; from Alice Powell, 70, 72; with Shipman, on Merrill garden, 55, 56; on wartime projects, 131

death, and eulogy to, 178–79

declining years of, 127, 129, 175

design skills of, 24, 40–41, 97, 105, 107–8

designs of: for Avison garden, 108, *109,* 110, *110, 111;* for Beebe estate, 97, *98, 99,* 100–101, *101,* 191nn11,14; for Breitenbush Resort, 57, *58,* 60; for Brown garden, 77–78, *78, 79;* in Cambridge School exhibition, 75–76; for Cooley's Gardens, 119–20, *121,* plate 21; for Deepwood Scroll Garden, 72–73, *73,* plate 11; drafting technique of, 38, 41, 50; for Gaiety Hollow, 86, *86, 91;* for Jarman garden, 50, 51, *52,* 53, plates 6–8; for Kingery garden, 105, *106,* 107–8, 192n30, plate19; at Lowthorpe, *22,* 24, *25, 26,* plate 2; for Merrill garden, *55,* 55–56; for Peterman garden, 122; for Robertson garden, 78–79, *80, 81,* 82, 173–74, plates 12–14; for Salem city parks, 159, 161–62, *162,* 198n20; for Shipman's practice, 29, 40–41, *42–43, 44–45,* 49, 186nn14,21, 187–88n14; for Tartar rose collection, *169,* 169–70, plate 25

education of, 16, 17, *17,* 18, *19,* 21–22, *23,* 24, 185n36

European and world tours of, 1–2, *4,* 28–29, *30,* 93–94, *94, 95, 96*

friends of, from Lowthorpe, 21–22, 40, 175–77, 185n8, 187n18, 201n14

Gaiety Hollow home of, 83–84, *84, 85, 87,* plate 26

as garden competition judge, 62–63, 133–34

garden lectures by, 103–4, 124

with Lord, *115, 139, 145, 172, 176, 178*

Lord's death and, 177–78

Lord's partnership with, 1–2, 7

Lowthorpe notebooks of, 21–22, 185n9

as OSLA member, 131–32, *133*

professional style of, 40, 66

pronunciation of surname, 14

on road trip to Salem, 46–47

at Seal Rock resort, 10, 74, 112, *178*

in Shipman's practice, 1, 24, 29, 32, 39, 40–41

See also Lord and Schryver, Landscape Architects (firm); Lord and Schryver projects

Schryver, Eleanor (mother of ES), 14, *15, 16*

Schryver, George J. (father of ES), 14, *15, 16,* 185n33

Schryver, Harry George (brother of ES), 14, *15,* 16, 178, 185n33

Schucking, Mrs. Bernard O. (Agnes), 46

Sciadopitys verticillata (Japanese umbrella pine), 139

Seal Rock (OR), 10, 74, 112, *178,* 179

"Sea-Side Garden" (planting plan, Schryver), 24, *25*

Second Dutch Reformed Church (Kingston, NY), 14, 184n27

Shelden, Mrs. Henry D., 41, 186n21

Shelden estate plan (Schryver), 41, *44–45,* 49, 187–88n14

Shelton Stream (Salem), 160–61

Shipman, Ellen, 3, 5, 18, 176

and ASLA, 194n2

Brook Place home of, 33, 186n1

garden design style of, 34, 36–37, 92, 123

Manhattan office of, *38,* 39

Merrill garden referral from, 41, 54–56, *55*

Platt's work with, 34, 54

Schryver's internship with, 24, 32

Schryver's projects with, 29, 40–41, *42–43, 44–45,* 49, 186nn14,21, 187–88n14

Strang hired by, 23, 37–38

as women's advocate, 37, 113, 186n2

Shipman, Louis Evan, 33, 34

Skidmore, Owings and Merrill (SOM), 177

Skiff, Ada, 57

Skiff, Mark, 57

Slabsides (NY), 16

Slotten, Hugh R., 103

Small, Virginia Harrison, 195n11

The Small Place: Its Landscape Architecture (Rehmann), 125

Smith, Clarence L., 77, 83–84

Smith, Mrs. Walter H., 175

Sorbus aucuparia (mountain ash), 160

Southern Oregon Myrtle *(Umbellularia californica),* 126

Spanish Colonial Revival style, 49, 50–51

Spanish gardens

European tour of, 2, *3, 4,* 29, *30*

irrigation of, 29

of Jarman project, 50–51, *52,* 53, 188n19, plate 6

Schryver's designs for, 41, *44–45,* 49, 50, 186n21, 187–88n14

"Spanish Garden Treatment, General Design Plan" (Schryver), 50, plate 6

Spears, Mrs. Frank, 149–50

Sprague, Charles A., 132, 175

Sprague, Mrs. Charles A. (Blanche), 149–50, 175

"Spring Flowers in the Garden" (lecture, E. Lord), 104

Sprouse, Barbara Barker, 147, 197n23

Stanton, Glenn, 61, 142

Statesman Journal (newspaper), 174, 175

statuary. *See* ornamental features

Stockbridge, Fanny Eliza, 8, 10, 13

Stockbridge, Henry, 8

Storrs, John, 61, 135–36, *136,* 195n25

Strang, Elizabeth Leonard, 3, 21, 22–23, 37–38

Streatfield, David, ix, 181

Stroh, Florence, 22, 185n8

Sunday Oregonian (newspaper), 82, 103, 124, 132, 145, 195n18

Sunset (magazine), 63

Swanley Horticultural College (Kent, England), 19–20

sweet gum *(Liquidambar styraciflua),* 138

Tartar, Mae, 169
Tartar Rose Garden (Bush's Pasture
  Park), *169*, 169–70, *170*, plate 25
Taylor, Mark, 163
terraces
  in Avison garden, *109*, 110, plate 20
  in Beebe garden, 97, 191n11, plates
    15–17
  of Cornish gardens, 35, 38–39
  in Kingery garden, 107–8, plate 19
  in Robertson garden, 79, *81*, 82, plate
    13,14
Thayer, Estelle, 47
Thompson, David E., 167, *168*
Thuja plicata (Western cedar), 148,
  195n30
Tree City Awards, 163
trees
  in Columbus Day Storm, 74, 165, *166*
  in eulogy to Schryver, 178–79
  in Lord's city street plan, 163
  at Marion County Courthouse,
    153–54
  at Portland Garden Club, 138
  in public parks, 160, 161, 162
  transition to ornamental, 114–15
  See also ornamental trees
Tucker, Ernest, 61, 97, 105, 107–8
tulip, 127
  Cottage, 117
  Darwin, *27*, 117
tulip tree *(Liriodendron tulipifera)*, 162

Umbellularia californica (Southern
  Oregon Myrtle), 126
Union League Ball (Baltimore), 8
United Brethren Church (Salem), 155
University of California Berkeley, 18

University of Illinois Champaign-
  Urbana, 18
University of Oregon, 103, 131, 195n9
Unwin, Mrs. Edward, 28

Viburnum
  opulus (highbush cranberry), 148
  plicatum (old-fashioned Snowball),
    148
viola, 122
violet, 10
Voisin, Andrien, 196n10

Wagner, Eulalie, 56
Wallace, Paul B., 163
walls
  in Beebe garden, 100, *101*, plates 16,17
  in Browns' construction plan, 77–78,
    79
  in Jarman's Spanish garden, 50–51,*52*,
    plate 7
  at The Oaks, 38–39, *40*
  Platt's use of, 36, 100, plate 5
  in Schryver's construction plan, 78, *79*
Walsh and Rainwater's Nursery
  (Marshfield, OR), 108, 115
Walton, James, 175
Walton, Kathryn, 175
Weatherford, Louise E., 104
West Side Restaurant (Kingston, NY),
  14
Wharton, Edith, 35
white birch *(Betula pendula)*, 138
wildflowers, 5, 10, 70
  See also native plants
The Wild Garden (Robinson), 194n42
Willamette Heritage Center (formerly
  Mission Mill Museum), 152, 175, 177

Willamette National Forest (formerly
  Santiam National Forest), 57
Willamette River, 46–47
Willamette University (Salem), 155, 167
Willamette Valley, 46–47, 114
Willson, William H., 159, 160
Willson Park (Salem), 159, 164, 165
Wilmsen and Endicott (firm), 165
Wiltwyck Cemetery (Kingston, NY), 14
Woman's Lewis and Clark Club
  (Oregon City), 141
women landscape architects
  advocates for, 37, 75–76, 113
  in ASLA, 185n12
  college programs for, 18–20, 185n3
  Depression's impact on, 65–66
  first generation of, 3–4
  horticultural knowledge of, 20, 113–14
  newspaper articles by, 62, 82–83, 132
Women's Veterans Society (Salem), 154
Wood, Rebecca Biddle (Mrs. C. E. S.),
  135, 138
Wooley, Mary E., 20
World Forestry Center (Portland), 135
World War II, 56, 105, 108, 131, 134
WPA (Works Progress Administration,
  later Works Projects Administration),
  155, 159, 198n9
Wright, Richardson, 31
Wyatt, William F., 50, 53
"Wynndie-Lea" (design, Schryver), 24,
  26, plate 2

yew, 97
Yoch, Florence, 3
Yturri, Anthony, 158

zinnia, 125